The Last of the Few

An Me 262 Pilot Remembers

By Hans Busch

Editor: Lance C. Frickensmith
Technical Advisor: Leon R. Frickensmith

Publishers Dedication:
To Hans Busch who as a pioneer of jet flight helped set the
standards for the young men of all nations who now seek to be
pilots, and to especially encourage Adam Edgar in fulfilling his
dream of becoming a pilot

DEDICATION

April 15, 2006

For my four children
Christian John
Rainer Charles
Renate Evelyn
Normann Marion

Now that I'm retired and I'm getting along in years I think it's about time to think back and record for the family, the children and grandchildren a few episodes, a few highlights of my very rewarding, and very interesting life. Of course, not everything went the way I had planned it, but then again I had a great life anyway. It's always good to follow the words of the German poet Eugen Roth who said: "A man hopes with idle wish and patiently that some day he'll get what he is desiring so much, until he finally succumbs, and just desires what he gets!"
Here I am in beautiful Southern California, where I enjoy the sunshine almost every day and live in great harmony with my sweetheart of over 55 years, my eternal love: Marianne.

CHAPTERS

FOREWORD

This book traces the career of the author from his early life in Germany, through his service in the Hitler Youth, on into a pilot's life in the Luftwaffe, culminating in his flying the fabled Messerschmitt 262 in combat – an unforgettable experience for any pilot. Mr. Busch then recounts his career in immigrating to the USA, and his many adventures in becoming a capable and worthy U.S. citizen.

His experience with the Me262 continues large in his life. He is called on to lecture America's youth as well as service groups about Germany's feat in creating the world's first combat jet aircraft. He never loses sight of Professor Messerschmitt's greatest creation, and his privilege of flying it into action.

Eminently readable and well written, this book is an absorbing personal history that I read twice – a rarity for me these days.

Trevor James Constable

The little boy Hans-Heinrich, August-Wilhelm Busch

When my father graduated from high school, although he lived many miles away from the nearest seashore, he was determined to become a naval engineer. He entered the Emperor's navy just as WWI broke out and was very fortunate to survive the only major engagement of the British and German fleet, the sea battle at Skagerrak May/ June 1916 (more commonly known as the battle of Jutland). Although torpedoed I'm glad his ship survived the battle. This way I had a chance to be born after WWI in the year 1924 in the city of Hamburg although I don't remember too much of my very early years there. When I was about four years old, my mother left for America. My sister Victoria, who was about 14 months older, and I now had to live with grandmother Auguste and grandfather Wilhelm (Gerstenberg) on a farm in Mecklenburg. Perhaps it was a little rustic, with an outhouse across the yard near a large manure pile and a pump to draw the water from for cooking and washing, we did not mind. The light of a smoking kerosene lamp was somewhat romantic for us city kids.

I was about six years old when father's mother, Oma (Luise) Busch, insisted that her two grandchildren had to go to school in the city of Neustrelitz where she and her husband Opa (Heinrich) Busch had been a school teacher for many years. Therefore a one-classroom village school was not proper for us. It must have been quite a task to take care of us two rascals because Oma was already 77 years old at that time. I never had the chance to be with Opa, because he had died in 1918 at the age of 57.

Prior to WWI , father's older brother Hans had studied to become a physician. He was said to be a very talented boy who played several musical instruments, painted and liked poetry.

When WWI broke out he immediately volunteered to serve his country in the military. He was a very dedicated medic who helped wounded soldiers in the "hell-battles" at the Somme. In 1916, during an especially severe artillery barrage he volunteered to rescue wounded soldiers out of the forward trenches. He succeeded in carrying 12 soldiers to safety and saving their lives; however, when he carried the 13th soldier out, he received a direct artillery hit, and was killed.

A monument in memory of Hans Busch was placed at the Neustrelitz graveyard, which we visited many times during our Sunday morning walks. From uncle Hans I was given my first name Hans which combined with grandfather Busch's first name Heinrich became my first name Hans-Heinrich. It was considered proper for a child to have a name from relatives of mother's family, too. Mother's sister's name was Auguste, voilà that became for me August. Mother's father's name was Wilhelm; with that I had my two hyphened double first names Hans-Heinrich, August-Wilhelm Busch.

For Oma it was a pleasure to watch over little Hans' scholastic activities. Because my first grade teacher had once been a student of Oma's, and over the years had maintained a close friendship I could not get away with anything at school without it all coming out at the next "Kaffeelatsch". In those days parents supported teachers in school 100%.

If I would have complained about a teacher I most likely would have received a reprimand at home and a check with the school to establish "corrective measures".

Corporal punishment in those days at schools and at home was the accepted rule. I don't think that I received too many beatings during the first three years in Grammar school. I do remember, however, that our Konrektor (Vice Principal) was the one who dispensed punishments. He had a very precise almost pedantic way of doing that, when arrangements were made for him to come to our class. He called the boy, the culprit (we had no girls in our classes) to come forward and bend over the bench in the first row. I very well remember while he stretched the seat of my pants he said. "What the human being needs, the human being shall get!, and wham his "pacifier" as he called his 2½ foot long and ½ inch thick bamboo stick came down on my behind. It really smarted! Whatever the "violation" was, I'm sure that I registered it in my mind not to do that again!

Naturally I would not mention anything about that at home or I would have received another punishment. Of course, I had to make sure that nobody saw the welts on my rear end.

Father never gave me a beating; he preferred to give me assignments to write a hundred times: "I shall always be nice to my Grandmother", or something like that. In a way I hated that even more than a beating, because the writing took me a long time, during which I could not play outside with my friends. When I say that father never gave me a beating I'm not quite correct because there was one, and one only really severe thrashing that I'll never forget.

Here is what had happened: A couple of my playmates and I we were romping around in Neustrelitz at the Zierker See (a good sized lake).

6

There was a dredge anchored a couple of hundred feet from shore. The workers had gone home and had tied their rowboat to a stake on shore. When we found out that the rowboat was not locked, we just could not resist the temptation to play a little "Skipper of an Ocean liner" with it. There were no oars but some long poles were good enough to push our ship back and forth. This was great! We had a wonderful time. As we became more daring we suddenly could not reach the bottom of the lake anymore, as we had drifted to where the dredge had worked, and where it was really deep. Now what? Frantically we tried to use the long poles as oars, but by then we were so far from shore that the wind pushed us further and further away from shore and towards the middle of the lake. All we could do now was to sit and wait until eventually we had reached the shore at the opposite side of the lake, a distance of more than a mile. Even then getting to dry ground was not so easy. A thick growth of reeds stopped us pushing the boat all the way to the shore.

There was no other way for us but to hop into water that reached almost to our chin, push ourselves through the water thicket, and leave the boat where it was. It was a long way home. Father was not there so I did not have to explain my damp clothes. Unfortunately in a small town everybody knows everybody, even the kids. Next day the dredge workers were a little upset that their boat was not there. Someone must have seen us and eventually my father was informed.

Father asked me: "Did you have anything to do with that"? Since nobody had stopped us I acted very surprised and denied any participation.

Apparently it was an established fact that I was part of that prank so I had to listen to a lengthy lecture about "truth", "honour", "responsibility" and the courage to admit when I had done something wrong.

Then I had to endure a royal beating with a stick on my behind. Again and again father said: "You don't get this for what you had done, -- you get this because you lied to me"! That was the only beating that I can remember father ever gave me.

And here I'd like to introduce the members of the Busch family:

My Grandparents photos from an old family album

Oma, Luise Busch, nee Marung   Opa, Heinrich Busch
1853-1934   1861 - 1918

My Father
Kurt Martin Busch
1893-1966

My Mother
Bertha Caroline Busch, nee Gerstenberg
1898– 1986

Oma Gerstenberg with 4 of her 9 grandchildren

In mother's family, there were five kids. Bertha, Willi, Grete, Guschen, and Johnny. When the children are young they all had to help with the chores on a farm. So they are needed, and even essential. When the children become adults, many times the farm will not support such a large family. That's the time the kids wander off to the city -- or as in the Gerstenberg family -- to leave Germany and emigrate to America. The first one to make that daring move was Aunt Grete around 1927. She found a job in Buffalo, NY, and wrote: "It's great here in America, there are a lot of German folks here and we live very well." That's when brother Willi, back in 1929, made the move. He did not speak a word of English so it was difficult for him to find a job, finally, he became employed by a sausage factory in Buffalo. It was great to get a regular pay check every week. After a year, his knowledge of the English language had not improved very much, although, he spoke Polish fluently as most of the workers in that factory had come from Poland.

In 1928, I was about 4 years old when mother departed for America. Supposedly mother was to pick up a loan from her sister Grete which they needed to start a chicken farm. We kids, sister Victoria and I, could not possibly comprehend what was going on. Father and the two of us saw Mother walking up the gangway of an awfully huge ocean liner. That was it, a very sad feeling!

Father could not work and take care of us two; therefore we were moved to our grandparents. Oma and Opa Gerstenberg who operated a farm near Zuehlen some 30 miles west of Berlin. Oma, I'm sure, did her best to care for us, as we certainly had plenty to eat and enjoyed the loving care of our grandparents. Farm life was a bit more simple and rustic than that in a city, there was no indoor plumbing; the outhouse was behind the manure pile. There was no electricity so kerosene lamps were lit when it turned dark. There was no bathtub in the house which meant that once a week, whether we needed it or not, we had to stand in a large bowl filled with warm water and were sponged from top to bottom. When it became time for us to start school, Oma Busch demanded that the kids had to live in Neustrelitz a city of some 25,000 where the schools were a lot better than in the village of Zuehlen.

Oma Busch knew what she was doing, after all she and her husband had been teaching there for many years. Oma accepted quite a burden when, at the age of 77 she had to care for us rascals.

When we had moved in with Oma Busch in Neustrelitz there was a bunch of neighbourhood kids who played together who loved Cowboys and Indians . When Uncle Willi wrote from America and asked me what I would like for my birthday I answered "A real Cowboy or Indian outfit"! How exciting when a package arrived and would you believe it, a complete Cowboy costume, chaps with fur, a bright chequered flannel shirt, cowboy hat, lasso and pop sounding six-shooter came out; but that was not all, an Indian Chief outfit with khaki trousers, a jacket with fringes on the sleeves a headgear with coloured feathers, a bow with arrows, a rubber knife and tomahawk, what a surprise! Now we really could play Cowboys and Indians I don't recall if the Cowboys or Indians usually won. I guess we got the inspiration to our games from "Tom Mix" mov-

The roughest - toughest Cowboy in Germany

ies, of which many played in the local movie theatres at that time. I had also mentioned to Uncle Willi, that I would like a football. Sure enough, a leather ball was also in the package. However, we were all very puzzled what to do with a ball that is shaped like a plum. Pumping it up really hard did not change the shape either. When we kicked the ball it would go every which way, but not where we wanted it to go. We thought how do kids in America play soccer with a ball like this?

After three years of grammar school a student could transfer to a Gymnasium (High School) or continue in the grammar school for an additional 5 years -- if the student was planning to learn a trade. Apprenticeship training started at about 15-16 years of age. For those who wanted to get a high school diploma and perhaps continue with higher education they had to enrol in the Gymnasium. However the student had to have fairly good grades and had to pass an entrance examination.

High school was not free in those days like it is today; monthly tuition had to be paid which was not easy for many families.

I started school at the Carolinum Gymnasium in Neustrelitz. In the first year, called Sexta, I had Latin, German, History, Biology, Chemistry, Geometry, Math, Physics, Arts and Sports. After a few years, another language was added usually English or French. These subjects were continued throughout the nine years of high school. Every student had to study the same subjects, there were no electives. Final graduation from a Gymnasium was called Abitur (High School Diploma) that is required for further studies at a University. (An Abitur is usually evaluated in the USA as a high school diploma plus two years of college.)

LIFE IN GERMANY

Life in Germany, in the years before 1933, when Hitler came to power was all-in-all quite miserable. In 1918, after 4 years of fighting, killing and suffering, WWI came to an end. The Versailles peace treaty also referred to as the "Versailles Dictate", imposed horrendous obligations and conditions on Germany. The demands were so severe that Germany just could not fulfil them. So for example French Troops occupied the Ruhr and seized industrial production and the British Royal Navy maintained its wartime blockade of German Ports to prevent the importation of food. During the Winter of 1918/19 many Germans died of starvation. Unemployment was high and the many political parties that came together in the Reichstag (Congress) of the Democratic Government the "Weimar Republic" were battling each other rather than working together on means and ways to get Germany out of the misery. The strongest party was the Communist party on the left of the political spectrum. Some moderate parties like Christian Democratic or Free Democrats of the Center also tried, but could not grasp the catastrophic economic situation. Overall industrial productivity dropped to 42 percent. Year after year it became worse and worse. When around 1923 the big crash with hyperinflation came, many people lost everything. The life savings of thrifty workers evaporated in a few weeks. The value of money steadily declined, yesterday a loaf of bread was priced at 100 Marks, today it cost 500 Marks. If you had money you had to take large bundles along to purchase a few groceries. In January 1923 the exchange rate of the US Dollar was 18,000 Marks, by October the same year it was 40 thousand million Marks = one US Dollar.

The story was told that a man had so much paper money along that he used a wheelbarrow to go shopping. He left the wheelbarrow with the money unattended outside in front of the store, when he came back the money was still there but the wheelbarrow was stolen.

To call that time "The Roaring 20's" for Germany, is a grotesque misnomer. However, there were also some entrepreneurs, especially those with access to foreign capital, who took advantage of this situation and scooped up fantastic riches for pennies on the dollar.

These are examples of the money used in the early 1930s

Postage stamps to mail a letter

These stamps illustrate how badly inflation ran away in Germany in the 1930s. The price rose from 300 Marks to mail a simple letter, to 500,000

RM [Reich Marks], to the astronomical 50,000,000 RM to mail that same letter only a few months later! Rather than print new stamps the postal authorities just over stamped them with the new higher values

Political unrest, and most miserable time in Germany

By 1930 we were fortunate that we could live with Oma who received her teacher's pension every month. That was enough to buy foodstuff for the four of us as Father tried to sell chemicals and lubrication products to the sawmills in the area around Neustrelitz. I say tried because he did not earn very much. Every day someone rang our doorbell and begged for food. These people did not ask for worthless money, they were hungry they asked for something to eat. Oma many times had cooked a pot full of soup and offered them some, which they devoured ravenously. They were ever so thankful. For us kids it was hard to comprehend that someone would go to a strange house and beg for food. I felt very sorry for them! Perhaps that was the first time in my life that I learned not to waste any food. Little did I know at the time, that after WW2 I would be in the same situation as the beggars of the early 1930's.

In the 30's, Germans became more and more frustrated. The political instability of the Weimar Republic, which had no less than 21 governments from 1919 until 1933, could not inspire the people. Then two major political parties tried to take the lead, the Communist party still the strongest and the new National Socialist party whose appeal to the German people since 1923 had gradually increased. In the 1932 election the Communist party could rake up more than 14 percent of the total ballots cast. Naturally the Communist regime in Russia since their revolution in 1917 very much in power now, gave considerable aid and support to the aspiring Communists in Germany; after all the Communists aimed at "World Revolution". It still seems strange to me that only "right wing" parties fully realised and took this threat seriously.

In 1932 I was only 8 years old and certainly had no interest or understanding of the political process. As the blue shirted Communists marched through town my friends and I followed them for a while on the sidewalk, especially when they had a band playing march music. It was the same when next time the brown shirts, the National Socialists marched to their rally.

Father was a true believer in the monarchy; he thoroughly disliked the National Socialists as well as the Communists. When in 1918 the Communists called out revolution he was stationed on the battleship "Bayern" anchored in the harbour of Kiel. His orderly, a very nice young sailor, made it possible for father to leave the ship at night by rowboat, thereby avoiding the embarrassing, distasteful and very degrading treatment by the Communist revolutionaries who ripped medals and officer emblems off every officer's uniform. Kaiser Wilhelm had abdicated and had gone into exile in Holland. Of all the political parties at that time, and there were many, one patriotic party called the "Stahlhelm", appealed to my father as all, or most of, their members were WWI veterans. He became the leader of the Stahlhelm-Navy section in Neustrelitz and from time-to-time he marched ahead leading his group whenever there was a patriotic procession through town.

Apparently the Communists did not like the Stahlhelm leader Kurt Busch and did what is typical for them; they tried to terrorise Kurt and his family. We certainly got the scare of our life when one evening when suddenly a brick came crashing through the window. Fortunately no one was hurt; however, Oma was quite upset and fearful for a while. The Stahlhelm also had a youth group for boys, which was called "Scharnhorst".

A shoulder patch with the old Teutonic Knights Cross emblem was sewn on the shirtsleeve of our olive drab uniform.

Naturally I joined the Scharnhorst and had a lot of fun with the other boys when we went on hiking trips or were sitting around singing patriotic songs. (Similar to the Cub Scouts in the USA) The little girl's branch, which my sister Victoria joined, was called "Kornbluemchen" (little corn-flowers). About 1932 Adolf Hitler, the Fuhrer (Leader) of the Nationalsozialistische Deutsche Arbeiter partei (NSDAP = National Socialist German Workers Party) increased his campaign activity considerably. He chartered an aircraft from the Lufthansa German Airline and addressed people in several cities all on a given day which had never happened before. Flugkapitaen Hans Baur was assigned to fly him. From that time on until

Arm patch from the uniform of the Scharnhorst

1945, Hitler flew only with Hans Baur. (I corresponded with Hans Baur after the war and also had a number of interesting conversations with him about table talks with Hitler at breakfast, lunch or dinnertime).

Hitler was saying what people wanted to hear, and he could fascinate people because he was a fantastic orator. I had the opportunity to listen to Hitler when he spoke to us Luftwaffe cadets in 1943.

There were 7 million registered unemployed workers in Germany at that time and 17 million in dire need. Of the 31 million so-called income-receiving workers almost 70% made only 1,200 Marks per year. At the time when Reichspraesident von Hindenburg on January 30th directed Hitler to form a new government, the economic and social situation in Germany had reached an unbelievable low.

For many workers, unemployment insurance benefits had run out and welfare provided only 55 Marks per month. More than 2/3rds of the population barely survived at a level barely above the minimum for existence. Many people even starved to death! Hitler's topics in his election campaign speeches were themes like this: "Give me 4 years time and I'll eliminate unemployment in Germany!" or "The German people have a right to exist!" or "We want our brothers and sisters in the Sudeten, in the Saarland, Poland and all the territories cut off from Germany as ordered by the 1919 Versailles peace treaty, to return back to the Reich".

After assuming power his peaceful revolution spread easily throughout Germany. He did not only impress the blue collar workers but also upper-class people in Germany, as well. When the election in 1933 was held, the NSDAP won with a significant, overwhelming lead.

Hitler became Chancellor and began his reign. The left-wing political parties like the Socialists and Communists were disbanded. At that time, some German politicians of the opposition parties actually contacted the British and tried to persuade them to attack Germany militarily while Germany was still very weak (the Army was allowed to have a strength of only 100,000 soldiers, no Air force or Navy) just to get rid of the most popular party, the National Socialists. However, the National Socialists now took the opposition "out of circulation", that's how the concentration camps were started in 1933 of which I and most people in Germany had never heard of until after the war. (These camps were similar to the camps established for US citizens of Japanese, German or Italian ancestry in California and elsewhere when the US entered World War II.)

In the USA, Japanese-looking citizens were thought to be a danger to the security of the country as in Germany known Communists, Social Democrats and other "opposition citizens" were thought to be a threat to the fragile new NS regime.

The kids in our neighbourhood came from different walks of life. I remember two kids of the owner of a modest shoe store around the corner, Bubi and Regina Rosenbaum were the only Jewish kids we played with in our neighbourhood. In our public elementary school we had religious Lutheran instruction. Naturally Catholic and Jewish kids did not attend those classes. There were no animosities or resentments among any of us, religion was totally ignored.

At home I never heard any derogatory remarks or discussions about Jews or Catholics. I was never taught to be Anti-Semitic, not in public elementary school or later in high school.

At that time there were not too many opportunities to encounter Jews in the daily life as there were only 0.6 million Jews living in Germany in 1923. Unfortunately Jews held certain positions of political and social power disproportionate to their total number of Jews living in Germany, which irritated some people.

With the National Socialist consolidation of power all the right-wing organisations , like the Stahlhelm were integrated into the NSDAP or the SA. The Scharnhorst, of which I was a member, was transferred as a complete unit to become "Jungvolk". (Jungvolk was like the Boy Scouts here in America) We changed the uniform a little bit, now it was a brown shirt with a black neck scarf, and black shorts made of corduroy, but did not change much in the conduct of the weekly meetings.

Singing of patriotic and folk's songs and listening to stories about the struggle of the party during the last 10 years were the main topics.

Father never joined the ranks of the brown shirts. He had been asked a number of times to become a member of the party but he staunchly refused. It most likely would have made it easier for him to advance at work but otherwise he was left alone. He always had some jokes and stories to tell ridiculing Hitler or the party, but apparently he always made sure not to tell them to the wrong people. I remember he had some correspondence with the Gauleiter (Governor) of Mecklenburg, who was a man who had no formal education, who chopped fieldstones into pavement stones but had joined the party at an early time. Can one expect intelligent decisions from a man like that?

For the government, and that meant all levels of government, the most urgent tasks were the activation of industry and the initiation of new projects which would immediately bring bread to the tables of the starving people.

There was the Autobahn (Highway), the construction of the most modern road system in the world. Many thousands of workers were required because nearly everything was built by hand with pick and shovel and hardly any heavy machinery or road-building equipment.

In addition to and parallel with the government's welfare programs the NSDAP went into action as early as 1933 to help the desolate and poor people. One such program was the Winterhilfswerk (Winter Aid Program). The popular slogan: "Nobody shall be hungry, nobody shall be cold" was all inspiring. The annual contributions to the Winterhilfswerk amounted to well over 400 million Marks ($200 million).

Once a month a Sunday was designated as "Eintopf Sonntag" (One Pot Dinner Sunday) to stimulate solidarity among all people poor and rich on that given Sunday, all families voluntarily ate no steak, pork roast, prime rib, etc., but instead cooked a stew-like meal. Volunteers went from house-to-house and collected volunteer donations. This money too was 100% used to help the poor. Money was also raised through a continuous street lottery as well as donations from industry or the newly formed NSV (National Sozialistische Volkswohlfahrt = N S Welfare). Many, many million Marks were collected by volunteers which then were really used for the benefit of the poor. No private agency or organization could skim off funds.

Programs like "Mutter und Kind" (Mother and Child) or "Kraft durch Freude" (Strength through Joy) all contributed to the general welfare of the country and the contentment of the people. For nearly 15 years Germany was in a shambles, but now there was light at the end of the tunnel. As the economy stabilized in Germany and as social reforms and programs became popular with the German people Hitler's popularity rose to open adoration. Even foreign dignitaries respected Hitler and his accomplishments. For instance: Lloyd George, Prime Minister of Great Britain during WWI said:

"I too say that Hitler truly is a great man. I have never met a happier people than the Germans and Hitler is one of the greatest men among the distinctly great men I have even encountered."

Viscount Rothermere, Director of the British Ministry of Information:

"I would like to say how I have found him. He conveys good comradeship. He is unpretentious, naturally and apparently sincere. He has a supreme intellect. I have known only two other men to whom I could apply such distinction – Lord Northcliffe and Lloyd George. If one puts a question to Hitler, he gives an immediate, brilliant clear answer. There is no human being living whose promise on important matters I would trust readily. He believes that Germany has a Divine calling and that the German people are destined to save Europe from the revolutionary attacks of Communism. He values family life very highly, whereas Communism is its worst enemy. He has thoroughly cleansed the moral, ethical life of Germany, forbidden publication of obscene books, and performance of questionable plays and films." and *"No words can describe his politeness; he disarms men as well as women and can win both at any time with his conciliatory, pleasant smile. He is a man of rare culture. His knowledge of music, the arts and architecture is profound."!*

The London Daily Mail, May 20 1938 reported:

"Hitler's political aim and policy is directed toward attaining his goal without loss of blood. He succeeded in ascending to the highest power position in Germany with very little spilling of blood or loss of human life in a land of 68 million inhabitants. Austria was annexed without one shot being fired."

When foreign dignitaries who communicated with Hitler and had the opportunity to experience and judge the man, made statements like the above should anybody ask Germans after the war: "Why did you vote for Hitler"? Should the average German citizens who were in dire straits have known him better?

Luebeck and Luebeck-Travemuende

In 1934 Oma Busch passed away, she was 81 years old. For me, the 10- year-old-kid, that was a shocking, a very sad experience. Suddenly Oma is no longer here! I really missed my dear Oma. Shortly thereafter Father accepted a position in the city of Luebeck.

After Father and Mother were divorced, he married Johanna, the daughter of a musician who lived around the corner from Augusta Str. 16., in Neustrelitz. The move to Luebeck meant I had to leave my friends and go to a different school in a different town, the second of a long list of transfers. Luebeck was a beautiful medieval city founded in the year 1143 and very well preserved with very attractive sights, seven churches and romantic remains of the Hansiatic League time city fortifications.

After a year or so father accepted a job at the Luftwaffe supply depot in Travemuende, about 20 Km north of Luebeck with a harbour on the Baltic Sea. For me, this again meant going to a different type of school. Until now I had to study Latin, now, however, this school in Travemuende had no Latin instruction; instead, the class for my age group which I was supposed to join, had started two years earlier with English. Now it was summer vacation time. In Fall I was told to participate with the English class. What did I do? Every day I had to study English, memorise irregular verbs and learn to pronounce "how now brown cow". I hated English! Why do I have to study English? I have no intentions to ever going to England. While all my buddies enjoyed summer vacation time on the beach or playing I had to visit an English teacher, a nice young lady Ms. "Muschi" Berndtson several times a week for private lessons.

Somehow it worked out all right, that is the way it was planned, in the Fall, I became part of the English class conducted by Mr. Wittern. (Certainly I was not one of the better students in English at that time.)

During the winter months the small town Travemuende was but a sleepy little fishing village on the Baltic Sea. During the winter months there were no tourists, no visitors and fishing came to a stand-still whenever the Baltic Sea froze over solid.

But during the summertime Travemuende became the spa of the world. Along the beachfront promenade there were many luxurious villas that were rented to wealthy people from around the world.

We boys marvelled at all those beautiful foreign automobiles, immaculate paint polished to perfection and sparkling chrome everywhere.

We loved snooping around the Rolls Royces, Bentleys, Duesenburgs, Pierce Arrows or Cadillac's, Mercedes Benz and Horch that were parked in front of the gambling casinos. On warm summer evening's, tourists went for a stroll along the well-lighted promenade of the beach or sipped a cocktail at a sidewalk cafe or bar, while enjoying the international hit tunes of the time.

My life in Travemuende became the most beautiful time of my entire youth. The four of us were like an inseperable four-leaf clover, Otto Langpaap, Otto Wittrock, Ferdinand Hummel and Hans Busch. We liked to hang around the harbour and talked to fishermen from whom we picked up Plattdeutsch, the Low German language spoken along the coastal areas of Germany. To this day I still have retained some of it, although whenever I try to speak it today, invariably I drift into English, an indication how closely related the two languages are.

At one time Otto L. and I made a bicycle trip of about 200 miles to visit relatives in Neustrelitz. In those days concern for childrens safety did not have to be of great worry to our parents, because criminality was very low at that time and automobile traffic was also minimal. After a day of pedaling along, we stopped at a farm and asked if we could work there, just for food. Yes, we were welcome. We helped with the harvest and did any job on the farm. After a couple of days we said "good bye" and moved on. That is how it was in National Socialist Germany, in those days it was safe for children to talk to "strangers"

At one time we slept out in a field in a grain hut. We did not have a sleeping bag, but there in the open that was really romantic! In the middle of the night I could hear mice rustling in the straw. Next morning we pedaled to a village and followed the scent of freshly baked bread drifting through the clear morning air. A great breakfast, still warm Broetchen (French rolls) and a quart of delicious cool milk. We happily pedaled along, made it to Neustrelitz and then went on to the grandparent's farm near Zuehlen. I could show Otto the church in the village of Zuehlen where I was baptized. Oma and Opa and Tante Guschen (Auguste Giraud), mother's sister, with her two daughters Margrit and Marianne were living on the solitary farm miles away from Zuehlen. This was the longest bicycle trip I had ever taken but we both enjoyed it very much.

In Travemuende, along the beach there were a number of jetties built into the sea to keep the entry channel to the harbour from being filled with sand. They were about three hundred feet long and had at the end a bulwark filled with heavy boulders. Naturally, because of the waters equalizing effect, whenever the wind pushed the water into the windward corner of the jetty there were sometimes strong currents, which could frighten an unfamiliar swimmer.

A large sign was posted: "Danger, no diving, dangerous currents" We boys, of course, swam there all the time so we knew how the currents were flowing. When some tourists wandered to the end of the jetty, to enjoy the feeling like being on a ship, we went out there too.

Then we wanted to show off. In spite of the warning sign we dove into the water on the windward side. Naturally the tourists expected us to resurface moments later. We, however, let the currents carry us around to the lee side of the jetty, where we quietly climbed up the ladder.

Meanwhile the tourists became concerned, where are they? Did they drown? While they were staring into the water on the windward side we stood behind them asking: "What happened?"

Ferdinand's father owned a nursery and a small farm near Travemuende. All four of us loved to roam around the barns and stables. Whenever possible we swiped a halter and went to the corral and became a daring cowboy. At first we had some difficulty riding a horse without a saddle, but after we had fallen off a few times, we learned. But we not only goofed off, we also tried to help wherever we could. We harvested potatoes or turnips, loaded or unloaded hay, fed pigs and chicken and even helped pulling when a cow had difficulty giving birth to a calf.

Ferdinand had a .22 rifle with which we went on a "big game hunt". One time when after two shots a rabbit still was sitting there we laughed so hard that the rabbit ran away before Ferdinand could get a third shot fired. My father had a couple of antique, muzzle-loading guns decorating the living room wall. We daredevils thought it would be exciting to shoot with a gun like they had used in medieval times. First we purchased some black powder (no problem). Then we designed a gypsum mould which we used to cast lead bullets. Well, they did not come out perfectly round but with a little bit of trimming with a pocket knife they did fit in the barrel.

Then came the question: how much of the black powder should we pour into the barrel? With trial and error we found out. A blank .22 round from a starter pistol happened to fit exactly so that the hammer of the antique rifle could hit it in the right location and fire it. For the first firing we wanted to play it safe, so we placed the gun between rocks, attached a long string to the trigger and took cover some 20 ft away.

With a loud bang and a lot of smoke the gun fired - no problem. Exciting! Now we became more daring. Finally we drew with chalk a target on the backside of a barn and fired at it in the normal standing up firing position. Luckily we had no problem with this hair-raising adventure; because we had no idea how much black powder would have been too much. Nobody at home noticed that I had appropriated the gun for our shooting experiments or I would have been bawled out royally for sure.

The new Regime makes Progress

Labourers and blue-collar workers usually lived in apartments in the city or a short distance from their place of work. Now the government made mortgage loans available to healthy young couples at their wedding for the construction of a home in suburban areas and furnishings to be repaid in small instalments. A great incentive was that the loan was reduced by 1/4 every time a baby was born.

It was the motto of the NS Ideology that the family is the smallest cell of the State. The State can only be healthy if the family is healthy, therefore the State must do everything to assure that the family is healthy. Now that Germany had good roads, Germany needed automobiles, too. "Just like Henry Ford put America on wheels, we will do the same" said Hitler. A new design by Professor Dr. Porsche was named "Volkswagen" (People's car). Mercedes, Horch, Maybach and all other manufacturers of luxury automobiles were totally disinterested in building a little car like the VW. Perhaps that might ruin the used car market?

A few of the VW's were manufactured and demonstrated throughout Germany. That's when a Volkswagen Savers Inc. was founded. People were encouraged to buy monthly 20 Mark stamps or whenever they could afford to do so, with the plan to have over a period of time 1,000 Mark (US $ 250.- at that time) in their account. That would have entitled them to accept delivery of a VW.

The money collected of course could be used to finance the construction of the VW factory. Unfortunately automobile deliveries could not be made to the public, as the war interrupted it. However, the VW factory started producing automobiles for the military, where they proved to be most reliable vehicles, especially under severe weather conditions like winter in Russia or in the hot climate of Africa. (During WW2 the VW factory received only 17% Allied bombing damage. American and British experts inspected the factory after the war and were in total agreement when they said: "It's not worth a damn!)

Meantime in a few years Germany became a favourite vacationland. During the 1936Olympic games in Berlin many people came to Germany and found that the country which had been in shambles in 1933 was now flourishing, was very industrious and was friendly and open to visitors. The world-famous aviator Charles Lindbergh, who crossed the Atlantic in 1927 in a single engine aircraft, was very much impressed. When he returned to the USA he gave speeches about his impressions and experiences when he visited and observed Germany. The American media, of course, promptly reprimanded him for saying something positive about Germany. Later, when he said that America should not get involved in a war in Europe he was black-balled for his politically incorrect statements and could never regain his acceptance as a good patriotic American.

Unfortunately, as soon as Hitler was elected, major London and New York newspapers proclaimed: "Jews of the world are declaring war on Germany" - and "Boycott all German goods".

Some financial analyst also thought: Hitler made the mistake not to apply for funds from international banks, which then caused a lot of resentment and hate as well as political problems down the road. However, until 1939 many statesmen and politicians from around the world continued to cultivate relations with Germany.

Youth Activity

By 1936 it became compulsory for all youngsters in Germany to be in the Youth Group unless they had a physical or mental handicap, for which they then were excused from membership.
The boys up to 14 years of age, the "Jungvolk" (similar to US Cub Scouts) had no specialization, but the 14-year and older kids of the "Hitlerjugend" (similar to US Boy Scouts) in many communities were given choices, such as Equestrian HJ, Motor HJ, or Marine HJ. In Travemuende there was a Flieger HJ group (Aviation-Youth). Boys of the Hitlerjugend had as part of their uniform a dagger with a 5-6 Inch blade which had the words "Blut und Ehre" ("blood and honour") engraved. In spite of that I never heard of a case where someone used it to attack or threaten someone with it. .

Not far from Travemuende was a Luftwaffe Base (Priewall). Almost daily I observed different types of aircraft fly overhead. Those machines fascinated me. In our crafts and woodworking classes in school we fabricated model gliders, which sometimes even flew the way we wanted them to. Naturally my decision was not too difficult, Aviation HJ was for me, knowing that real glider flying was offered.

Germany by edict of the 1919 Versailles treaty was not allowed to maintain a military flying corps nor design, build and fly powered aircraft, military or commercial. That gave aviation enthusiasts the motivation to develop the art of flying without a motor which was not prohibited. Fourty years earlier Otto Lilienthal (1848 - 1896) had made hundreds of flights, for scientific studies which he recorded and constantly modified his gliders.

Building upon experiences the young German flying generation went to work and developed first gliders which where only in the air for a distance of a few hundred feet, but then improved the design and built high performance sailplanes that established again and again world records in endurance, distance and altitude. In 1928 there were some 200-glider clubs in Germany which made in that year 10,000 flights and short glides.

The interest in glider flying increased year after year so it was not surprising that the HJ picked up glider flying as one of their sponsored activities. Now after 1933 the government-supported glider flying, assisted in any way possible, including manpower and material support. (Many years later I thought that it was unfortunate that glider flying did not become popular in the USA as it did then in Europe.)

While the general HJ continued to wear the brown-black uniform, we in the Aviation HJ, however, had a uniform in light blue – grey colour similar to the Luftwaffe uniform that in our young minds made us better of course!

Once a month, there were still general meetings during which we listened to talks about the early history of the party, National Socialism in general, and the life story of some famous fighters or leaders in the movement. We practiced to sing patriotic songs the same as or similar to the songs we sang in the Scharnhorst, or we learned how to execute some drill commands so that we could participate in May Day parades, etc.

What I really liked best was the once-a-week crafts and workshop meetings in the public school basement. A qualified adult instructor showed us how to saw, cut or glue pieces of wood together that were needed to fabricate the components for a full size primary glider.

Although we wasted some material; eventually the critical eye of the instructor passed our handicraft. With great enthusiasm we could see how the aircraft began to take shape.

Every one of us boys had a log book in which each workshop hour was recorded. The instructor had to sign the entry off. When we had a certain number of hours accumulated in the book we were entitled to participate on a real flight activity.

The first of my glider-flying encampments I remember especially well. It was during the summer vacation time. A truck, probably volunteered by one of the boy's father took me and some 30 boys to the camp site located about 10 to 15 Km from Travemuende. There were gently rolling hills and young pine trees all around us.

Tents were pitched and straw was placed in each tent for us to sleep on. If we would have had such crude bedding at home we probably would have rebelled, but here in a tent it was just great. There were no tables and benches or chairs, instead we dug 1 1/2 ft wide trenches about 1 1/2 ft deep. These trenches were arranged in a large square, about 20 ft by 20 ft. The idea was to sit on the outside edges of the trench put the feet in the trench, place the mess gear on the inside rim of the trench in front of us and thus consume our meals with the rest of the gang sitting side by side. For washing and bathing there was a lake nearby.

There was one more important job to accomplish, we needed a latrine. With spade and shovel we dug a large hole in the ground, perhaps 10 ft by 3 ft and about 3 ft deep. Then we mounted one sturdy tree trunk roughly hewn and de-barked horizontally about 1 1/2 ft over the edge of the pit and a second trunk about 2 1/2 ft high as a back rail. The lower trunk we sat on and the higher one we leaned on. Voilà! That was our latrine. Old newspapers cut to toilet paper size were good enough as toilet paper. Periodically chlorine powder was distributed into the pit as disinfectant. We called this whole contraption: "Donnerbalken" (Thunderbeam).

Early morning, a shrill whistle sound and the loud commands of the boy in charge made us stumble out of our tents and "fall in!" A quick check made sure that everybody was there. Then came a cross-country run through the forest, all in the world was peaceful and quiet. It was great to breathe the fragrant dew- fresh forest air. At the lake we all had a quick dip (nobody needed to shave yet), a short swim and then back to the camp. In a jiffy the tent and our few belongings were straightened out and we were dressed and ready for breakfast. Adults were operating a "Goulaschkanone" (Field kitchen on wheels) with some assistance from some of the boys. Most likely this kitchen was on loan from the military.

A typical breakfast was: Kommisbrot (black whole grain bread), with margarine and jam or artificial honey (made from sugar). With that we had coffee made from roasted and ground barley called "Ersatzkaffee" or herb-tea. After all of that, we finally began to proceed towards the location of our flight activity. After a short march from the camp we came to a knoll at the west side of the forest. There were no trees or shrubs, only some grass on top of the hill and down the slope for a thousand feet. The slope was ever so gradual, not very steep at all. On top, facing the wind sat a SG 38 Schulgleiter (primary trainer), the type of glider we had worked on during our weekly workshop activity, this one, however, was ready to go into the air.

Our flight group of about 15-17 boys assembled around the flight instructor who awaited us. We listened to a thorough explanation of the aircraft, the various parts and functions. How is it possible that this piece of assembled wood and fabric can fly? We absorbed what a Querruder (Aileron) a Seitenruder (Rudder) and Hoehenruder (Elevator) is, so we could follow the flight instructor's terminology. Now came the most exiting part.

"Hans Busch, sit on the seat at the nose section of the aircraft!" It looked like a simple card table chair and had no cockpit enclosure. One wing was resting on the ground, which the instructor now picked up and held horizontally. I had to buckle up, the belly strap and the shoulder strap really tight. Feet were resting on the rudder pedals.

With the right hand I held the stick, oh yes - we had also a leather-padded crash helmet, neat! The trick was now to use the stick to move the ailerons quickly when the flight instructor let go of the wing. I learned that very fast.

If enough wind was blowing up the hill, I could keep the wings level, no problem.

If the wind slowed, of course, a wing would eventually drop down. "Now Hans: look way over there at the horizon and pick a point. When the aircraft is moving downhill you use your feet on the rudder pedals and steer the aircraft precisely toward that point. Understand?" "Yes sir!" With the stick you not only control the ailerons but also the elevators." Now listen carefully, put the stick in a neutral position!"

I pushed forward and then pulled back until I found the neutral point. When he looked back he could tell when the elevators were in the right position. He did not want me to start gaining any altitude during take off, nor did he want me to scrape the ground with my wooden skid and not get airborne at all. (There were no wheels on this aircraft)

The pilot gets ready

Flight instructors last words

The launch crew is ready

Our glider flight training was real teamwork, no one could fly by himself, and we needed each other. Now came the take off. An elastic one inch thick rubber rope, about 150 ft long was laid out downhill so that the metal ring in the centre could be connected with the hook at the nose of the aircraft thereby forming two 75 ft ends. About 7 boys now grabbed the rope on one end of the elastic rope and 7 on the other end. The two teams had to spread out forming a large V. Meanwhile the Flight instructor appointed two boys to sit on the ground at the tail of the aircraft and grab two heavy ropes with knots in them that were fastened to the frame of the aircraft. They had to dig their heels into the ground and wait, making sure the aircraft would not move an inch. Now loud and clear came the flight instructors voice: "The towing crew OK?" answer: "Ready!" -- "The holding crew OK?" answer: "We are ready" -- "Is the pilot OK?" -- "Jawoll, the pilot is OK!" well then let's go! To the towing crew on the elastic ropes came the command: "Ausziehen!" (Stretch out) They held onto the elastic rope and started to walk downhill. Then came the command "Run!" now the boys ran as fast as they could.

When the elastic rope was stretched to the limit the flight instructor gave the order to the hold-down boys "Let Go!"

What a feeling -- first a crunching sound as the wooden skid scraped over the dirt, but then quiet! "Watch the point on the horizon! Keep the wings level! And don't climb too much!" In my mind I repeated all the instructions.

"I am flying!"

The aircraft shot about 15 ft in the air, but not higher, it just followed the contour of the terrain. No noise, only the wind blowing by my ears as if I was racing downhill on my bicycle. After a couple of hundred feet I ran out of speed or altitude. With a crunching sound the wooden skid scraped to a standstill. Now be quick and react to the least movement of the wings, the wings stayed level until, that is, there was a lull and the ailerons just could not respond anymore, one wing dropped to the ground. The first flight in my life, what a thrill! I could scream with joy! I unbuckled myself and stepped aside. Boy was I proud!

By that time, all of my buddies, the launching crew and the hold-down crew came running down the hill.

They brought with them a two-wheeled dolly with a long handle and a vertical pin between the wheels, which fit in a hole of the skid of the glider.

Everybody "heave- ho"! and the aircraft was placed on the dolly. With lots of pushing and pulling the aircraft was back at the starting point in a jiffy. A short de-briefing by the flight instructor and the next boy had his turn.

Can anyone not imagine how each boy was full of enthusiasm, full of thrill and excitement?

Time was just zipping by. In no time was it time for lunch. We returned to camp and ate our lunch which was usually a very simple but tasty stew, goulash, etc.. In the afternoon more of the same flight activity. We all learned of each other's minor mistakes. None of us had ever flown before but nobody made any major mistakes.

"Which goes to show you: flying is really very simple" said the flight instructor. He was of the opinion that: if one person wants to learn to fly who had no previous contact with aviation, and an other person wants to learn to ride a bicycle the flyer will be way ahead of the bike rider mastering the skill. One thing is sure: nobody had any difficulty or caused any damage to himself or the aircraft. The whole thing was just great joy for all of us.

After a day of launching and retrieving the aircraft we were all very tired. After dinner we usually had a brief gemuetliches (cozy) get together at our eating-place with a nice fire burning in the middle. A long day of physical exercise or exertion was over and none of us needed a lullaby to fall asleep.

The night before our departure day we had a special entertainment evening after dinner. In the middle of our eating trenches, a beautiful campfire threw a flickering light on the spectators and performers.

We sang traditional folk songs and humorous enlightening catching tunes (like "Hamburger four mast ship", "Columbus discovers America" or "Our pastor's cow", etc) we had a great time. Then someone showed some magic tricks and someone else told a really funny story. Everybody liked this "Kameradschafts-abend" (an evening of comradeship).

The next day it rained. How lucky for us now that we were going home anyway. Standing on the open truck we sang all the way home on our trip back to Travemuende, in spite of this little moisture in the air. I'm sure that I like everybody else was ever so inspired by the first exposure to real flying! A weekend of this activity belongs to one of my fondest memories.

Teenage life in Travemuende

One day the local Protestant pastor came to our school and asked us: "Who wants to be Confirmed ?" Everybody signed up except one boy who was an atheist (He was considered to be a little odd but nobody teased or ridiculed him). After attending the prescribed number of religious instruction classes and after passing the final examination we were all Confirmed. This also constituted the acceptance of a 14-year-old as a full-fledged (semi) adult among the members of the congregation.

Church and state had agreed not to interfere in each other's domain. The HJ meetings were usually held on one evening per week. During Sunday church hours the HJ was not allowed to conduct meetings. The only exception was of course whenever there was a major event on that day like the May Day parade.

Great things were happening. Radio and newspaper reports brought 1938 the exiting news of the "Anschluss", Austria and Germany were finally united again. Since 1919 Austrian politicians, Social Democrats, Labour leaders, Communists and the clergy all pleaded with the WWI victorious Allies to allow a union with Germany, but to no avail. In 1938 German troops were greeted with great joy, flowers and kisses as they marched towards Vienna.

Later the world media spread the misinformation that Germany was out to conquer the world. Was it unreasonable for Germany to try to get the 10% of the German states territory back that was cut off from Germany by the direction of the 1919 Versailles Treaty? In many of his election speeches Hitler campaigned for Germany to get those territories returned which made him very popular with most people.

In 1938 a young Jew shot and killed a German diplomat in Paris. That triggered some rabble-rousers, the bouncer type in the SA to go overboard and initiate a revenge action. Enticed by some news from the propaganda ministry releases by the minister of propaganda Dr. Josef Goebbels, these hoodlums felt like heroes when they threw rocks in the windows of businesses and stores owned or operated by Jews. This even resulted in some killings and the arson burning of synagogues. It was later referred to as the "Kristallnacht" (Crystal Night). At the time when this happened I was not aware of it at all. It might be that in Travemuende no businesses, homes, shops or synagogues were damaged or destroyed. Obviously this was a very stupid thing to happen. A typical lynch mob action one could expect from low intelligent SA members.

Years later, I read that Hitler was furious about this affair, and gave immediate orders to stop that nonsense at once, but by then it already was too late, the damage had been done already. The irony was, since most of the damaged or destroyed businesses had been insured, all the damage repairs had to be paid by the insurance companies and that meant by the German people.

Whenever Hitler gave a major speech the entire school was assembled in the auditorium. A loudspeaker was set up on the stage and we kids, teenagers that we were, had to sit there and listen. Not too many kids really paid attention. (I wonder how many teenagers here in America are glued to the television whenever national conventions are broadcast or the President is speaking?)

I had the crazy idea to make the dull listening a little more interesting. When I had to help with the laundry on washday at home, I had experienced that a little dust of the laundry detergent always made me sneeze.

I took some of the white powder to school when the next speech was announced. This time I sat upstairs on the balcony. When Hitler's oratory echoed through the auditorium I put a little bit of detergent in my open hand and blew at it. A cloud of dust settled down on the students sitting below. It took only a moment and I heard the sneezing below. Had I stopped at that everything would have been OK. However, I got carried away and with a strong blow sent a whole lot of powder drifting downward. Unfortunately there was also a teacher sitting straight below who noticed that his dark suit suddenly turned white. Naturally he realized where this white stuff had come from and immediately rushed upstairs. He caught me red-handed. I'm sure I received an appropriate punishment.

Then came the news about the German demand to reunite with the Sudetenland, which had been granted to Czechoslovakia from Germany during the Versailles Peace Treaty. People in the Sudetenland were predominantly German (3.5Mill) but in 1919, their area was given to the newly formed state of Czechoslovakia, in spite of US President Wilson's promise of self determination. Naturally there was some high tension in Europe. A last minute meeting with Neville Chamberlain and Adolf Hitler in Munich defused the situation.

Some people, my father included, thought that Hitler was too impatient and moved too fast and that Germany might find herself suddenly at war. We 14-year-old kids were not too concerned about all the politics etc., for us life went on as usual and we enjoyed every day of it.

One day a rumour made the round that Hermann Goering

31

(Supreme commander of the Luftwaffe) was to visit Travemuende. Apparently this was not an official visit but only a brief inspection of a new Luftwaffe air crash recovery boat. I remember it looked like a PT boat and was docked in the commercial section of the harbour. Naturally many peeople immediately many gathered around to try to get a glimpse of the Reichsmarschall. (Who was "slightly" overweight, which means that he was fat) There were also a number of civilians with cameras trying to take a picture of this event. Suddenly Goering saw out of the corner of his eye a man with a camera who tried to take a picture of him from the side. Right away he turned towards the photographer and said to the people: "please step aside for a moment!" and to the man with the camera:" Now go ahead, -- you know, I don't want you to take a picture of my fat ass!" -- a roaring laughter broke out, as he was known to be jovial with common folks.

Travemuende had a beautiful park in the middle of town. Trees, lawns, flowerbeds and a little lake. In the wintertime when the lake was frozen solid (ice 12 Inches or thicker) the local brewery harvested some of the ice for cooling the beer during the summertime. Workers came with saws and cut chunks of ice, loaded them on a wagon and hauled them to the cellar of the brewery. Refrigeration probably was too expensive in those days. After the thick ice was gone the water froze over quickly. A little bit of snow made it difficult to distinguish the thick ice from the thin ice.

In the wintertime we boys liked to go to the park after school was out and play ice hockey. Nobody had real hockey equipment like kids have today; we simply "borrowed" a walking stick or cane that we found at home in a closet. We had clamp-on skates, I and my buddies could not afford the special boots with screwed on skates. A roughly shaped piece of wood was good enough as a puck. We had great fun chasing back and forth over the ice and what we lacked in skill, we made up in energy. At one time the puck flew way over where the ice had been taken out a couple of days before. I was the closest and took off after the puck like a whirlwind. In my excitement I had completely forgotten that, somewhere near the shore, there must be some thin ice. The snow made it look all alike. With full speed I hit the thin ice and splash I was all the way up to my neck in the freezing water. Fortunately I was not too far from shore and swam and waded to dry land. I was shivering a bit and by the time I was home my clothes had frozen stiff. At home I changed into dry clothes, hung the wet ones over the bathtub to dry and 30 minutes later I was back in the game. Lesson learned: From that day on I always made sure that I knew exactly where the thin ice was.

War with Poland

September 1. 1939, war broke out with Poland! For us boys this too was an event that I think we really could not comprehend. The old folks, especially the one's who had seen the misery of war during WWI were worried or at least very concerned.

There was no jubilant "Hurray - Hurray!", only "I hope this will be over soon!" However, we boys were thinking:" I hope the war lasts long enough so we can have a part in it!" When reports about the military success came in, and the ministry of propaganda was very effective and efficient, the mood of the people changed to a feeling of relief, maybe even a feeling of great accomplishment. After all, the whole war with Poland was over in a few short weeks. However, now England and France declared war on Germany.

Why did this war have to start? One major factor for England to destroy National Socialism in Germany was that Hitler was able to rehabilitate Germany and build a modern industrial and military force without considerable loans from British banks. Certainly England had economic reasons to be jealous of Germany, but weren't they minimal in view of the risk to start a world war over a German commerce rivalry? Certainly the results of WW2 clearly show how unnecessary this war was for England and for the world.

Of course the seed for a future conflict was already planted at the peace treaty in Versailles after WWI in the year 1919. Germany was ordered to give up territories like the Saarland, Eupen-Malmedy, Silesia, Egerland, the area around Memel and the territory of West Prussia referred to as "the Corridor" the area between Pomerania and East Prussia in which a predominantly German population was living.

The 1000-year-old German city of Danzig was now controlled by the League of Nations and Poland. In order to travel to East Prussia from Germany it was now necessary to go through the sovereign country of Poland or take a ship on the Baltic Sea. I still cannot understand how stupid those people were who would dictate such a condition, unless there was a plan behind it(?). (Perhaps: the world planned ahead and created a reason to start another war soon). For the German minority living under Polish control, life became unbearable. Daily persecution was everywhere. Polish terror and atrocities like the bloodbath in the city of Bromberg where several thousand Germans were killed escalated hate and tension in all former German areas in Poland.

When the first edition of a collection of documents went to press in New York, November 1939, 5,437 cases of murder committed by soldiers of the Polish army and by Polish civilians against men, women and children of the German minority had been definitely ascertained. During the last few days before Germany marched into Poland and the days when the war was in progress it was reported that some 58,000 Germans perished. German proposals to solve this idiotic situation were among others:

1. Let people in the Corridor vote and decide if they want to be part of Poland or of Germany.
2. In case they want to belong to Germany the harbour of Gedingen on the Baltic Sea would be assigned to Poland and a connection for traffic from Poland to the harbour would be established.
3. In case people want to belong to Poland a railroad and highway connection from Germany to East Prussia would be guaranteed and established.

During numerous meetings and conferences between October 1938 and March of 1939, Germany made very reasonable suggestions to Poland to solve the Corridor problem, but of no avail; England gave Poland strong encouragements not to conduct any discussions with the Germans.

Unfortunately, Poland with enormous encouragement from Great Britain promptly rejected all proposals. From March until August 1939, England made sure that no agreement was reached between Poland and Germany. When Germany insisted to find a resolution, a reclaiming of the former German territory by force apparently was the only option left. The moment German troops marched into Poland, England declared war on Germany. The assistance England had promised Poland failed to materialize. Poland was facing the German military invaders all alone.

Not only that but Stalin in agreement with Hitler had his Red Army march into Poland and occupy the Eastern part of Poland. Strangely no English declaration of war to Russia resulted and till 1993 Russia still occupied the Eastern half of Poland. The Russian military government controlled and ruled in a typical communist barbaric fashion with round up's and deportations of all perceived enemies of the "workers paradise".

Later when Germany and Russia were at war, German troops who

EDITORS FOOTNOTE: Germany invaded Poland for the exact same reasons NATO made war on Serbia over Kosova, to stop the persecution of a minority up's and deportations of all perceived enemies of the "workers paradise".

Later when Germany and Russia were at war, German troops advanced into the region of Katyn and were told by farmers to check the area of a forest near Katyn. It turned out that the Russian secret police , on the orders of Stalin, had murdered thousands of Polish officers and buried them in mass graves in that forest. In total some 15,000 Polish officers were killed by the NKVD.

Our lifestyle in Travemuende now had a few changes. Food ration cards were issued to each person in Germany. Although there was not an abunance of foodstuff, enough calories were available so that nobody was hungry. Pregnant women, babies and children were issued special rations. For workers who had especially long working hours or very hard work to perform, upon request additional food tickets were issued. A story was told at that time: Women standing in line to request additional food tickets. The first women: "My husband is a brick layer and has to work 10 hours a day 7 days a week!" Well of course here are the Zusatzmarken (extra tickets). The next woman steps up: "My husband is an engineer in an aircraft factory." "Sorry" said the bureaucrat, does not qualify." The woman:" But he is working on a project of national importance!" "Sorry" the bureaucrat again. She, "But he is working 12 hours a day!" "Sorry" the bureaucrat says once more. The woman leaves. The colleague of the bureaucrat asked him: "Why did you not issue food tickets to that women, she qualifies?" The bureaucrat: "Do you know how to spell Engineer?"

In all of Germany. "Verdunkelung" (black out) was ordered immediately. The local police constantly had to conduct patrols throughout the city to check on total window coverings, not a crack of light was allowed to be seen from the outside. Automobiles, and my bicycle, too, had to have special headlight covers, which allowed only a small slot of light to cast on the street ahead.

At the high cliffs north of Travemuende next to the golf course, an anti-aircraft battery (Flak) moved in to position. It worked together with a set of huge listening devices like giant ears to detect the sound and to locate enemy aircraft if they should approach the area.

A "Sicherheits und Hilfsdienst" was formed. That was something like air raid wardens and civil defence emergency help crews. Somebody had the thought: what if the telephone and communication systems are interrupted, how do we get messages delivered? (Cell phones had not been invented yet) That's when it was decided to have "Melder" (messenger) attached to the various posts. But where do we get the messengers? -- From teenage school boys of course! Someone came to our school and asked, "Who wants to volunteer?" There were several boys who wanted to sign up right away. However, first a check with the school was conducted to see if the boy had good grades. If not -- sorry!

The only other requirement was that a Melder had to have a bicycle and had to be of normal build and good health. Well, that's how I became a melder. Really this was a goofy job, but we liked it. Naturally my two friends Otto and Otto were in the team, too; but because Ferdinand had a slight speech impediment he could not join us.

Our "job" consisted of being at the Sicherheits und Hilfsdienst post, which was a requisitioned beautiful villa right at the Baltic Sea oceanfront. We were given specific duty time after school, because during the school hours we had to be in our classes. While on duty, we usually did our homework first. Then we played ping-pong or played cards. After curfew we hit the sack -- that is we each had a bunk-bed where we slept until the morning. For morning wash-up and breakfast we went home and from there to school.

First we wore our HJ uniform but then we received a brand new black sharp-looking uniform with a green Sicherheits & Hilfsdienst armband (no swastika) and a narrow band with the word Melder on the lower sleeve. To our great surprise we found out that we were also getting paid. It probably was not very much but enough that later I could buy myself a new bicycle and a few other things and still had money in my savings account.

Sicherheits und Hilfsdienst

36

Sicherheits und Hilfsdienst

War at our doorsteps

One day we heard a loud boom! We found out that a Finnish coastal freighter coming into port at Travemuende had run on a mine, one of the many, which the British had dropped at night from aircraft all along the coast. The ship sank about a mile off shore in fairly shallow water, so that 1/4 of the masts were still sticking out of the water.

One afternoon Otto W. and I had the idea to take our little kayak and paddle out to the sunken ship while we really were supposed to be on duty. We had no problem getting there as the wind was blowing out to sea. We inspected the ship and climbed into the rigging and looked down at the ship, which we could see clearly below. There was nothing we could salvage or take along as souvenir, so we headed back to shore. Now however, paddling was a little more difficult against the wind and a little higher waves. Some of the waves began flooding our boat, so one of us had to paddle and the other scooped out the water. We were still a distance away from shore when we heard the air raid sirens hooting. That's the time we were supposed to be at our post. Well, there was not much we could do now, but to paddle as fast as we could. Fortunately there was no emergency in our absence but nevertheless we were supposed to be on duty. Naturally we were duly reprimanded for our irresponsible behaviour.

Apparently the sea mines that had been dropped in the Bay of Luebeck were magnetic mines. This type of a mine was dropped from an aircraft and was then sitting on the bottom of the ocean and each time a ship sailed overhead the mine made one click. After so many clicks, and each mine was set for a different number of clicks, the mine rose from the bottom and exploded when it made contact with a ship. That was the time when I saw a Ju.52 (three engine aircraft) fly very low in a grid pattern back and forth over the water. This aircraft had a large ring mounted from the nose to the wing tips, and then to the tail. We found out that this ring emitted a very strong magnetic field, as if a ship were sailing by. There was also a mine-sweeping operation going on. A wooden hull motorboat like a PT boat was towing two unmanned boats, which apparently had some magnetic-field-emitting devices on board. They too were able to detonate some mines.

Although we heard an occasional boom we did not see too much from shore, but we heard an occasional boom. If the wind was blowing in the right direction we discovered hundreds and hundreds of dead fish that had washed ashore.

The message travelled fast, because in no time there were many housewives on the beach to pick up fish, free of charge. At one time there were so many fish on the beach, that people could not use them all, for in those days not too many people had refrigerators in their home. That's when I saw that people picked up only the roe from the fish, which could be heated and used for frying and cooking. Fishing with an explosive device like a hand-grenade was strictly against the law but here it was different. For a change this was a by-product of war that was good for the people.

From time-to-time when British bombers flew overhead to drop bombs on a city somewhere, the heavy flak at the Priewall airbase fired a number of rounds. We liked to observe the spectacle and were thrilled when we heard flak grenade fragments rain down to earth. We always made sure that we were standing under some cover. I once found a shrapnel piece the size of a fist that had easily pierced the tile roof and landed on the floor of the attic.

A very inexpensive radio receiver called "Volksempfaenger" (Peoples receiver) was on the market for 35 RM (less than $10). Most people could listen to the news and some very popular programs like the "Hamburger Hafenkonzert" (a musical show from the harbour in Hamburg) which had been broadcast for many years before and after WW2 and became the longest continually running radio program in the world, or the "Wunschkonzert" (requests by listeners).

The news was followed by a brief report with the latest information from the military, first broadcast in German and right after that once more in English.

Mister Wittern, our English teacher, insisted that we listen to the German and the English version, which was an exact translation of the German. He was not interested that we listen to the news so much, but wanted us to comprehend the translation and learn from the English version the proper pronunciation. I still remember the opening words of each broadcast: "Germany calling, Germany calling, here are the stations D J A on the 31 meter band; you are about to hear news in English; the supreme command of the German defence forces announces!........." Today, I think that it probably did help us some in our studies of the English language.

The principal of our school, his name was Hendricksen was huge, built like the former German Chancellor Helmut Kohl. We referred to him only as "Mister Big". He taught our German and History classes. He liked to start the history class by asking : "What happened in the year 9 after Christ?" then he pointed at a student who had to get up and say the right answer : "the battle in the Teutoburger Wald!". Or he had a student pick a date or event in history and he would then point to another student who had to say the correct answer. After five or so minutes everybody was awake and we had memorized a few more dates.

In his German class we had to learn by heart a number of poems, which we had to recite in front of the class. When my father checked if I had memorized a poem and I spoke the lines correctly but in a very monotonous voice he explained to me how I should recite the poem. Now I had to also learn the proper accentuation to please my father. However, next day in class I stood in front of the class and recited the poem in the usual monotonous voice -- I felt silly to say it in a different way than everybody else, it wasn't until years later that I tried to recite poems with the right emphasis.

Mr. Big was a stickler for punctuality. On my shortest way to school I had to cross some railroad tracks. I usually left home on my bicycle with maybe a minute to spare before the beginning of classes. Unfortunately once in a while there was a freight train blocking the railroad, crossing by, moving back and forth for 5 minutes or more. Of course then I was late for school. In his class that resulted in an assignment of extra homework, because he said, "you could have taken another way not crossing the railroad to school and with that you would have been here on time -- the railroad is no excuse!" True, I could have taken the other road to be on time, but that would have meant for me to leave every morning 3 to 5 minutes earlier, and who wanted to do that?

Our class teacher was Kuddel Hass. He was a teacher with talent and great enthusiasm. We all liked him because he seemed to be more a friend than an authoritarian. The whole class, of 9 girls and 9 boys, all adored him.

He had been in Paris, France, and had learned the French language quite well. When he said to us: "French is a very beautiful language, wouldn't you like to be able to speak it?", and after he had given us a few samples we all agreed we would learn French! Unfortunately a year later he was reassigned to somewhere else -- we were all very disappointed to say the least. A women took over the French class, but she conducted the lessons so uninteresting and so boring, that we all quit at the end of the year because French was not a compulsory subject.

When I was a boy between 10 and 18 years old I was very much filled with enthusiasm to obtain the various badges and medals for sports achievements. When I was 6 years old I was enrolled in a swimming pro-gram. When the instructor thought that I and some other kids were ready to take the final test, we were ordered to swim across a lake and back. Of course he accompanied us in a rowboat. The object was to swim for a whole hour. With that accomplished we were allowed to sew a scull with crossed bones badge on our swimming trunks. A little later I acquired the Jungvolk Leistungsabzeichen, a badge I received after completing several sports events. A follow-up was the HJ Leistungsabzeichen, which had similar requirements only more demanding for the older boys. A DLRG (Deutsche Lebens Rettungs Gesellschaft = Proficiency certificate from the German Life Savings Association) was issued in three classes: Bronze, Silver and Gold. As the name says it, this organization has the purpose to save lives from drowning. The applicant had to demonstrate his (her) ability to swim a certain distance, swim under water a certain distance, dive and pick up objects from a certain depths, rescue and tow someone "lifeless" a certain distance and perform resuscitation efforts. After the bronze pin the silver and gold pins required more demanding criteria. I qualified first for the bronze and then the silver emblem.

1. S.A Para-Military   2. HJ Shooting Badge   3. HJ cap emblem
4. NSDAP Membership Party lapel   5. HJ uniform patch
6. Men's sport badge   7. HJ Accomplishment badge / silver

In later years the HJ offered shooting practice. The gun was a .22 rifle and targets were the same as internationally used. Before being allowed to start shooting an adult gave us thorough instruction in safety rules and weapon handling. Although I do not recall what the requirement was I was able to get the badge.

Much later when I was close to 18 years of age I fulfilled all requirements for the Maenner Sport Abzeichen. (men's sports badge) which were all of the field and track type. For the Maenner Sport Badge my last event was swimming, the goal was a 1,000 meter swim in 24 minutes. That was normally easy for me to do, however, in late 1942, the swimming facility was about to close up for the winter, and the water was a bit cool. In addition I had to run 3,000 meters the day before, a requirement for the SA Wehrsportabzeichen which caused me to have sore leg muscles.

Well, I thought, I'm a hard guy, so off I went. After a couple of hundred yards I had a cramp in one leg. Shall I quit now? No way! It slowed me down but I could continue. Then I got a cramp in one of my toes of the other leg. This swim really was not very comfortable, but I pulled myself together and continued. I finished this swim just under the wire at 23:30 minutes. Well that was the last test to qualify for the Maenner Sport Abzeichen, with that I had fulfilled all the requirements.

In the last class in high school I had a Biology and Chemistry teacher who was a big-wig in the N S party. None of us was a member of the SA, but with his influence, several of my friends and I qualified in all events and received the SA Wehrsportabzeichen (military pentathlon badge).

Back to Travemuende. Whenever we needed some groceries I hopped on my bicycle and rode the half mile to the store and did the shopping as ordered. Once, on a late afternoon, it was during winter time, there were about 6 inches of snow on the ground, and it was dark already, I had the choice to ride my bicycle on the street which had not been cleared and automobiles left nasty ruts, or ride on the sidewalk where a snow plough made it easy to pedal along. Of course it was "verboten" to ride a bicycle on the sidewalk. As nobody seemed to be walking there I took the easier road.

Everything went fine, I bought the groceries and was on my return trip when near a house perhaps 30 feet away from the sidewalk a policeman with a blue flashlight blinked at me and shouted: "Halt!". I thought, "By the time he gets over to the sidewalk, I'll be long gone;" so I stepped on it.

Unfortunately there was a second policeman who had just checked the next house for proper blackout and had returned to the sidewalk. Suddenly, he appeared in the very dim shine of my headlight. As it sometimes happens when two people walk towards each other and both move to one side and then both move to the other side until they bump into each other, as the policemen and I tried to avoid each other, we both ended up in the snow. He was furious.

After I had received an appropriate lecture from both policemen, all information was recorded on a citation slip, I gathered my groceries and went home. A 5 Mark fine came to us by mail a few days later. I had reported the incident at home, so father knew about it. That was it!.

Memel

In 1941 my beautiful life in Travemuende came to an end. My father had accepted a job in Memel. Memel was a German city located at the northernmost corner of East Prussia. After WW 1 the city and the Memel territory was cut off from Germany per the Versailles Peace Treaty and made a Free State similar to Danzig which the Lithuanians then exploited to incorporate into Lithuania. When the war with Poland had come to an end Memel was returned to Germany in exchange for free Lithuanian use of the port. .

There was one shipyard in Memel and that was contracted to perform certain repair or alterations work on German Navy ships, which were operating in the Baltic Sea. Father was the representative who had to authorize, assign and accept the tasks for the German Department of the Navy.

Where did that leave me? My ideal time with my dear friends in Travemuende had to come to an end. I was devastated! I pleaded with father to let me stay in Travemuende and continue school there; perhaps I could live with one of my buddies? All to no avail! I had to resign myself and move to Memel. It was a very sad farewell.

It was a long journey, some 1,000 Km of a boring railroad trip. It was bad weather, rainy and windy when I arrived in Memel. Everything looked drab and unfriendly to me. We settled down in an apartment and I went to school with 25 other boys. The classes were similar to my previous ones, but in English I was suddenly better than the class average. Not knowing anybody in Memel and not even having any interest to meet someone I spent the first weeks pretty much to myself.

I liked to take the ferryboat to the peninsular Kurische Nehrung. From the landing to the Baltic Sea side of the peninsular it was a 20-minute walk through a beautiful pine forest. One day as I strolled along, minding my own business I suddenly got a frightening shock. I had not seen it before and here just a few yards away a huge animal rose to its feet; an elk as big as a horse. When I had recovered and hidden behind a tree, the elk majestically walked away. What a relief! I found out later that elks over there are usually harmless, except during mating season, when they might get aggressive.

I liked to walk along the seashore of the Baltic Sea, sometimes for miles Occasionally the surf was quite high and the thundering waves and the mist from the ocean spray, were quite enjoyable. One day, I saw on the beach what looked like a yellowish little pebble. I found out that this was Bernstein (Amber). East Prussia is the only place in the world where amber is found and a little further south it is even mined. Amber is the sap from trees which during a sudden ice-age-change millions of years ago were submerged in the Baltic Sea and became petrified. Some amber pieces even had little bugs or insects entrapped, which then became very valuable.

One day the whaling ship "Walter Rau" which had been requisitioned by the German Navy was in port for some work to be performed by the Memel shipyard. When there was an opportunity my father asked me if I'd like to get a guided tour of the ship. Of course I would like to!

During peace time the Walter Rau, we were told, would sail accompanied by several whale-catching ships into the South Atlantic. The little ships brought the whales they had caught to the mother ship. The whale was pulled over a ramp at the stern end to the deck. A crew with spiked boots walked on the wooden deck and cut the blubber in chunks and dropped them through shafts directly into the vats of the factory below. The blubber was converted into oil and the meat was cooked and canned. The bones were ground and pulverized. Nothing of the whole whale was wasted. When empty, the fuel tanks became storage tanks for the whale-oil. The ship had the most modern navigational equipment and ocean-depth-measuring equipment. Crews had the opportunity to make telephone calls home. All-in-all, it was for me a very interesting, a very impressive tour.

The former cruise ship Odin with Captain Luedke came to port. For me it was interesting to listen to the "old salt's" stories. Captain Luedke told how he had a ship which had many Jewish passengers on board who wanted to emigrate to Palestine. Some asked him, "Why is Hitler so stupid, why does he not accept money from us and thereby assures his safety in the future?"

**The Navy ship
"Odin"**

The Odin was used for living quarters for Navy personnel. Several times when I picked up Father after work, I had an opportunity to meet some sailors and officers who were stationed on PT boats, submarines and destroyers. One day I was asked if I would like to go out on a destroyer that night. The assignment was submarine torpedo-shooting practice. Well, of course, with pleasure, I said. I reported around 11 pm to the designated destroyer. The ship was really old, it had been in service around WWI, but for a torpedo-catching job she was still good enough. We steamed into the pitch black Baltic Sea.

I was told that I could go wherever I wanted to. That was great! I went into the engine room and was impressed by all the levers and wheels and dials. The noise was considerable. I also went to the bridge and observed the operation. A target ship was steering an irregular course, following her were two or three destroyers. Out there, somewhere in the dark night submerged, were several submarines waiting for an opportunity to fire a torpedo at the target ship.

When a torpedo was launched by a sub it was set at a depth to pass under the target ship and then come up to the surface. The first destroyer in line following the target ship would then steer towards port and search for the torpedo, which by then was floating vertically in the water and only a little bit of the head would stick out. In order to see the torpedo at night a chemical started to burst into flames the moment it came out of the water. Now all that had to be done was to lift it out of the water and bring it aboard. The destroyer would then fall in line behind the other destroyers and wait for another torpedo to be retrieved.

One place on board ship that I liked to visit very much was the galley, because the cook was a very friendly man and had good things for me to eat. In the early morning hours we returned to port. This was a very exciting and interesting adventure for me. Which I still can recall vividly.

War starts with Russia

Suddenly in June 1941, an immense military build up was apparent in Memel. We were amazed how many horse and wagon teams, loaded with fodder or military equipment rolled through the streets. Obviously there was something in the making, but what? Perhaps a military manoeuvre? It seemed like a last-minute, helter-skelter action of sorts. A few days later the radio broadcast that German troops had marched against Soviet-Russia, captured a huge number of prisoners and seized a fantastic large amount of military equipment. Were the Russians having a picnic so close to the Russian / German border?

It was not until many years later that I read what the Russian general staff officer Victor Suvorov had found in his research (his book: "Stalin's Prevented First Blow"). His information leads to the conclusion that Stalin was planning to attack Germany. This pre-emptive German strike foiled Stalin's plans and stopped the grand invasion plan by the Soviets of all of Europe. This was of course one goal towards the long-range plan the "Communist World Revolution" which meant the entire world, naturally.

A short time after the beginning of combat a few miles to the east an "Air Raid" alarm was sounded. A small formation of Soviet twin engine bombers flew over the city and dropped bombs indiscriminately into the city. No military targets or the shipyard were hit--only some apartment buildings in town.

A group of French prisoners of war who were heading back to their barracks had some casualties when a bomb exploded near where they were walking. I wonder if were not perhaps later, after the war, reported as "murdered by the Germans".

Mecklenburgische Annenschule

Father was reassigned to be the Department of German Navy representative in Toulon, France. A moving van came and transported our whole household from Memel to Hamburg, Zimmerstrasse 3. This was the fourth move since we had left Neustrelitz. Apparently it was difficult to find a high school that I could get my Abitur diploma in Hamburg so I was enrolled in the Mecklenburgische Annenschule, a boarding school in the city of Wismar. Wouldn't you know it, this school had in their curriculum Latin, for my grade that had been taught for two years already! Like a few years earlier in Travemuende where I had to catch up with English I now had to struggle with Latin to get to the level of the class.

The school buildings were idyllically located, near a nice little lake and surrounded by lots of greenery. Four boys had one living room and one bedroom together. This was a private school, so we wore civilian clothes only, no uniforms. Only whenever we had HJ duty we had to put on a uniform. Most of the boys came from rural areas of Mecklenburg where there was no high school nearby for the boys to attend.

Wake up during the week was usually around 06:30. After roll call, where we were stood there shivering in the cold air of the gigantic hall-way downstairs, we ran once round the lake for our morning exercise.

If it was warm or cold, if it was windy or snowing, we ran; only when it rained we did not have to go. After a shower and breakfast, we were ready for classes.

By the way, after the whistle had awakened us from our slumber the teacher on duty inspected each room to make sure that everybody was healthy and awake. In my room one of the boys had a phonograph and a stack of records. Each day one of us had the duty to wind the machine up and put a record on. I remember one American record in particular which was called "Flat Foot Floozy" or something like that. We all thought it was neat, just cool, but when the teacher came to inspect, the first thing he would say was: "Turn this stupid music off!" Which we did of course, only to start it again the moment the teacher had left.

Subjects every boy in the school, had to take were: German, English, Latin, Biology, Chemistry, Physics, Geometry, Algebra, Geography, Music, Art and Sport. During the winter months, sports classes were held in the large gymnasium. .

When the younger sports teacher was drafted into the military our old Latin teacher, who was considerably older, had to fill in for him. One day we were all more or less unable to do anything right on the 8-ft high horizontal bar when he became irritated so much that he said: "Here, hold my jacket" then he pulled his pocket watch out of his vest, "Hold this, too!"; with that he leaped up to the horizontal bar, swung back and forth a couple of times and wham! he made a "giant" which seemed to him effort-less. Gee whizz ! We were impressed! This "old man" (probably 60 years old) from then on really had our respect.

Our Biology teacher, whom I mentioned before, had a high position in the NS party. He was the one who arranged it so we could qualify for the Sports Badge without being in the SA. He seemed to be very tolerant, because when we made a remark criticizing something of the National Socialist System he listened, smiled and gave us a logical answer. When we became aware that he could be distracted by politics and led away from the school subjects, we were encouraged to ask more questions. My buddy Rudolf Seiderer, at times, was outright disrespectful and I thought he should better slow down a bit or our teacher will get mad. But, nothing like that happened - he just defended National Socialism very calmly and very intelligently.

After the war, anti-German propaganda proclaimed that under Hitler, the German youth was brainwashed in the feeling and belief that Germans are a "Master Race". However, neither our NS party official Biology teacher, who perhaps could have been motivated to impress on us thoughts like that, nor any other teacher during my school years in Germany ever taught us such things.

One night, British bombers attacked the "open city" of Rostock, not the Heinkel aircraft factory a few miles from Rostock. Next morning, my class of about twenty teenagers went by train to Rostock to help in salvage operations. From the distance we could already see huge trails of smoke over the city. A truck took me and a group of boys into the city. It was a windy day and the closer we came to our target the more dust and smoke was in the air.

In a street which looked pretty desolate, we stopped in front of an apartment house, which was still burning except for the ground floor apartment. Our task was to move everything we could, furniture, dishes, bedding, etc., from the apartment onto the truck. We were all strong boys and willing to help salvage whatever we could, so the truck filled up quickly. It was high time we got out of there, because the fire which was still smoldering from the four-story apartment building was then lying on the ceiling of the ground floor apartment in which we were working. The white ceiling had already turned brown and it felt like being in a baking oven.

As we were preparing to leave, one particularly slow friend held us up; we climbed on the back of the truck, shouted for him to hurry, and waited. The next house down the street also four-stories high was totally burnt out, only the rear wall of bricks of the building was still standing. It seemed that every gust of wind made the wall sway. Then we saw three men on the street coming towards us. They were about 50 yards away from us when suddenly that huge wall toppled over and completely buried the three men under a high pile of bricks.

Immediately we jumped off the truck and wanted to run over and dig the men out, however, our leader shouted "NO"! The men could not have survived and another wall was dangerously close to collapsing, too. We realized how lucky we were, we certainly had a guardian angel watching over us; had we pulled out just a few seconds sooner, we would have been under tons of bricks. At another salvage mission we were to see if there was anything useful left in a burnt-out food and vegetable store. This single story building was totally destroyed. As we were poking around in the ashes we noticed some condensed milk cans stacked up three feet high. The heat had boiled the milk and the top layer of cans had exploded. The 4th or 5th layer of cans below, however, had not exploded. At the bottom, the milk was OK. In another corner of the store there were five gallon buckets of jam. The same was true here as with the milk. The bottom layers of the stacked-up buckets were perfectly good. We were able to salvage a lot of foodstuff under mountains of ashes and debris.

Around the year 1943, boys from our school were assigned to railroad protection. I had already left the school when the 16 and 17-year-old ones were trained to operate an anti-aircraft machine gun. All trains in Germany especially during the last years of the war were targets for low-flying Allied aircraft.

To give the trains some protection, a flatbed railroad car was hooked to the last wagon. On that flatbed a quadruple 20 mm gun was installed, which was manned by the boys. They probably saved a few people's lives, because enemy aircraft very much respected these anti-aircraft defence systems.

Vierlings flak aboard a German train.

Father once sent me a letter, which oddly enough had on each page a large hole. He explained it: low flying enemy aircraft attacked the train he was riding in. The train immediately stopped and everybody looked for cover in a ditch nearby. A machine-gun bullet had gone through his suitcase and the writing paper inside thankfully nobody was killed. Unfortunately some Allied aircraft pilots found great pleasure in using a farmer plowing a field with his oxen's for target practice. On a wide-open meadow in the Bavarian Alps I later saw a sign "In memory of" which the family placed on the spot where such a "hero" pilot killed a woman with her little daughter pedalling with their bicycle on the dirt road five days before the end of the war.

"In silent memory of Mrs. Elisabeth Schwink and her daughter Ruth who lost their lives at this location on May 3rd 1945 as victims of war. Forgive us our sins as we forgive those who sin against us"

Volunteer Luftwaffe

Late in 1942 I knew that after graduation at the beginning of 1943 I would be drafted. As a "seasoned" glider pilot in the Flieger HJ, after all I had already a handful of take offs in a SG 38. I, of course applied to the Luftwaffe for an assignment as a pilot. It did not take long and I received a reply. The letter informed me that I had to report to the Luftwaffe test centre in Hanover for examination, tests and psychological evaluation; a free railroad ticket was included. Great! I was thrilled! Although a little bit apprehensive what was expected? Would I pass the tests? I did not have the faintest idea what those tests consisted of and there was no one that I could ask.

When I arrived at the test centre there were some 15 other boys with me in my group who all wanted to become pilots. It started with a thorough physical examination. Nobody was told the results except the ones who were found to be colour blind. For them a pilot assignment was immediately terminated; however, they could enlist in the Luftwaffe ground forces, I did not have an eye problem.

Then there were endurance tests, like climbing up a 8-foot-high wall with some weight strapped to the back at least 10 times, or tests of courage like jumping from a high horizontal bar with a squat vault or straddling a vault, etc, and of course a number of written and oral examinations. A brief speech, a quick picture of my group, and off we went. I had the feeling that I probably did not fare too badly, but went home with great anxiety and full of wishful thinking.

Applicants at the Luftwaffe Officer Acceptance test Centre in Hanover

I thought to myself: "Keep your fingers crossed!" while school continued as usual. Every day I anxiously looked forward to the mail delivery. No letter telling me that I had been accepted or rejected! Then one day a very official looking letter from the Wehrbezirkskommando (draft board) arrived.

Surely this must be the notification that I should report at a Luftwaffe base. However, I was totally shocked when instead there was a draft notice: "You are to report at the Wehrbezirkskommando for induction into the heavy field artillery of the army". Now what? Did the Luftwaffe reject me? That most certainly was not what I had expected. I was pretty contrite.

About a week later another letter arrived this one from the Luftwaffe. Hurriedly I read the words until I came to the: "You are accepted!" Hurray! ,Hurray! The next day I went back to the draft board with a feeling of great satisfaction and presented my letter from the Luftwaffe. My file was pulled and my draft notice to the Army was filed in the waste paper basket.

At the beginning of 1943 there was a brief ceremony at our school, the Director gave a short speech, wished all of us well and handed us our Abitur graduation diploma. The Abitur was a requirement for an active officer career in the Luftwaffe, so now I was all set. Shortly thereafter, I received an order to report at the Luftwaffe base at Oschatz in Saxony for basic training.

Boot camp at Luftwaffe Airbase Oschatz

As I was passing the time until the departure of my connecting train in Leipzig, I spotted a bookstand. A little book caught my eye, the title was "Palmstroem als Flieger" (Palmstroem As A Flyer). It was a collection of verses by Christian Morgenstern, the famous German poet and writer about flying during WWI. Naturally, I had to buy it. I loved those funny poems and could not help but learning a number of them by heart. The little book accompanied me throughout the war and today I still can recite a number of the humorous verses by heart.

At the airbase Oschatz, the boot camp had a slow start. We were assigned our rooms and our bunk beds. A couple of days later we checked out our fatigues and uniforms from the quartermaster. The sergeant threw a bundle of clothing at me with a terse "They'll fit!"

However, when I tried them on I found them much too small for me. So, I had to go back and exchange them. When I said "They are too small!", he barked back at me: "What do you mean, they are too small, the Government had them made, so they are of the correct size, the problem is you are not of the right size, you are too big!" -- "Yes sir!" -- No more argument I got another set which did fit.

I packed up my civilian clothes and shipped them home. For us soldiers, postage was not required. The next few days we were still sitting around in our rooms without any assignment. I heard for the first time the saying: "Half the time of his life the soldier waits in vain!"

We all wanted to be good soldiers, so we went to work and started to polish our boots (Knobelbecher). We wanted to get them really shiny a customary spit polish, after hours of brushing with a lot of "elbow grease" and shoe polish we were really proud of our accomplishment, the Sergeant came in. One glance at our boots and he blew his top: "Are you crazy? This is sabotage, you are destroying government property." What we did not know was that the boots were soaked in whale oil to keep the leather flexible and water proof, our shine definitely was not desired, that was not allowed!. That was a lesson learned: do not do anything in the military unless you are ordered to do so.

The army had barracks that dated back before WWI but all Luftwaffen bases were built between 1934 and 1940. At Oschatz all buildings were located in a forest and attractively designed and well constructed.

In peacetime each room was laid out for 4 soldiers; now in wartime there were bunk beds so each room had 8 recruits. During my entire time in the military I never had to sleep in a large room with many other soldiers.

Finally! The daily drill started. Hour-after-hour we marched and made left turns and made right turns, about face and attention!. The drill instructors were never satisfied. During any march, short or long distance we had to learn how to sing. For the rest of my entire military life we always had to sing. Drill instructors always shouted at us but they were not allowed to touch us. If any superior wanted to close a button on a soldier's uniform or adjust the tie, he had to ask first: "May I touch you?"

The philosophy of the New Germany was to break down class and caste distinction and weld the whole nation into a conscious "Gemeinschaft"(a folk brotherhood). The German military now was more a People's Army than ever before. The old Imperial Army was a vastly different institution, made up largely of peasant boys and common lads commanded by "blue blooded" Junker squires.

However, heel clicking, keeping a good posture at all times and saluting smartly, all ranks from a corporal up were as punctilious as they ever were in the olden days.

Initially, our battalion of recruits was supposed to have our training done in France, but for whatever reason it was decided to stay at Oschatz air base. Unfortunately the kitchen facilities were not prepared to handle so many hungry soldiers.

The food was generally wholesome and good tasting but for active young men there was never enough. I was always hungry and there was no food supplement available at the base.

I was looking forward to the day when the officials felt we were able to walk and stand and salute properly in public. Finally the day was there! I went with some of my friends into town, not to a movie theater, but to a restaurant. We did not have any food ration tickets, but most restaurants usually had one dish without meat of course, but with vegetables and potatoes that did not require a ration ticket That felt good, the stomach brim full for a change.

Each recruit received a rifle, a Carbine 98K. It was impressed on us that we were to treat the weapon as if it was our "bride". "Handle it gently, keep it dry, keep it polished and never let it slip out of your hand and drop to the ground."

I really enjoyed target practice with the carbine 98K. Keeping track of the rounds fired and to have an accurate account was a major undertaking. If the number of shots fired and the ammunition on hand did not balance properly, a small panic broke out. Everything had to be precisely accounted for.

The uniforms had something not one of us had seen before "Kragenbinden". The collar of a jacket usually gets soiled first; in order to protect it a strip of white material about 1 1/2 inch wide and about 12 inches long was fastened with buttons inside the uniform collar.

Every couple of days we had to wash and scrub the Kragenbinden because spot checks were made to see if we kept them clean.

Another item new to most of us was "Fusslappen." When wearing boots we first put on our regular woollen stockings and then a piece of flannel-type material about 14 inches by 14 inches which was wrapped around the foot. That gave feet a snug fit in the boots and was very comfortable, and especially warm in the winter time. The base laundry washed our fatigues but stockings, handkerchief and Kragenbinden we had to wash ourselves. All of us had to learn how to mend the holes in our socks.

It took me some time to get used to having to wear long-john underwear, but it was ordered when we wore the blue uniform. The reason was to keep that uniform clean, as dry cleaning facilities were not available very easily in those days.

We wanted to keep our pants neat and pressed but did not have an electric iron to do it with. As we slept on straw mattresses on plank beds we learned the easy way to press the pants of the blue uniform -- which was by carefully placing them on the bunk beds wooden boards and placing the mattress that is the straw sack on top of them, then we slept on them for the whole week. When the weekend came we were sharp-looking soldiers (we thought). Well at least we had neatly pressed pants.

Part of our basic training included familiarization with intense infantry exercises in the countryside around Oschatz. We did not have any practice hand-grenades, but we wanted to surprise the "enemy" by throwing a hand grenade at him. In the forest we found some broken off branches. With a pocket knife we whittled them into the shape of a hand grenade. I don't remember if that made us win our infantry battle or not.

Infantry training with homemade hand-grenades, I am on the left

During one of those "battles", our sergeant realized that he and his team were lost. We did not come right out and make a remark, but enjoyed seeing him in his predicament. The enjoyment, however, was very short lived, because he, in still trying to find his way back to the base, ordered double time marching and finally jogging as we were supposed to be back at the airbase for lunch. I was assigned to carry a light machine gun and really had to struggle with that weight on my shoulder; and discovered it was not light at all. We made it, which was the only time ever that I was so exhausted that I was close to collapse.

Nearly all the recruits in my room got along very well. However, there was one young man who caused us some displeasure. He was a nice guy, but apparently he did not like to take a shower. After a few days he really smelt awful. We urged him to take a bath, we even pleaded with him but to no avail. So, we asked the sergeant, what can we do? The sergeant's answer was: "Give him the Holy Ghost!" What was that? We had never heard about that. He explained it to us and in the next night we sprung into action. When our "buddy" was sound asleep we jumped him, turned him on his belly, held his head down so he could not make any loud noises, pulled his pyjama pants down and gave him about half a dozens of whips on his behind with a leather belt; then we took some shoe polish and painted his behind black. That was all he needed, from then on he took his showers regularly, and everybody was happy!

It was important that every soldier had the proper haircut, so we were ordered to go to the base barber to get the standard haircut. It was not allowed to have long hair but it was also not allowed to have a butch haircut or even a shaved head. The hair had to be the length of a match stick. Of course the barber knew and would not consider special wishes anyway.

Finally after eight weeks, boot camp came to an end. Our unit company, platoon or room mates broke up and everybody went home for a brief furlough. I never saw any of them again I was the only one who was ordered to report to the LKS IV (Luftkriegsschule No 4 + Air Academy #4) located at Fuerstenfeldbruck near Munich in Bavaria.

Before we were allowed to leave the base we all were issued our "Soldbuch" (pay book / passport Identification).

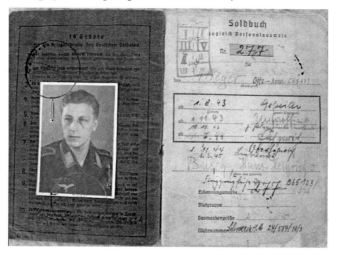

The first pages of my Soldbuch, with my photo stapled to the front

The first page that is the inside of the cover page had the "10 Commandments of the German Soldier During the Time of War". It is interesting how precisely the do's and don'ts are spelled out.

10 Gebotefuer die Kriegfuehrung des deutschen Soldaten

1. Der deutsche Soldat kaempft ritterlich fuer den Sieg seines Volkes, Grausamkeiten und nutzlose Zerstoerung sind seiner unwuerdig.

2. Der Kaempfer muss uniformiert oder mit einem besonders eingefuehrten, weithin sichtbaren Abzeichen versehen sein. Kaempfen in Zivilkleidung ohne ein solches Abzeichen ist verboten.

3. Es darf kein Gegner getoetet werden der sich ergiebt auch nicht der Freischaerler und der Spion. Diese erhalten ihre gerechte Strafe durch die Gerichte.

4. Kriegsgefangene duerfen nicht misshandelt oder beleidigt werden. Waffen Plaene und Aufzeichnungen sind abzunehmen. Von ihrer Habe darf sonst nichts weggenommen werden.

5. Dumm-Dumm Geschosse sind verboten. Geschosse duerfen auch nicht in solche umgestaltet werden.

6. Das Rote Kreuz ist unverletzlich. Verwundete Gegner sind menschlich zu behandeln. Sanitaetspersonal und Feldgeistliche duerfen in ihrer aerztlichen bzw. Seelsorgerischen Taetigkeit nicht gehindert werden.

7. Die Zivilbevoelkerung ist unverletzlich. Der Soldat darf nicht pluendern oder mutwillig zerstoeren. Geschichtliche Denkmaeler und Gebaeude, die dem Gottesdienst, der Kunst, Wissenschaft oder der Wohltaetigkeit dienen, sind besonders zu achten. Natural und Dienstleistungen von der Bevoelkerung duerfen nur auf Befehl von Vorgesetzten gegen Entschaedigung beansprucht werden.

8. Neutrales Gebiet darf weder durch Betreten oder Ueberfliegen noch Beschiessen in die Kampfhandlungen einbezogen werden.

9. Geraet ein deutscher Soldat in Gefangenschaft, so muss er auf Befragen seinen Namen und Dienstgrad angeben. Unter keinen Umstaenden darf er ueber Zugehoerigkeit zu seinem Truppenteil und ueber militaerische, politische und wirtschaftliche Verhaeltnisse auf der deutschen Seite aussagen. Weder durch Versprechungen noch durch Drohungen darf er sich dazu verleiten lassen.

10. Zuwiderhandlungen gegen die vorstehenden Befehle in Dienstsachen sind strafbar. Verstoesse des Feindes gegen die unter 1 - 8 angefuehrten Grundsaetze sind zu melden. Vergeltungsmassregeln sind nur auf Befehl der hoeheren Truppenfuehrung zulaessig.

Translation of the Ten Commandments
For German Soldiers in Time of war

1. The German soldier fights chivalrously for the victory of his people, he is unworthy of cruelties and unnecessary destruction.

2. The combatant has to be in uniform or must be wearing a special publicized insignia which can be recognized from far away. Fighting in civilian clothes without such an insignia is prohibited.

3. No enemy who surrenders shall be killed, this includes terrorists and spies, they will receive their punishment in due process of law.

4. Prisoners of war shall not be mistreated or offended. Weapons, plans and documents are to be confiscated. Personal property shall not be taken

from them.

5. Dum-Dum ammunition is prohibited. It is also prohibited to modify projectiles to make them into Dum-Dum projectiles.

6. The Red Cross is inviolable. Wounded enemy soldiers are to be treated humanly. Members of the medical corps and chaplains shall not be hindered in the performance of their medical or clerical activities.

7. Civilians are unassailable. The soldier is not allowed to plunder or destroy wantonly. Historical monuments and buildings used for religious services, for art, science and charitable functions are to be respected. Payments in kind and services from the population are only allowed if so ordered by superiors and against compensation.

8. Neutral territory may not be drawn into war action by walking into it, flying over it or shooting at it.

9. If a German soldier becomes a prisoner of war he must if asked state his name and rank. Under no circumstances is he allowed to make statements about the military unit he belongs to and about military, political and economic conditions on the German side. Neither promises nor threats may alter his position.

10. Violations of the above orders are punishable. Violations by the enemy of #1 through #8 are to be reported. Retaliatory actions are only permissible if so ordered by the high command.

[English translation by Hans Busch]

This little booklet, called Soldbuch was easy to carry in a pocket, about the size of today's American passport, contained all essential information, not only to identify the soldier and the unit he was attached to, but also a complete record of all other personal details:

       Page 1. 10 Commandments
       Page 2. Dates of promotions
       Page 3. Soldier's physical description
       Page 4. Promotions / units signed by authority
       Page 5. Listing of military units assigned to

Luftkriegsschule LKS IV, Fuerstenfeldbruck Bavaria

Full of enthusiasm and with great expectations to immediately start flight training I reported in May 1943 as ordered at the Luftkriegsschule IV. This Fuerstenfeldbruck Air Academy was constructed 1935/36 with the use of top quality material and superb architectural design fitting beautifully into the Bavarian countryside.

It was an expensive project at that time at a cost of 35 million Reichsmark. (Americans later compared the base with the US Randolph Field). I was very much impressed how beautiful clean and neat everything looked. It was now 1943, 4 years of war and not a single bomb had been dropped on the base yet.

The soldier at the gate directed me to the "Kilometerbau". A building one kilometre long, in which among others our unit was housed. The first time we were all assembled, perhaps about 240 young soldiers one of the permanent staff non-commissioned officers barked at me: "You attracted my attention before you even got here!" "Jawoll, Herr Unteroffizier"! (Yes sir!) It took me some time to realize what was serious and what was BS.

Our anxious questions "When do we start flying?" were usually answered with some ridiculous statement. Instead, we were informed that we were now part of "Vorfliegerischer Lehrgang". (Pre-flight training course) under the command of Capt. Grass. Soon we only referred to it as "Circus Grass". It was a disappointment when we realized that flying was not part of this pre-flight training program. From the very beginning we became aware that we really had to pull ourselves together so we would not get washed out before we even had a chance to sit in an aircraft. Military discipline and military drill were the most important subjects here.

The Vorfliegerische Lehrgang was composed of units which were named simply Aufsicht "A" (Unit Anton), "B" (Bertha), "C" (Caesar), etc., with each unit of approximately 40 soldiers (all airman basic). I was assigned to Aufsicht Caesar. If I had thought that I had been through enough military drill activity when I left Oschatz boot camp, I was totally mistaken.

"Circus Grass" was military drill to the umpteenth power of drill compared with Oschatz. However; so far no flight activity at all. The soldiers came from all parts of Germany and most of them were sadly aware how many civilians had been killed by Allied air raids in their city. We all had pretty much the same opinion and that was: "to hell with all this military activity, let's get on with our flight training so we may help in the protection of the open German cities!". For us it was most important to keep our mouth shut, do everything to full satisfaction of Cpt. Grass and just stick with it. Our daily routine was:

Very early wake-up, shave, shower, get dressed and make the bed, all very hurriedly. Making the bed was an art we had to learn first. A linen sheet and a woollen blanket had to be arranged in such a way, that the bed was absolutely straight and level without wrinkles. The head end had to have a precise vertical step about 4 inches high and then level again over the head pillow. It was not allowed to use any devices like a piece of cardboard or wood to produce this step, that would have been too simple. By squeezing the linen sheet with the fingers, a sharp crease could be produced with a little bit of practice, but without a hot flat iron how do we get the wrinkles out? We found a way. When the bed was made we ran to the wash room down the hall, took a mouthful of water, ran back to the bed and spray-vaporized the water over the linen. When the spray of water had evaporated the wrinkles had disappeared.

We were told the story about a drill instructor at a boot camp who looked cross-eyed. He walked up to a line up of soldiers and asked the first one: "What is your name?" The soldier standing next to the soldier he wanted to ask replied: "My name is Mueller, Sir!" The D.I. looked at him and barked: "I did not ask you!" where upon the third soldier in line said: "I did not say anything, Sir!"

Singing while marching was an absolute must, whether a very short march to the mess hall for breakfast or a lengthy march to the shooting range, we always had to sing. The one in charge of the Aufsicht would command: "Ein Lied"! (a song!) The first three in the marching unit had to come up with the title of a song quickly, which was passed to the rear from row to row until the last soldier heard it and would loudly shout:

"Lied durch!" (Song through!)

The first three would then shout in cadence with the march: "Drei - vier!" (Three - four!") which was the command for the whole unit to start singing at once. Our repertoire was already quite extensive, as we all had sung in school in the Scharnhorst and in the HJ service; therefore most of us knew the same songs. We did not sing any political songs but folk songs and now that we were soldiers, songs about leaving the sweetheart behind or conning the innkeeper out of another beer. (The type of songs were similar to the British "I Got Sixpence" or "It's a Long Way to Tipperary") Usually we sang pretty well, but if it did not sound too good we were ordered to run and who wanted to do that? So we really tried to sing good and loud.

Our days were filled with, what we thought unnecessary gobbledygook -- we wanted to fly!!! But flying was not on the agenda for a long time yet. We found it strange that a Captain was standing around inconspicuously just watching, whether in a classroom during a lecture, in the mess hall eating a meal, marching or drilling. He never spoke to anyone. Apparently he was observing each one of us at all times. We called him the "Seelenspion!" ("Soul Spy"). It was rumoured that he knew every one of us by name. I don't know if his observations were important to our general evaluation, but we did not want to take any chances and made sure that we appeared especially alert and active when we realized he was around.

At one time, I think they wanted to test our endurance; we were ordered to fall out. We were surprised, because it was raining cats and dogs. Well, an order is an order, here we assembled in fatigues with helmet, gas mask, and rifle. For about two hours we marched, we ran, we crawled through the mud and we stood at attention.

We were soaked by the rain on the outside and thoroughly wet from perspiration in our underwear. When after an especially exhaustive run we were ordered to stand at attention -- we were close to giving up. After several soldiers collapsed, just keeled over; as they had passed out the "drill" came to an end. "Dismissed!" We were all so muddy, that we walked right under the shower, helmet, rifle and all, and washed the mud off.

The following day, a Saturday of course: "There had to be rifle inspection at 13:00". This way no one could go into town. After taking the rifle, the carbine 98K, completely apart and cleaning and oiling every part, we fell out for inspection. The sergeant looked at each weapon but did not even inspect it closely and declared: "This is filthy! go back, clean that thing and present it to me for inspection at 14:00". Naturally we went back to our rooms and cleaned any imaginary speck of dust that might have been left on the rifle. When at 14:00 we fell out and presented our really clean weapons to the sergeant and he again barked at us that the bore looked like an old toilet pipe, we realized that all this surely was only to harass us. We returned to our rooms, laid the rifle aside, chit chatted about anything and fell out at 15:00 as ordered to present arms. This time after not having touched the rifle, we were praised how neat it now looked, why did we not clean it like that in the first place?

One day, Aufsicht Caesar was assembled at the football field for sports activity. Capt. Grass said to one of us: "Move them out!" After the command, "Right face", we expected the command "Forward March"! however, nothing happened. Everybody stood at rigid attention, nobody would dare to turn his head to look around and see why no further order was heard. Capt. Grass walked around the rear of the unit and apparently noticed that one soldier, although he did not move his head, turned his eyes to detect what was going on in back of him. Capt. Grass noticed that. Immediately he had the Aufsicht Caesar make a, "Left face!", Soldier Bayer, step forward: "I hereby punish Soldier Bayer with a strict reprimand because while under the command "Attention" he did not keep proper eye discipline!" (This punishment was entered in his personal file). We were all flabbergasted and could not believe it!

Naturally, we tried very hard to avoid getting any sort of reprimand, we tried to keep our nose clean, the danger of getting washed out was always imminent. Then there was "room inspection." Well, we cleaned the floor, had beds neatly prepared and had the wall lockers in ship shape. However, when Captain Grass came into the room he found everything "dirty" and "disorderly". At that time, we were determined to make it impossible for him to find anything wrong in our room at the next inspection. Sleep was ordered and not sleeping at that time was considered violating an order. Nevertheless in spite of the danger we decided to take a chance and prepare our room after bed check was over so it would be immaculate for inspection. Somewhere we "acquired" some steel wool, moved all furniture to one side of the room, scrubbed the hardwood parquet floor and moved the furniture back to the other side of the room. Now, the floor was really clean. From then on, until the next inspection we did not dare to walk on the floor with our shoes or boots on. We also made sure, that the helmet on top of the locker was measured to be exactly

in the precise location on top of each locker, the same with the gas mask.
I'm sure the Capt. noticed how clean the floor was, but he had to find something at the inspection. He tried and tried, and then finally he found something that really showed how "dirty" this room was. He wiped our dust pan and the whisk broom over his white gloves and exuberantly proclaimed: "This place is Filthy!", of course again we were all flabbergasted. For the next inspection we washed the dust pan and the whisk broom thoroughly. When then the Capt. really could not find anything to complain about this time, not even dust on the angle iron of the bed frame under the mattress, he took his ornamental dagger out and poked in a crevice between the floor molding and the wall. Naturally, he found some dust! I don't think he impressed anyone of us, we just found that most ridiculous. One day when we returned to the barracks from the shooting range we were not dismissed to our rooms, instead we had to form a single file and walk past a row of tables the Capt. had set up behind the barracks. What was the reason? Throughout the barracks we had trash barrels, each marked with a label, like "Paper", "Metal", "Dust" or "Garbage". Apparently some of the trash had not been properly sorted. The Capt. saw that and had the contents dumped on the tables for us to inspect. A piece of paper was mixed in with the metal barrel or a paper clip was in the dust barrel, anyway a "terrible crime"! As punishment, we were not allowed to walk one step at normal walking speed, only running was allowed, regardless when or where. If in the middle of the night one had to go to the toilet, running was the only speed. If caught walking, the soldier was put on report and another minus point was recorded in his file. At each trash barrel a double guard with rifle had to take position 24 hours a day. (This duty was required in addition to the regular duty.) Also, no one was allowed to leave the base. After a whole month finally the Capt. seemed to be satisfied. "The sky is blue again"! he announced jovially.

Hamburg is the city where I was born. Hamburg was and still is the second largest city in Germany with 2 million people living there. The city was founded some 1,200 years ago and is called "The Gate to the World". (In 1951, Marianne and I sailed from Hamburg to America) However, back to 1943:

From July 24 1943 until August 3rd 1943, Allied terror-bombing air raids were flown day and night continuously against the people in the city of Hamburg. Some 26,000 high explosive bombs and 3 million incendiary bombs including canisters with liquid phosphorus rained down on the open city. Half of all apartments were destroyed, and 55,000 people, mainly women and children were killed, many burnt alive. Of course there were anxious times for me too – worried about what had happened at home? Finally I received a letter and found out that the apartment house we lived in miraculously was spared, our apartment was still intact but most buildings in the neighbourhood had been reduced to rubble. Our little Terrier-dog, Lumpi, became so frightened by the tremendous noise and continuous explosions that he panicked and ran away, never to be seen again. This was the most severe raid, but there were many other raids which the city had to endure.

Naturally, in our discussions, we the aspiring pilots could not understand it, we were shocked, we were appalled, how can military leaders in England and America commit such barbarism against the civilian population? Meanwhile not a single bomb had fallen on our airbase Fuerstenfeldbruck. News about these terror bombing raids against all major German cities created in each one of us a strong feeling of urgency, of a desire to get going with our training and blast the terror bombers out of the sky. But our training went on in the prescribed manner.

Flying, real flying: at least with a glider

Finally -- Aufsicht Caesar was ordered to report to the Luftwaffe base, Landsberg, on the river Lech. The most exciting news was, that we would now start flight training, not with powered aircraft yet, but with gliders. To get away from the Circus Grass, that alone was great news, and to fly gliders was just wonderful. A short train ride from Fuerstenfeldbruck to Landsberg and a march to the Luftwaffe base; we moved into our barracks and looked forward to flying.
Next morning we proceeded from our barracks to a large hanger on the fight line. We pushed a door open and surprise, surprise there it was: our aircraft a good old SG 38, the primary trainer type that some of us had a few hops with when we were still in the youth organization. We pushed and pulled the bird to the end of the runway. This aircraft too had no wheels, only a wooden skid We used a two-wheel dolly to move it around with. However, the launching of the glider was a little bit more efficient now. A motor-driven winch was placed at the west side of the field. We set up the glider starting point at the east end. We did not take off on the paved runway -- instead from the grass parallel to it. Local farmers were assigned to cut the grass and keep it short, thereby harvesting the grass as

feed for animals.

The 'luxury model' SG 38 Boot had
an enclosure around the pilot.

Now we listened to the instructions of our flight instructor. After
explaining the functions of the controls he demanded that: "First of all,
look at a point on the horizon and keep the nose of the glider heading towards it; don't deviate even a little bit, while keeping the wings level.
Don't pull back on the stick; leave it where it is; that's all" -- practically
the same words that our instructor had said to us back then in the HJ
glider flying camp. The cable from the winch was hooked up to the nose
of the aircraft and a flag signal to the winch operators gave the O K. We
followed the instructions and no one had any difficulty; neither those who
had some previous experience as well as those who did not have any. The
winch operators knew how fast to reel in the cable, just long and fast
enough to get the glider some 20 feet off the ground. Then they stopped
the winch so that the pilot had to set the aircraft gently down on the grass
with the wooden skid. The field was long enough to repeat this exercise 3
or 4 times. The aircraft and the cable then had to be pulled back to the
starting point with a clunker of an old automobile and the next student
pilot had a chance.

We all thoroughly enjoyed this great activity in the setting of the
beautiful foothills of the picturesque Bavarian countryside, snow capped
high mountains in the south and that great summertime weather of 1943.
How lucky we were! As we experienced really exciting moments which
we all shared, naturally we all became closer friends, too. That's the time
when the special friendship with Jochen, Rudi and I started, a friendship
that lasted for more than 60 years thereafter. Jochen was the one who inspired and encouraged us most when at night he took his notes that he had

written during the day at meteorology or navigation classes and other subjects and transcribed them into neat diaries. We tried to follow his good example, but for sure we envied him.

After a good many hops we were trusted to be able to take off in a very steep ascending launch. The moment the winch started pulling we pulled the stick back, the elevators responded and the aircraft shot up at a 45-degree- angle. When we had reached several hundred feet of altitude, we were to drop the nose, pull the cable release knob, and release the tow cable. Of course we had no instruments in the aircraft, so we had to watch the winch operator and wait for his signal with a flag, which then told us, "Now is the time." This, then was really flying, first a left turn, then a couple thousand feet downwind, we felt free like a bird!

After passing the take-off point I continued a short distance, made a left turn to base and another left turn to final. I had no difficulty with the aircraft or the procedure and tried really hard to set the bird down right at the starting point.

At one of those flights, I was going downwind when I saw the flight instructor give me a signal. He had told me that I should watch him and if I should see him waving circles with his signal flag, I should fly a 360-degree circle before making my final approach. Well, if he felt that I was high enough to fly a circle, so be it -- I did it -- I looked down again and I got another signal and a third one after that. Then I proceeded and made my landing. What had happened? I guess it was beginner's luck. Along my flight path there were some black-tar-roofed buildings; the sunshine apparently had heated the roof, which created an updraft of air, and that made me maintain my altitude for a while. When all of us were quite familiar with this type of flying we progressed to the next phase. The more advanced aircraft we now had to fly was the Grunau Baby, a single-seat, high-performance aircraft. With a winch we could not be brought to a sufficient altitude to stay aloft for a while, so we used tow aircraft instead. To be sure that we could stay behind a tow plane without endangering ourselves or the tow plane, we were given instruction in a two seat "Kranich" aircraft. The student pilot sat in the front seat and the instructor pilot sat in the rear seat.

From then on I had no problem with the "Kranich" or the "Grunau Baby" and performed the required number of take offs and distance flights required for the "Luftfahrerschein Kl 2". (International "C" certificate.) Learning to fly a glider stimulates the pilot's "aviator nerves" which could become very important and advantageous in the pilot's future while

A "Kranich" two-seat trainer glider. I had my first flight with an instructor in this type of glider.

flying powered aircraft. It certainly helped me several times later in my flying when I had to make a dead stick landing after my engine had quit.

When our Aufsicht Caesar marched on the base we usually sang and we sang quite well. On our way from the barracks to the mess hall we passed -- singing loud and well -- a two-story barracks. Suddenly all the windows were opened. To our greatest joy we realized that there were many Nachrichten-helferinnen (WAC's) leaning out of the windows, listening to our singing. It is not hard to imagine how much better we sang and which best sounding songs we selected from then on. We heard that at this base there were several hundred WAC's stationed and in training. Unfortunately we did not have a chance to meet them personally !

We must have really impressed some people, because one day the base commander, who heard us sing passed on to us the word that he would like for us to sing a song he had composed. It turned out that he had composed a song as a gift to his beloved wife. We should have felt honoured to be allowed to sing his song. Unfortunately we did not like the melody at all, yet we could not refuse this honour either. What could we do? Nothing. We learnt the song and sang it a few times.

At Landsberg, we noticed from time-to-time that there was a very strange noise, way up in the sky. It was a sound that none of us had ever heard before like a rushing continuous thunder. Today any child knows what a jet aircraft sounds like and what noise a propeller aircraft makes. The odd thing was, that when we looked up to where the sound came from there was nothing there. Only occasionally we detected far ahead of where the sound came from something that looked like an aircraft -- although hard to make out -- as it was very high in the sky and of a shape that nobody was familiar with. We asked our flight instructors, but they did not know anything either. It was a mystery to everybody. Little did I realize at that time that this was the last aircraft that I would fly in the Luftwaffe many moons later, the first operational jet aircraft in the world, the legendary Me 262 which at that time was in flight testing at Lagerlechfeld, an airbase some 20 Km to the west of Landsberg.

One morning at wake up time, at 06:00, the private on duty, which was one of us, was just going through the barracks blowing his whistle, when the telephone rang. It was Capt. Grass, who looked at his watch as he heard the whistle in the background and found it to be 06:02. He left a message for the private to call him back. When he did, he was informed to call him again at a given time, dressed in the blue dress uniform and the helmet on his head. During that call Capt. Grass barked at him over the telephone: "Attention!" and then punished him with a strict reprimand because he had not awakened the unit at 06:00 as ordered but instead two minutes after 06:00.

Fahnenjunker / Air Cadets

On August 1, 1943 those of us who did not get washed out completed the "Circus Grass" program. The sad thing was, that some of the very best most enthusiastic boys were washed out because of rinky-dink infractions, and not because of an inability to fly. And that at a time when the Fatherland was in desperate need of pilots! At that time we were also promoted to "Gefreiter O.A." (Private First Class and Officer Candidate) and transferred to the first Fahnenjunker (cadet) company at Fuerstenfeld-bruck. Now life really made sense to us. No more of the idiotic drills and harassing inspections. Instead , finally the beginning of flight training. Because of the flight traffic congestion at Fuerstenfeldbruck some of the students were stationed at Fuerstenfeldbruck and others were sent to the auxiliary landing field Neu Ulm, some 100 Km or so to the west located a couple hundred yards from the river Danube. That's were I began my power-flight training.

The grass landing field of this auxiliary base was large enough for our primary trainers, perhaps even for smaller twin-engine aircraft. There was a hangar for the aircraft maintenance work and the usual standard wooden barracks for us. Everything was very simple, no permanent stone buildings, no villa for the base commander, or detachment of soldiers for guard duty. It was more like a country club atmosphere and therefore very much to our liking. For flying personnel there was one nice arrangement and that was "Startverpflegung" When we were expected to fly that day, we received, one egg, 1/2 ltr (1/2 Qt) of milk, a little butter, sugar or marmalade and some cookies. For all of us who were always hungry that was a very welcome food supplement. When we had to undergo a high altitude test in a decompression chamber, one of the four of us had severe abdominal pain, so the test was broken off. Next day, we encountered the same situation. Now the Doctor who conducted the test inquired what food we had eaten that morning? Well, the regular black bread, etc. as we were not on flight status that day. He immediately gave orders to feed us Startverpflegung the next day. Result: All of us completed the test.

One other test we all had to take was the oxygen-starvation test. We had to put on an oxygen mask, sit at a table write the numbers from 1000 backwards on a sheet of paper and make notes indicating our feeling. A Doctor sat next to me and checked my heartbeat and made other notes. Breathing the air with the oxygen content of an altitude of 17,000 ft., I gradually became altitude sick due to oxygen starvation. First I did not notice that I had made mistakes in the number sequence; that is I suddenly got mixed up in a number totally out of sequence without realising it. I felt a little tingling in my fingertips but that was all. Finally after about six minutes when I passed out without realizing it, the Doctor briefly opened the oxygen valve. I took one breath and immediately I was wide-awake again. We all thought that this is a good test for all pilots who fly at higher altitudes.

Oxygen altitude test

70

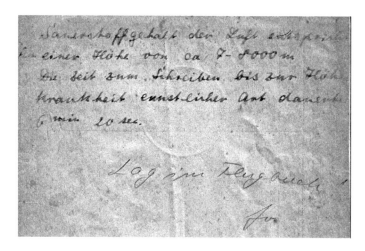

Powered Flight

At the beginning of August 1943, our Aufsicht Caesar was ordered to start the first phase of flight training at the auxiliary base at Neu-Ulm, in beautiful Bavaria. My log book says that on August 3, I had my first flight in a powered aircraft. I remember this exiting moment very well.

I climbed into a Buecker 181, (a single engine low wing 100 hp trainer, two seater, side by side seats, enclosed cockpit) with Staff Sergeant Richter as my flight instructor. This was very different from a glider. There was a very peculiar smell about the aircraft, dope, because it was fabric-covered but also the smell of hydraulic fluid, gasoline and oil. And then there were the "many" instruments -- how can anyone control all of them? In gliders we had none or just a few. Listening to the calm explanations of my flight instructor I gradually lost my tense anxiety and was able to absorb all the essentials.

Again as in glider flying, we started with rule # 1: line the aircraft up in a take off position, pick a point on the horizon, rev up the engine and keep the nose of the aircraft heading straight ahead, not the least bit of deviation to the right or to the left is allowed. And then as the aircraft accelerates, push the stick lightly forward which lifts the tail of the aircraft up; and with the increased speed pull the stick back which makes the aircraft leave the grass field and head into the sky. Staff Sergeant Richter was in command but he let me handle the controls part of the time.

The first flight lasted 14 minutes and gave me an introduction to the base location and the surrounding terrain, the city of Ulm on the other side of the Donau river, with the Ulmer Muenster built in the year 1529 which is the highest cathedral (528ft tall) in Europe, a great landmark for us beginners to always find the Neu Ulm base. The next 22 flights each lasted about 5 - 6 minutes and concentrated on flying the traffic pattern. Usually we made only 5 to 6 take offs and landings after which the next student had his turn.

The rest of our group sat in the grass and observed the friend who flew. This way we could watch what manoeuvre was not executed too good and learnt from the mistakes of others. During the waiting time we became relaxed and had a fresh attitude for the next set of flights.

Now that we were "real pilots" we also became accustomed to aviators' terminology. For example, when someone did not execute certain manoeuvres correctly or sloppy we said, he is an "Uhrmacher" (watchmaker) or if someone really did not fly good we said, "der fliegt wie eine gesengte Sau" (he flies like a singed pig). I don't know where those expressions came from but everybody used them. When a student made a sloppy landing and the aircraft made several hops before it stayed on the ground, we called that "eine Wochenlandung" (week-landing like Monday, Tuesday, Wednesday etc.) there was also the "Eier-landung" (egg-landing meaning a greased on, or perfect landing) and so on.

The Buecker 181 was an aircraft which was very easy to control. It was fully aerobatic and had inverted flight capability. Of one thing we were warned: do not let the aircraft get into a spin because it was very difficult to get it out again. To bail out is very difficult at that time or perhaps even impossible as the aircraft rotates around the vertical axis the pilot is glued into his seat with the force of 7 to 9 G's.

The Buecker Bue 181
Bestmann Trainer made by Buecker Aircraft Co. Engine: 105 hp
Weight: 1,600 lb Max speed 215 km/h Range: 800 km Crew: 2

Five days later I was given an introduction to certain flight dangers and emergency landing procedures. For example, if you are flying cross country and have power failure look for a field, an unobstructed flat terrain, try to land into the wind, a dust cloud from a ploughing farmer or the smoke on the roof of a farm house will tell the wind direction as will a herd of grazing cows lined up with the wind.

Now I was considered to be ready to fly with Oberfeldwebel Barry (Master Sergeant Barry) the group's head-flight instructor and prove to him that I was able to handle the aircraft.   After a check ride with him I was signed off to fly solo. Hurray!

I had made 25 take-offs and landings with my flight instructor, I had logged at that time a total of 2 hours and 57 minutes in a powered aircraft.   I was very happy. Now I was really on my way to becoming a pilot. In addition to our flight activity -- which we all thoroughly enjoyed -- we had to attend a lot of classes on Meteorology, Aircraft and Engines, Navigation and Military Communication which included Morse code transmitting and receiving.

Typical flight coverall

When I had made 42 flights with the Bue 181 I was scheduled to fly the Buecker 131. My total air time was at that time not quite 4 hrs. The aircraft was similar in size and weight to the Bue 181 but this bird was an open cockpit biplane.   In this aircraft, I had to wear not only a flight suit but also a helmet and goggles. It was like flying in WWI days. I really liked the aircraft, especially when I stuck my head out of the cockpit and the wind was hitting my cheeks. I felt like a bird high above all those earthlings. Humans looked like ants from up here, and trotting along the dusty earth down below.

Flying aerobatic manoeuvres was especially beautiful and thrilling. The controls of the Bue 131 were so light that it felt as if the stick should be handled with as much force as you would handle a raw egg. At one time my flight instructor said, "Practice a few more slow rolls!" (aileron rolls) So I went up and flew slow rolls from one end of my assigned practice area to the other end, back and forth then a chandelle or half a loop and again rolls to the left and rolls to the right. I really enjoyed myself. When I reported back to my flight instructor he growled at me, "I did not mean that you should fly rolls only, so go back up and practice the other manoeuvres, too!" "Yes sir!", and with pleasure I went up for another half hour of fun.

After about 6 hours of aerobatics flying the head flight instructor, Oberfeldwebel Barry, had to evaluate my flying. He stayed on the ground but closely observed all of my manoeuvres. Apparently he was satisfied with my performance because he wrote in my logbook that I passed the aerobatics flight test with a "plus".

I had a buddy who amazed all of us, Airman Malsch I remember was his name, he completed the prescribed number of aerobatic flights and passed the final examination; but each time after he landed he taxied the aircraft behind the hangar because he had become air sick, so he had to take a bucket of water and clean the inside of the aircraft.

One day Capt. Vester, in charge of the flight activity at Neu-Ulm, had some business to take care of at Fuerstenfeldbruck. I got an assignment: "Now let's see Private First Class Busch if you can fly me to Fuerstenfeldbruck!" Naturally, I was a bit worried, would I find Fuerstenfeldbruck without getting lost? The Capt, however, was very jovial and I lost my nervousness and concentrated on the terrain below and my map on my lap. That flight was recorded in my logbook as "Introduction to cross country flying". The Capt. was satisfied and I recorded a flight of 45 Min to Fuerstenfeldbruck and a return flight with 30 Min back to Neu Ulm in my logbook. I probably had a good tailwind.

A little story circulated about two student pilots who were lost on their first cross-country flight: They could not match the terrain below with their map. When they spotted a railroad station they decided to fly very low and try to read the name of the station. The pilot concentrated on his low flying and the observer tried to make out the name of the station. The first pass: "Did you get it"? "No, but it starts with the letter G." Both searched on their map for a railroad station with the first letter a G, but there was none. "Try to fly lower!" The next pass was a little lower. "Now, did you get it?" , "No, but the last letter is also a G of this long word". The map did not have any name like that. Now the pilot flew daredevil low. With a loud laughter the observer shouted: "I made it out, the sign says GUETERABFERTIGUNG!"   (F R E I G H T D E P O T)

In addition to flight training, we had classroom instruction in Meteorology, Navigation, and Aircraft and engines, especially whenever the weather restricted our flight activity. Those subjects were very important for our cross-country flights.   We became more and more alert to high pressure or low-pressure weather phenomena and the inherent dangers of sudden weather changes in which we had no flying experience, yet.

To give us a little more variety in flying different aircraft we now used the Klemm 35. It was a tandem seat, open cockpit, low wing aircraft. Like the others, it was fully aerobatic with extended inverted flight ability.

The Klemm 35
Trainer Made by Klemm Aircraft Co 1935 Engine 80 hp
Weight 1,150 lb Max Speed 132 mph Range 413 Miles Crew 2

After about a month in Neu Ulm we returned back to Fuerstenfeldbruck. It was customary in landing the aircraft to try to touch down in a three point attitude, that is main gear and tail wheel all at the same moment, right next to the landing cross laid out on the ground.   This landing cross consisted of two large sheets of heavy white tarpaulin about 6 ft wide and 15 ft long which had lead pellets sewn into the edges so the wind would not blow it away.   The two pieces were displayed on the ground in the shape of a large letter "T", pointing in the direction of landing.   Requirements for precision spot landings   close to the "Landekreuz" (Landing T) from overhead 180 degrees or 360 degrees gave us new challenges.

The Buecker Bue 131 primary trainer.
Made by Buecker Aircraft Co.1936 Engine 100 hp Weight 1,474 lb
Max Speed 114 mp/h Range 400 miles Ceiling 14,000 ft Crew 2

Again it was time to introduce the next aircraft to us. In September 1943 I just had made my 76th take off I sat with my flight instructor Uffz. Richter at Fuerstenfeldbruck in a W 34. This aircraft was designed and built by Junkers Aircraft in 1926. It was used as a freight and transport aircraft or could carry six passengers. Now this was a more substantial aircraft, I thought.   All the aircraft I had flown so far (Buecker 181, Buecker 131, Klemm 35, Arado 66, Fockewulf 44) had 100 - 150 Hp engines; the W 34, however, had a 660 - 700 Hp engine.   The take-off weight with about 7,000 lb was four times as heavy as the previous aircraft. I liked the feeling I had when I moved the throttle forward and the aircraft accelerated at once, quickly, which pushed me hard into the seat. In addition to the familiarisation flights, with this type of aircraft we also started our basic instrument flight training.

Hans takes command of a W.34

During our classroom instruction we already had learned all about the cockpit instruments, but to control the instruments so that the aircraft would be in the proper attitude, that was not so easy. When I thought that I had a vague idea how to keep the aircraft on course and keep it at the required altitude, Uffz Richter removed the curtain so I had outside visibility. He then directed me to fly straight and level but smack into a large cloud. I thought: "Nothing to it!", but then I was suddenly totally in the soup, white all around me. It did not take long at all and the airspeed increased. When the aircraft flies faster all I have to do is to pull back on the wheel I thought. But that increased the airspeed even more. The compass started to turn and the turn and bank indicator was all out of control while the altimeter showed that I lost altitude rapidly. I was all fouled up!

Uffz Richter knew what he was doing and had planned this demonstration very well. While I was still thinking that I was flying right side up, I already was flying inverted. Suddenly I dropped out of the cloud and saw the ground not below me, but instead above, on top of me. With visibility re-established it was no problem to get the aircraft back under control without the help of Uffz Richter. This exercise made me realize how important it is to learn to fly by instruments.

By Sept. 30, I had 10 flights in a W 34, when Uffz Richter said, "Let's go and fly the W 33." All right, off we went. There was not much difference between the W 34 and W 33, except the latter one was a bit older and not as powerful.

Junkers W. 33 light transport
Made by Junkers Aircraft Co 1926 Engine 660 hp Weight 7,056 lb
Max Speed 165 mph Range 559 Miles

We were on our 5th traffic pattern flight, had made our climbing turn and were flying downwind when suddenly, without any warning the engine quit. Silence! Was I glad that this happened to me while my flight instructor was still aboard. He right away said "I got it!" so I could let go of the controls. All I could do now was to watch the expert get the aircraft back on the ground.
He did not have many options. We were heading towards a meadow, which, was way too short with a forest at the end with tall trees.Richter did an excellent manoeuvre. He changed the direction of our aircraft descending some 45 degrees and headed straight for a road on an elevated roadbed, which ran across the meadow. As we were going too fast to

stop the aircraft before we reached the road he dropped the nose and picked up speed, then let the aircraft touch the meadow, but quickly pulled the controls back, which made the aircraft jump up again and over the road.

Unfortunately there was a small pile of gravel for road repair on the road, which the right landing gear did not clear. A loud "bang" and the gear sheared off, but we made it over the road and under telephone lines and came to a quick stop on a ploughed field. It was stupid of me to think that it would be better if I would pull my legs back from the rudder pedals to protect them in case the engine got pushed into the cockpit. The very sudden stop, however, made my legs snap forward and hit the bottom of the instrument panel. Nothing serious happened, only my shins smarted for a little while. Uffz. Richter did not have his shoulder straps tight enough and got a little bump on his forehead. That was all. The aircraft sustained 17 % damage caused by the engine malfunction. That was my first (of four) emergency landings I survived during my flying life.

In addition to the classroom instruction, especially the practical instruction in the aircraft included: instruction in cockpit emergency situations, recovery from unusual attitudes, practice of emergency landings, diving instructions, aerobatic flying, cross country flights, formation flying, spot landings, slipping, etc.

A rendezvous with Adolf Hitler, The Fuhrer

Early one morning we heard a special announcement: "The entire cadet training unit has to assemble after breakfast in dress blue uniform equipped with shaving gear and tooth brush for a march to the railroad station and a trip to somewhere unknown!" Naturally our curiosity was very high, what was the purpose, what was the destination to travel to? We asked anybody and every-body but no one had any clue, not even a vague guess.

At the Fuerstenfeldbruck railroad station we heard an announcement, a strict warning not to call anybody and not to communicate with anybody while on this travel assignment. Of course our curiosity increased yet more yet, 'Where could we possibly be going?', but nobody had any logical and plausible answer. The locomotive whistled and we started moving in an easterly direction. This special train was transporting only the soldiers from the LKS IV. After Munich the train headed north. At some little railroad station there was a stop, probably for the locomotive to take on water or coal.

One of the cadets suddenly remembered that he still had a postcard addressed to his parents in his pocket, which he had forgotten to drop in the mailbox at the base. He saw a mailbox at the platform of the station, so he quickly jumped off the train and dropped the postcard in. Unfortunately an MP (Military Police) saw that, immediately the cadet was arrested, the stationmaster had to get the mailbox opened and his postcard was retrieved. After a careful examination, I guess it was found that the message on the postcard was indeed quite harmless, so the train could continue. The cadet came very close to being court-martialed. All of this made us wonder more and more: Where are we heading and why all of the security? After Nuremberg the train went in an easterly direction. Then came Prague, in Czechoslovakia, with no end in sight. Finally, the train pulled in the main station at Breslau in Silesia. "Everybody out!" the command finally came to tell us that this was our destination, Breslau, but still no word yet why are we here in Breslau? Now we realized that we were not the only soldiers disembarking from a train, because several more trains had arrived at the same time.

It was dark and it drizzled a little as we formed marching units which instead of the customary three abreast, we were now in march columns 10 abreast, so as to be able to move so many soldiers through the city. As far as I could see there were soldiers marching through the streets of Breslau. Each unit with soldiers from an academy tried to out-perform the unit ahead and the unit behind by singing better and louder too. Many people lined the streets but still nobody knew what was this all about? Quarters had been prepared for us at some barracks at the edge of town. After an evening meal we hit the sack falling asleep -- knowing only that something important was going to happen the next day -- but what..?

Next morning we marched to a large, a huge assembly hall, the world- famous Century Hall. When seated we heard for the first time the reason for our being there. Adolf Hitler was going to speak to us. I was very fortunate, because I was given a seat in the 15th row of seats in the middle, right in front of the stage. First several Generals like Goering, Raeder, etc., gave brief introductions, and then Hitler spoke. I remembered that Hitler's speeches, which we had to listen to in school, were all very boring to me, but this was different. Hitler wanted to address the entire next generation of officers of the German military, Luftwaffe, Navy, Army and Waffen SS. In essence he stimulated and inspired us young soldiers and left a feeling in us: "Let's try harder, we will each do more as it is our duty and responsibility to save Germany". I was very much impressed and I think all of the soldiers present had similar feelings, because on our march back to the barracks and even later nobody made any negative remarks, which was normal after speeches like this. Now could understand why there was all the secrecy about this gathering. We we could imagine that if the Allied bomber command had known about this assembly, they probably would have sent a couple of thousand bombers and tried to wipe out Germany's future officer corps with one blow.

And now a twin engine aircraft

So far I had flown seven different aircraft. Light to medium / heavy straight and level, on instruments, in aerobatic manoeuvres and in forma-tion. Here now Uffz. Richter took me to a Caudron, C445 a French de-signed and built aircraft. I liked the looks of the aircraft and that it had two engines. It's uniqueness was that the propellers were counter rotating; therefore I felt no torque when I lifted the tail of the aircraft during take off. It still had a tail wheel like all other aircraft at that time, but it had a retractable landing gear. The aircraft was a pleasure to fly; however, the engines were a bit of a problem at times.

A Luftwaffe Caudron 445 that belly-landed.
Trainer made by Caudron Aircraft Co. in France

My buddy Haenschen Jaeschke and I were assigned to fly with a radio operator from Fuerstenfeldbruck to Nuremberg, Regensburg and back. The weather was not too bad, a broken layer of clouds was just above our assigned flight altitude. We were right on course, but here and there we had to fly around some lower clouds. We had flown about one hour when both engines lost power. Fortunately we were close to the air base of Ansbach and right away set course to land there. We had no communication with the base, but felt that we had to get down somewhere. So the base was the best place. However, as we approached the field they fired a red flare. That was an order: "Do not land!". We understood that, but what could we do? We just continued our approach. Immediately several more red flares were fired. We landed with no difficulty and were able to park the aircraft at the flight line. As we climbed out of our aircraft, we did not even have a chance to explain anything. The officer on duty, with a red face and highly excited started yelling.
"This field is the base of a fighter unit which is flying missions in defence of the Reich – the grass is muddy from the recent rains – we have no paved runway - therefore we can not allow any other aircraft to use the field - period!" When finally we were allowed to speak he accepted our decision as an emergency situation. We then turned the aircraft over to the ground crew to fix it, called Fuerstenfeldbruck and reported our dilemma, ate dinner and went into town to a movie theatre. Next day: the aircraft was not ready yet so we enjoyed the leisure time, the food and the movie theatre. Next day: the aircraft is ready but the weather was lousy, maybe tomorrow it would be better. It wasn't and it looked as if the weather would keep us there for a few more days. Then came a message from

Fuerstenfeldbruck: "Grab your parachutes and come home by railroad!"

First we thought that order was stupid, that we had to carry the bulky parachutes with us, but then when we waited at the train station with the parachutes over our shoulders we realized how many admiring looks we received, especially from young ladies who surely thought, "Those are real pilots!"

I suppose at that time, the beginning of 1944, enemy aircraft were not in the area around Munich yet, so we could conduct the required night flying. For the citizens a total blackout was the law. We, however, needed runway lights on the ground, position lights and landing lights on the aircraft; without those, we would not have been able to fly.

One night, already close to the end of the exercise for that night, a friend didn't watch closely where he was taxiing and bumped a light post with the wingtip of his W34. The result, no major damage but still a noticeable dent. As until then we did not have any accident or damaged aircraft, this would ruin our clean record. An investigation, reports and punishment would cause a major commotion. We had to find another way out. Quickly we collected a lot of cigarettes and found a mechanic who smoked and could do the repair work during the night. It worked out beautifully; the next morning, the aircraft was parked at the flight line, ready to go, no blemish.

My favoured Neu Ulm

October 1943 we were back in Neu Ulm. The city of Ulm had a very famous citizen a long time ago. A tailor by the name of Berblinger had the idea that he could be able to build a device with which he could fly like a bird. Well, he was so enthusiastic, that he used his sewing talent and fabricated a flying machine, well, at least a set of wings. He then went to the high shore of the Danube River on the side of the city Ulm, set up his wings and proclaimed, that he would cross the river and land on the south shore. Unfortunately his wings were not sturdy enough and he fell into the Danube. Instead of praise and admiration he had to endure lots of ridicule and laughter from the crowd. I was standing on the same spot where he had started his flight, which a bronze plaque nowadays certifies to the visitor.

I think food at Neu Ulm was always a little better than at Fuerstenfeldbruck. With one exception, that exception is the dish called "Saure Lunge" (Sour Lung) which was unknown in Northern Germany.

This dish consists of lung from beef, chopped up like hash and cooked with a shot of vinegar. This is served with noodles or potatoes. I did not like the taste at all and many other soldiers did not like it either. Because many said to the cook :"Only half a scoop!" there was always some left over. However I could ignore my dislike for Saure Lunge and was ready when the cook yelled: "Who wants some more!", because I was always hungry.

Breakfast was pretty much standard, regardless where and at which base. Usually it consisted of strictly rationed: a couple of slices of black bread (Kommisbrot) a little margarine, marmalade or artificial honey and coffee brewed from ground and roasted barley. Real coffee was practically non-existent during the war years, very little for the military and none for the civilian population. The four fruit jam was considered the cheapest on the market. That led to the joke we liked to tell imitating Hitler's voice: "For the German soldier the best is barely good enough -- therefore after an in depth study and with great and thorough determination I have decided to introduce the four fruit jam as the standard bread spread in the German military!" hurray and "Sieg Heil!"

Our cross-country flight training had one great advantage. We planned flights to small airports in southern Germany especially Bavaria and Schwabia. There are a lot of apple trees in that region and we could use the W 34 for many supplemental food roundup flights. Neither Neu Ulm nor Fuerstenfeldbruck had a paved runway. I found landing on a grass field is so much softer than on concrete. Neu Ulm had one problem and that was weather. At certain times of the year there was a persistent layer of ground fog in the Danube valley. That restricted our flight activity many times. We looked desperately up to the sky, but only grey fog, at 8 AM, 9, 10, 11. Then the sun became visible, everybody got ready with flight planning. At noon the sun was shining! The weather bureau, however, announced that the fog would move back in within an hour. No chance for a cross-country flight.

Sometimes, when it became a little colder, frost formed on the wings of the aircraft parked in the open. One day, a clear but cold day, two of the student pilots of the neighbouring unit wanted to take off with a W 34. They ignored this little bit of frost on the wings, which was hardly noticeable. In their take off they rolled and rolled but could not get airborne. Too late did they realize that the aircraft did not develop any lift. They chopped the power and slammed on the brakes, but too late. They hit some obstacles at the field and were killed. If they had fastened their seat belts and shoulder straps a little more tight they probably would have survived. I registered that as a warning: Make the straps as tight as possible (it saved my life at a later time) and have great respect for even a little bit of frost on the wings!

The "Cadet-Father" was Capt. Mahlmann, he was a real gentleman and was admired by us all. At one time he gave us some advice for our future love life. He put it this way: "There are two types of aircraft A.) the flight trainer and B.) the combat aircraft. The flight trainer is a very well maintained aircraft but it is to be used by many to learn how to fly. The combat aircraft, however, is an aircraft that is assigned to you and you only. You will become so close, so intimately familiar with this aircraft that you don't even need an instrument, you'll sense the aircraft's condition before it shows up on an instrument." "Now you see, the same is true with women, it is important for you to know what is the right women for you!"

I had a mate in my room whose name was Murr, his flight instructor had great difficulty with him when he started instrument flying. He was able to keep the altitude precisely on the mark, without deviating a bit. However, when he was told to watch the compass heading he concentrated hard on that, but lost total control of the altimeter. His flight instructor became very frustrated and did not know what to do. One Sunday afternoon we were all sitting in our room, reading, sleeping or writing letters the door opened and Capt. Mahlmann walked in. Immediately someone shouted "Achtung" (Attention). Everybody jumped to his feet, except Murr, he just sat there reading his book. The Capt. walked over to him and touched him on the shoulder. Suddenly Murr reacted and got up. It was later found that Murr could concentrate on one thing at the time and that 100% but not on something else simultaneously. That made it impossible for him to fly on instruments, he was therefore washed out.

One Sunday afternoon we were all quietly sitting in our room reading, writing or sleeping, when the door opened and Captain Mahlmann entered. He was very surprised and said that we behaved like young girls in a dormitory school and commented: "When I was a cadet we always had something going on!". With that he left and went to Ulm. This inspiration was all we needed, in no time someone had the crazy idea to go to the officers' barracks and play a trick on our Captain. The other officers were also gone, so nobody noticed it when we took all the furniture, bed , chair, table and wall locker to one of the classrooms and set everything up as if it was in his room. We then blocked the door to his room from the inside and left through the window.

When Aufsicht Dora heard what we were doing they thought that was great and so they did the same to the room of their Captain. Little did they know how their Captain would react, Captain Mahlmann came back to his room about midnight. He gave up trying to find his bed, so he just used the bed of another officer who was on leave. That was it, no fuss!

The Captain of Aufsicht Dora, however, did not think there was anything funny when he opened the door to his room and his shotgun was pointed at him with a sign "Haende hoch!" (Hands up!). He immediately ordered all cadets to fall out and very angrily demanded to know : "Who did this?" No one from our Aufsicht had anything to do with this so nobody answered. He was furious and he angrily shouted that those step forward who were responsible for that. Although only a few cadets from the Aufsicht D had anything to do with it, the entire Aufsicht made one step forward. That was the beginning of a very strenuous night. It started with a run around the airfield, but in sheepskin flight suits, and a second and third time. Now the rooms in their barrack had to be cleaned, again and again with lots of water. Aufsicht Dora did not get to bed until 5 a.m., wake up call was then as always at 6 a.m.

In the months of November and December we flew from both Fuerstenfeldbruck and Neu Ulm a lot. On the 1st of November I became Staff Sergeant and Officer candidate. On November 2nd at Fuerstenfeldbruck I climbed with Uffz Richter on board a French C445. This was the first twin-engine aircraft that I had to fly. In addition to the take off and landing practice with all of the various types of aircraft we also continued instrument flight training, cross country flights, single engine flights, night flying, aerobatic and formation flights. Whenever weather restricted our flight activity we had plenty to learn about Navigation, Aircraft and Engines, Meteorology and Communication. Pilots were supposed to be able to decipher Morse code messages and if necessary transmit in Morse code in case the radio operator was unable to do it.

During peacetime so we heard, cadets learned to drive an automobile, to ride a horse, learn to sail a sailboat and learn to dance. Now, during the war all the extracurricular activities were discontinued, only dancing instruction was still given. That was a welcome interruption of the monotonous air base life. Arrangements were made for young ladies, girls about our age to come by train from Munich and dance with us for a couple of hours every week. Afterwards, although in those days there was no danger for a young lady to walk unescorted through the forest, we enjoyed the "duty" to escort the ladies back to the train station. Lessons were also given in the fine art of etiquette. "How do I have to light my commander's cigarette; who sits down first at a party; where does the junior officer and where does the senior officer walk as they are escorting a lady, etc., etc." It was customary towards the end of the program at the academy that a formal ball would be held with cadets and their dance instruction girls and the officer-corps with their wives or sweethearts and of course the base commander with his wife. We enjoyed ourselves with our dance course girls and more or less ignored all the "old folks". It was tradition during the course of the ball that one of the cadets would very courteously request a dance with the Commandeuse, the base commander's wife. My buddy Horst Netzeband probably was one of the better dancers if not the best and was urged to take that assignment. Horst was quite nonchalant about it and walked over to the table of the Commandeuse lady and very elegantly requested the honour to have the next dance. She very graciously accepted. The music came to an end. There was a short pause and Horst got himself ready. The music started playing the next melody and Horst walked straight over to the Commandeuse. "May I have this dance, please"? The two walked over to the dance floor and started to dance. The music played a fast waltz;. Horst danced as he would have with his young dance partner. Unfortunately the Commandeuse happened to be a little corpulent and when Horst rotated round and round the centrifugal force of the Commandeuse was greater than Horsts which made her slip right out of his arms and "bang", she sat in the middle of the dance floor on her behind. Naturally Horst was very embarrassed, assisted her in getting up escorted her to her table and apologized profusely. The rest of us who observed this spectacle would have liked to laugh out loud, but we controlled ourselves kept quiet und saved our laugh for later. Horst was a dear friend with whom I shared quarters until he was killed in March of 1945.

As we were close to completing our flight activity in Neu Ulm, our Capt. Mahlmann arranged for a party in the base mess hall. First we all had dinner together and then a little "Happy Hour". It was not easy to find some brandy or for that matter any liquor, but our Capt. somehow had acquired some. As we were sitting together, chit chatting Capt. Mahlmann broke out his brandy. Apparently he had another reason to offer someone a drink and that was to see how his boys would behave after a couple of drinks. I think none of us were accustomed to consuming alcoholic beverages, as it was not easy to obtain and we were really not too interested in alcoholic beverages anyway. The Capt. had some of the boys in mind whom he wanted to observe a little more closely so he addressed the candidate with a cheerful: "To your health!" Immediately the soldier jumped to his feet lifted his glass and downed the drink. After a while the so-saluted soldier had to go back to the Capt. with a full glass and say: "I request permission to return the Captain's salute!" The Capt. jovially raised his glass and as before sipped on his drink while the soldier downed his drink "bottoms up". This made some of the otherwise somewhat timid soldiers a little more relaxed. Odenthal was one of the men Capt. Mahlmann wanted to say something or do something. Odenthal did not have any story to tell but announced that he would sing for us. Unfortunately he was not able to hold a note. As a matter of fact he sang so terribly bad that we were all roaring with laughter. To this day I don't know what became of Odenthal, did he make it through the course or did he eventually get washed out?

In December the cross-country flights became a little more challenging. The entire countryside below was white, covered with snow, and dead reckoning navigation was to be practiced very precisely. On the 23rd of December 1943, I was assigned to fly a triangular course over southern Germany and return to Fuertstenfeldbruck. The flight was no problem: I landed back at Fuersten-feldbruck just before darkness, after a flight of 540 Km in 5 hours and 25 minutes. Everything went very well. My dear friend Jochen, however, who had been given a pass to go home and visit with his family in Breslau, had a different experience.

Jochens Christmas experience (as he recorded it)

"On December 23rd after duty hours I was given a pass to go home. On the morning of that day, the clouds had broken up, Capt. Mahlmann said to me: "I know you are expecting to go home tonight, but as you can see the weather has improved considerably, so if you like to, you could still get your triangular cross country flight taken care of today." Naturally we all wanted to get all of our prescribed flights accomplished as soon as possible, so I said "Yes, Sir; gladly!" Now everything had to be arranged a bit helter-skelter. Günter Hoffmann was to be my observer / navigator. Günter had already made plans to spend Christmas with his girlfriend and their parents in Maisach (which is near Fuerstenfeldbruck).

Uffz Schulz was assigned to be our radio operator. I went to the flight control office and asked Guenter to find Schulz and get the W 34 ready. I checked the weather and planned our flight, from Fuerstenfeldbruck to Straubing, then to Nuremberg and return to Fuerstenfeldbruck. At that time I had some instrument practice flights but certainly was not qualified to fly entirely on instruments. We were instructed to turn around at once in case we should encounter clouds at our assigned altitude or lost sight of the ground. Naturally we flew through a few clouds here and there, but we maintained sight with the ground all the time. We made it to the navigation station at Straubing and thought that we would not have any problem making it on our new course to Nuremberg. Still busy with the radio fix from Straubing, we suddenly found ourselves "in the soup." We expected to have visibility again momentarily . Now I had to fly strictly on instruments. Guenter thought that we were on course to Nuremberg and would pass Regensburg a little to the north. After about 15 minutes on course heading for Nuremberg the engine quit. We had plenty of fuel supply so it could only be the typical BMW Bramo motor problem. In snowstorms or very moist clouds this engine had the tendency to lose power. Our altitude dwindled away rapidly.Our life wasn't worth a nickel anymore if we did not get visibility of the ground quickly. I thought, "The only way to save our lives now is to jump out with the parachute." So I gave the order, "Get ready to jump!" The radio operator came up to me shaking like a leaf and white as a sheet, "I have no chute!" I said to Guenter, "You jump and save your life, I can't leave the radio operator alone in the aircraft!" Guenter, however refused, "Maybe you might need me yet!" I then tried to keep the aircraft in the normal flight attitude and lose as little altitude as possible without the engine running. This was a miserable feeling to sit at the controls of that aircraft and have no way of knowing if we would hit a mountain or another obstacle at any moment. Some beautiful moments of my past life flashed into my memory and culminated in my thoughts that tomorrow, on Christmas Eve, when I was supposed to be with my dear parents they instead would receive the word that I had been killed. There was not even time enough to say a brief prayer. Suddenly Guenter grabbed the controls and without a word got the aircraft into a sharp left turn. I was shocked! "Are you crazy?" I shouted at him, "Did you see something?" At the same time I tried to get the W34 back under control. The altimeter showed that we are only 90 feet above ground, which meant the three of us would be gone in a few seconds. Suddenly Guenter shouted, "There's the earth below us!" -- at the same moment I saw ahead of us some sort of a dam, I pulled up but the aircraft was losing too much speed -- don't stall -- I pushed the controls forward: "There's water under us and ahead of us." I got the airspeed under control again. "There's a field in front of us; thank God!" I pulled the controls back some more to keep the aircraft from flipping on its back and there we sat down on a rough frozen ploughed field. After a short distance, the W 34 stopped. We three jumped out and checked to see if gas was leaking out, but everything was in order -- except the tail wheel, which had broken off.

I don't remember how the other two looked but I had cold sweat pouring off my forehead and I was trembling all over. That was my flying experience on the day before Christmas Eve around 11:30 am.
If Guenter had not jerked the controls out of my hand, we found out later, if we had maintained the heading, we would have crashed a few seconds later, on the north bank of the river Danube, a short distance from the city Woerth. When the fog lifted a little more and we had better visibility we also realized that our landing field was anything but good. Directly in line with our approach was a large pile of rocks that had been deposited there for future highway construction, so we were told. To our right, at about 150 yards away and parallel to our final approach heading, ran a high-tension power line.   To make it even more dangerous, there was a road lined with tall poplar trees, which ran towards the rock pile.   The ploughed field where we touched down was at that time lightly frozen, which made it possible for the aircraft to roll along. A little while later the ground became so soggy, that we would not have been able to make a smooth landing. Instead we most certainly would have flipped the aircraft on its back and that in all probability would have killed all three of us.

I can only faintly recollect the name of the town where our sergeant went to use the telephone to report our situation to our home base, Perhaps it was the town of Altach? Anyway, the local constable was assigned to guard our aircraft. My crew disappeared, too. The radio operator took the next available train back to Fuerstenfeldbruck and Guenter went to his girlfriend or fiancé at Maisach.   I had received the order to remain with the aircraft until the salvage crew took over; which I was told would not happen until December 24th. I went to find a place to stay that night. I was lucky and found a nice place.   I remember that the farmer's wife was very friendly; I remember also, that I had some difficulty eating the soup I was offered because both of my hands were still trembling so much that I spilled most of the soup before I could get the spoon in my mouth.   I waited there until the morning of Christmas Eve when the salvage crew arrived. With my furlough pass in my pocket I proceeded to go home. Christmas Eve, I spent at the railroad station in Nuremberg. Finally on Christmas Day I rang the doorbell at our home in Breslau, Kronprinzenstr. 76. Aunt Lore opened the door and screamed with joy: "Jochen is here!" Father and both of my sisters rushed into the hallway and hugged and kissed me. Mom, however right away asked me: "Jochen, what happened yesterday? I had a very strong feeling as if you were very close with me!" I then told my whole story. The family prayed together and thanked God for having saved me out of this terrible danger. That was Jochen's remarkable and miraculous experience, Christmas 1943.

Festtagsurlaub

I too had received a pass to go home. My Soldbuch has it stamped under Beurlaubungen (leave of absence) from Dec 24. to Dec. 30 as Festtagsurlaub, (Holiday-leave) combined with a free railroad ticket from Fuerstenfeldbruck to Hamburg, 814 Km to the north. Great! On the 24th I was on my way home. The city of Hamburg, the second largest city in Germany with nearly 2 million inhabitants, had already been severely damaged.

The most devastating aerial bombardment happened in July and August 1943 when, for 10 days in a row, Allied aircraft dropped 1,200 heavy bombs, 25,000 high explosive bombs and 3 million incendiary bombs on the city. The phenomena of a never-before-experienced firestorm of gigantic proportions caused 55,000 people killed, many of them burned alive.

Apartment blocks in Hamburg reduced to rubble piles.

I was shocked when I arrived and saw the area around the Main railroad station. Whole sections of formerly 4 - 5 story apartment buildings now looked like a moon landscape. I found it strange, that a number of German cities had been destroyed by that time and none of the Luftwaffe bases I had been stationed had any damage. Naturally I had a revolting feeling, "don't waste any time -- get going -- finish the flight education and then battle the bombers to protect the German homeland".
Streetcars, however, were functioning again after a few days. I made it to Zimmerstrasse with ease. The house we lived in miraculously was not destroyed, it was one out of only five buildings of the whole block, which still stood. Father was also able to leave his job as representative of the German navy at a French shipyard and spend a few days at home. Father, who was always outspoken and highly critical of the National Socialist system and I had a few discussions about the chance of winning the war. Naturally he was older, wiser and more experienced than I, so he had many reasons for his prediction that it would be doubtful for Germany to win this war, where I only had youthful enthusiasm as a reply. I thought at that time: "Let's win the war first and then we will throw the incapable bureaucrats out and replace them with decent, capable and honest managers." Especially after I saw the immense destruction of civilians living quarters I was anxious to complete my flight training and then do my best to stop this terror bombing.

After the war I heard the "excuse" for the Allied bombardments: "Well, the Germans started the bombing of British cities -- so the Allied forces only retaliated!" Unfortunately that is not true. British bombers started to bomb German cities in May 1940 and continued in spite of German warnings during the following months. (German aircraft only dropped bombs on the highly industrialized city of Coventry about 5 months later.)

I am certain that my father had never heard of any German war crimes or crimes committed by Germans in Germany or outside of Germany, or he certainly would have mentioned it during our discussions. He must have been in a good position to hear something, because he was assigned to several French shipyards by then. Apparently he had very good rapport with the French authorities, because when he had to assume an assignment at a different shipyard, French staff arranged a very nice farewell party with speeches and farewell-presents. Apparently the old saying, "The way you shout into the forest, is the way it will echo back to you!" still holds true. All that is necessary is that people respect each other.

The word "Concentration Camp" was not in our vocabulary at that time. Discrimination of Jews, yes, we were aware that there was some, but very little. I remember that during my last year of high school 1942 in Guestrow, I frequently saw people with a yellow star on their clothing, which Jews were obligated to wear, walking in and out of the apartment building across the street. In school or otherwise, we never discussed anything about the Jews and I never heard any lecture about anti-Semitism, from grammar school to high school. The mentality of "Herrenmenschen" (super men), that the media nowadays tells people the Germans supposedly were afflicted with, I also never heard about in my younger years. I can imagine that some simple-minded soldiers as occupier of a conquered country were conceited of "their" accomplishment and acted in an arrogant manner. There were a few and that did not only happen with some in the German military. I can remember some not-so-nice American-occupation forces soldiers after the war.

The few days of leave came to an end only too quickly. Although the railroad system had great difficulty operating and running on time because of many damages and destructions in cities I was able to catch a train back to Bavaria. It was not the most direct route, but it got me where I wanted to go. From Hamburg I caught a semi-fast train to Berlin and from there an express train to Munich. Like most trains during the war, this one too was filled to capacity. All compartments were fully occupied and in the passageway we were pressed together like sardines in a can. The steam-heating system was apparently set for full blast. After a while everybody was gasping for some fresh air. Then the train stopped somewhere at a small station for no apparent reason. In the distance we heard the rumbling of heavy anti-aircraft guns and saw the reflections on clouds of some burning city in the distance. After some other soldiers and I tried to open the window, we had pushed and pulled on the window release bar in vain, I went outside while there was a chance because the train was still standing there and I pushed against the glass from the outside while others pulled up inside. We tried and tried, but the window was stuck. One last try and -- crash-- the window broke. Now we had more than enough fresh air. I went back inside to my spot in the passageway. Because of the danger of night bombardment, trains had a total black out. I noticed that I had cut my right hand with the window glass but could not determine how much. Then one of the soldiers brought out a flashlight and then we could see that I had about a half a dozen or so-deep cuts in my hand from which the blood was pouring. Someone had a first-aid-kit with a long bandage and wrapped my hand tightly. To stop the bleeding I held my arm high above my head. Then when someone got off the train and vacated a seat in the compartment, everybody offered it to me. That was great because I could rest my arm on the windowsill and as a bonus I sat next to a very attractive girl who was also travelling to Munich.

Back at Fuerstenfeldbruck I went to the base hospital and had my hand professionally cared for. Therefore because I had some difficulty using my right hand, much to my displeasure, I could not fly for a couple of weeks. But finally then on January 14 the Doctor allowed me to fly again. I could perform another cross-country flight.

A recaptured Luftwaffe C.445, back in French service.

My Luftwaffe pilot's badge.

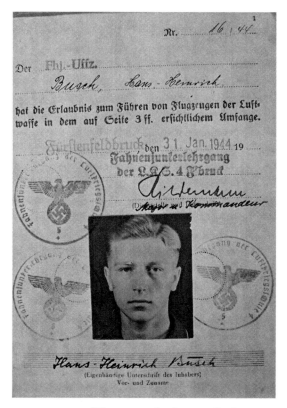

Flugzeugfuehrerschein

    I wanted to become a fighter pilot, but certainly not a bomber pilot, that was too tedious, too dogged for me. My flight instructor Uffz Richter, however, wanted to do me a favour and tried to change my mind.

95

"You are pretty good flying on instruments, why don't you instead fly destroyer type aircraft like the Me 110, Me 210 or Me 410? The missions are flexible like bomber escort, night fighter or fighter-bomber for special targets. With a fighter aircraft you have only one engine; if that conks out, down you go! A destroyer aircraft has two engines, if one fails you, there is still the other one to get you home on."
Well, he talked me into volunteering for destroyer mission assignment.

Flugzeugfuehrerschule B31/Blindflugschule 1 Brandis

We all were anxious to complete our flight training as quickly as possible in order to get to fly combat missions. Shortly after my choice was recorded and reported I received my order, "Report to Flugzeugfuehrerschule B 31 / Blind-flugschule 1 (multi-engine C-School and Instrument School) at Brandis near Leipzig!" I thought that I would go to a combat unit right away. Some disappointment! A consolation for me was that my friends Jochen and Rudi, Horst, Alex, and Klaus also received the same order. Altogether we were 20 Fahnenjunkerunteroffiziere assigned to Brandis, 10 from our former Aufsicht Caesar and 10 from Aufsicht Dora.

It took a while for the train to make it from Munich to Brandis. Again, as always, we travelled by train, no transportation was available by bus or even by truck on the Autobahn. Whenever the train stopped during our slow journey, and that happened quite frequently, we all opened the windows and looked at the traffic on the station's platform. It could be that there was an attractive girl walking along. One of my friends brought a megaphone, which he had swiped from his flight instructor. Just as the train started to move out he used the megaphone and blared out some commercials like, "Drink daily Schoenebergers fruit juice and you'll always stay healthy. All of us then made a loud gong sound "boooong". Today I think that it was a bit silly, but at that time we all had great fun with it, especially when we competed making up new commercials for the next station, some of them I'm sure were a little bit disreputable, somewhat risqué, which we only dared to say when the train started to move out.

At Brandis we were directed to a prefab, standard wooden barracks, the type we were used to at Neu-Ulm and the same kind that prisoners of war used in Germany. The first thing was to get acquainted with the base, where are the aircraft and where is the mess hall -- not necessarily in that order.

We now ate our meals at the officers' club. The food was probably the same as in the enlisted-men's mess hall with one difference; bread was in baskets on the tables and was not rationed. For most of us, me included, there was usually not enough food, and I could have eaten a lot more. When dinner was over, the base commander, Col. Aue got up; and of course everybody had to get up also. That was the time when the hungry cadets suddenly emptied all the breadbaskets. In our rooms we had iron potbelly stoves that now functioned very well as a toaster. Roasted Kommisbrot (army -black- bread) tasted pretty good especially when one is hungry and here it was a welcome food supplement for us.

But first we had to attend classes on aircraft we were about to fly. We had to learn all the idiosyncrasies of each, the hydraulic system, the fuel system, the electrical system etc., etc., and remember what to watch for and what not to do. Finally it was the end of February; I climbed aboard a Ju 86 with the marking VA+GV, together with my flight instructor, Ofw Kaufmann. Naturally I was full of expectations to fly this awfully big aircraft. The overall shape was similar to, but a little larger than the American Douglas C – 47.

My postcard to home – showing the aircraft I had just learned to fly.
Bomber Made by Junkers,2 BMW Engines 810 hp each Weight 19,078lb
Max Speed 224 mp/h Range 870 Miles Ceiling 24,610 ft. Crew 4

I had flown twin-engine aircraft before, so I thought this would be the same but just a little bigger than the C445 I had flown at Fuerstenfeldbruck. Very quickly I found out that this bird had a mind of its own. As I taxied towards the end of the runway I had a terrible time keeping the aircraft rolling along on a straight line. First it wanted to move to the right side of the taxiway, so I quickly reduced power on the left engine only now to find that the aircraft swung over to the left side. Moving the throttle forward a little bit -- nothing happened -- adding a little more power -- nothing happened -- adding a little more power yet -- suddenly engine RPM's increased a lot! With braking and alternately applying and reducing power on one or other of the engines, I zigzagged along. I felt awful and my pride was hurt, I could not even taxi the aircraft. How would I be able to fly it? Finally I was in take off position. I applied full throttle, the aircraft accelerated, I pushed the control column forward until the tail came up, concentrated on a point at the horizon, pulled the control column back and away we went. Flying the Ju 86 was no problem at all and shortly I got the hang of it taxiing on a straight line, too. After 7 take offs, 6 min. to 15 min. flights each, around the traffic pattern, I was signed off to fly solo.

The next aircraft for me to fly was the Siebel 204. This utility aircraft and multi-engine trainer was smaller than the Ju 86 but a lot more modern . The Ju 86 had been in production since 1937 and the Sie 204 entered service in 1942. With its two 600hp engines it had a maximum speed of 230 mph and an endurance of 1,118 Miles. In addition to the pilot and co-pilot it could transport 8 passengers. It was a very sturdy aircraft of which some 1200 were built primarily in Czechoslovakia and France.

My third multi-engine aircraft at Brandis was the Ju 52 tri motor. This aircraft had been in service mainly as the German Lufthansa commercial passenger aircraft. Designed in 1930 it was not changed much in its 15 years of production. Initially each engine had only 725 hp. As time went on more powerful engines were used. The Junkers factory in Dessau had a number of aircraft built by Ateliers Aeronautiques de Colombes in France and in Spain by CASA.
Nearly 5,000 were produced. Airlines around the world were using the so very reliable old "Tante Ju" (Aunt Ju) until many years after WWII. This very dependable aircraft was very easy to fly, it was really fun, too. During the landing maneuver it was important to have the aircraft at the right speed in a three-point position, a foot off the ground and then chop the power and pull the control column back. We all had no problem with it. The base commander Col Aue used to fly for Lufthansa airlines before the war. He never advanced from the Ju 52 to any other aircraft. Col. Aue was a relatively short man but had a large beer belly, that's why he was

generally referred to as "Kugelblitz" (Ball of Lightening).

The venerable Ju 52, with the familiar Edelweiss insignia.
Transport Made by Junkers Aircraft Co. 1934 Engines three BMW 725 hp each. Weight 23,146 lb Max Speed172 mp/h Range 620 Miles Ceiling 19,360 ft

Rumors had it that "Kugelblitz" came in to land with a Ju 52 and wanted to make a perfect three-point landing. At the time when he should have pulled back the controls, his belly was in the way so he announced: "I'll make a wheel landing instead" (touching the ground with the main landing gear only and then cutting power and let the tail settle down). At Brandis, Bomber wing # 1 "Hindenburg" was retraining to fly the 4-engined He 177. I had never before seen such a big aircraft.   On each wing there were two engines (2,700 hp each) coupled together which drove a huge four bladed prop. The wingspan was 103 Ft and its weight was 66,000 lbs. It still had a tail wheel, which goes to show how slow the nose wheel configuration was accepted.   The landing gear seemed to be the weakest part of the aircraft and I observed a couple of dramatic landings when the main landing gear collapsed. The crew was lucky in each case.

One day, a Heinkel Company test pilot came to Brandis to demonstrate the He 177 to pilots of KG 1. That was quite a show! Flying over the base, he wrung the aircraft out as if it was a little primary trainer. Now it was apparently time to find out how good our eyes were. Once more we had to look at a device to test our depth perception. The three dimensional pictures were shown on a screen through tightly fitting goggles.

Heinkel's huge He 177 long-range bomber.

Then the light was dimmed and more dimmed until I could barely see anything, then suddenly a very bright light was flashed in my eyes, blinding my vision completely. The time it took for me to recover and be able to see anything again was recorded. I passed that test "no problem". For another eye examination we were taken to a basement room with absolutely no light. After sitting there in total darkness for 30 minutes I had to arrange 10 chips of different fluorescent brightness in an ascending order. The number one compared to number ten was no problem but all the other ones in between took a bit of time to order accurately, but I passed this test too and received a stamp in my Soldbuch "Test for night vision passed with: excellent".

Our group 22F was busy with lots of take offs and landings; we did some of our touch-and-go flights at the auxiliary base Moertiz, nearby.
One day it was getting close to dinnertime. There was no flight instructor around anymore, but 5 or 6 of our buddies were stranded with one Ju 52. At that time it was an order that nobody of our group should fly with student pilots on board as passengers unless a flight instructor was present. Nobody wanted to be late for dinner, so everybody piled in the Ju 52, which we all had been checked out in. We were always horse playing around, so when we were heading home we suddenly all went to the rear of the aircraft. The buddy who flew, of course had to react quickly and push the controls forward. Everybody laughed – ha – ha – ha! As we were not buckled down in our seats the pilot wanted to get even with us

and suddenly "porpoised" with the aircraft, which made some buddies suddenly float on the ceiling, only to hit the floor a moment later. Normally that was quite harmless, however, just as two guys were inspecting the hole in the top of the fuselage back in the rear of the aircraft where there used to be a machine gun at one time, the bottom dropped out for the one standing under the opening. Barely was he able to grab the edge of the hole and hang on for his life's sake while his buddy clung to his legs. That all lasted only for a brief moment, but made everybody realize how close we came to losing one man without a parachute.

We did not have too much regard for "Kugelblitz." I remember one day, we were having dinner in the officers club. At the head table sat Col. Aue, seated to his right was a visiting Major and to his left a visiting Captain. A waitress served all of us the measured ration of butter, cheese and sausage on a plate. Col. Aue, as fat as he was, spoke at length about his weight problem and that he ate almost nothing and still maintained his weight. He then asked his guest to his right:, "May I offer you some of this ration?" The Major said very politely: "No, thank you very much, Sir." His guest to his left declined also. Across the table from "Kugelblitz" some of my buddies were sitting and now expecting the offer. However, "Kugelblitz" overlooked them completely instead called the waitress and said, "Save this for me for tomorrow's breakfast!"

The most powerful aircraft for me to fly now was the Junkers Ju 88. This aircraft had entered service in 1939. It was initially powered by two 1,200 Hp engines but that increased during the war. The Ju 88 A had a maximum speed of 280 mph, a range of 1,000 miles and carried some 4,000lb of bombs. The crew consisted of a pilot, navigator – bombardier, mechanic and radio operator. Taxiing was no problem at all. Take-off was most impressive. When I pushed the throttles forward and the engines with 2,400 horses pulled the aircraft forward, I felt the tremendous power that pressed me into my seat. That was a great feeling, a real thrill!

One night there was a severe terror bombing of the people of the open city of Leipzig. It must have been about 3 or 4 o'clock in the morning when our flight-training group Lehrgang 22F was awakened and ordered to fall out immediately.

Germany's best medium bomber, the Ju 88.

Made by Junkers Aircraft Co 1939 Two Jumo engines 1,200 hp each
Weight 22,800 lb Max Speed 280 mp/h Range 1,056 Miles Ceiling 26,250 ft
Bomb load 3,960 lb Crew 4

The assignment was to go by bus to Leipzig and assist citizens to rescue and salvage whatever we could before the fire would consume everything. I was assigned to work with half a dozen of my buddies in the Brandvorwerkstrasse. In that street there were many buildings consumed by fire. The four-story building I worked in first had the stairway burnt out from top to bottom. The only way to salvage anything was to climb up with a ladder and through a window into an apartment. Time was of the essence, so we threw pillows, blankets, mattresses, clothing, tablecloths, etc., out the window. There were people down on the street that knew whose items we had salvaged and who sorted everything out. Further I never heard of any stealing or looting in situations like this.

When we opened the door to another room we had to close it quickly as a large flame leaped at us. It was time to abandon this apartment. Someone, however, had the crazy idea: "Let's see what it sounds like when a piano falls from the 2nd floor to the street?" The apartment had a small balcony, maybe about two-feet by four-feet. We used the piano as a ram and broke the railing; down went the piano and made one indescribable loud bang. Ha, ha, ha! Is there anybody in the world who has heard a sound like that?

Around noontime the city suffered another air raid, which we just ignored, and which it luckily, turned out affected another part of the city anyway. The inhabitants of a large 4-story apartment building came to us and begged us to help them. An incendiary bomb had ignited the attic of the building. People poured water from buckets passed from hand-to-hand to the attic, but the very dense smoke made it impossible to get close to the fire. The fire already had burned a large hole through the attic floor, but as burning debris fell into the apartment below it was immediately extinguished. The only way to save the building was to stop the fire in the attic. Wherever we soldiers went we always carried our gas masks with us. I thought, "I can put on my gas mask and then I can get close to the fire." That surely worked, my eyes did not water and I could deliver each bucket, which people handed to me directly into the fire. We stopped the fire and saved the building. Nobody brought us anything to eat and when it was afternoon we were quite hungry. Finally the bus picked us up and we headed back to Brandis. This chucke-di chuck bus did not move very fast because it was a "Holzvergaser" bus. (Chunks of wood were burned in a stove like device; the gases from the smoldering wood were directed to the regular combustion type engine, which propelled the bus.)

Gradually I experienced severe pain in my lungs. Everybody immediately said: "Stupid -- a gas mask is good for mustard gas or blue cross gas, but not for carbon monoxide gas which is in smoke." That did not help me much. From the owner of a store some of my buddies had received , as a thank you for their help , a couple of bottles of spirits from which they offered me a drink. This helped me with my pain a little. Suddenly the bus stopped, there were not enough wood-chips left to produce the fuel for the vehicle. We were still a mile or so from our base, so we had to walk the rest of the way. The fresh cold air really made my lungs hurt. If it had not been for Jochen and Rudi I would have just as well laid down right there in the snow and rested. My buddies dragged me back to our barracks; I saw a Doctor, got some medication (no Schnapps) and recovered after a few days. Lesson learnt: gas masks are no good for fire fighting.

The preparations and classroom instructions prior to flying the Ju 88 were most extensive. When we were able to answer all questions correctly we went to a hangar where the cockpit of a Ju 88 was set up like a flight simulator. While the flight instructor observed closely we demonstrated that we could handle all operations. Loud and clear we recited step-by-step the starting of the engines, the warm up, ignition-magneto check, etc., the taxiing, take off, climbing, horizontal-flight-approach and landing. When we could do all that blindfolded, and reach for the correct knob, switch or lever, we were ready for our first flight. My flight instructor, Ofw Kaufmann, a typical Viennese, on the ground an easy-going man, but in the air very demanding, went up with me until I could satisfy him and he could trust me with this great aircraft. I thought the Ju 88 was easy to fly; it behaved, as one would expect it, not temperamental at all. Our agenda called for so many take offs and landings, cross country flights, high altitude and low level flights, formation flights and instrument approaches. During a formation flight training Jochen suddenly saw his right engine lose the propeller, it just whirled a little ahead of the aircraft and then disappeared downward. Jochen shut the engine off and made a fast return to base. The single-engine performance was not too good, as now the left engine was strained at its maximum. Jochen made it to within a few hundred yards of the runway when the left engine gave up. He had no choice but to make a belly landing (the landing gear stayed retracted) in a field. Fortunately everything went quite well, nobody got hurt; but of course the aircraft had some damage.

Ju 88 A-4 "Weisse 58" after a rather exciting 'notlandung'.

Rudi, on the other hand, also had a problem with a Ju 88 while he was on his 5th solo take off. As he was just off the ground he retracted the landing gear and boom, the right tyre blew. He realized what had happened and had to decide how to land the aircraft. As we had no voice communication with the tower -- we did not even have a radio operator on board for local touch and go flights -- he decided to shoot a flare to get the attention of his flight instructor who was observing the flights at the end of the runway. That worked very well. He then wrote a note on a slip of paper, stuffed it into the empty flare casing and while making a very low pass for the flight instructor to see his tyre; he threw his message overboard near where the flight instructor was standing. Fortunately the guys on the ground saw it falling down and the flight instructor read: "My right tyre blew, if you want me to make a wheel landing shoot a red flare, if you want me to make a belly landing (retracted landing gear) shoot a green flare!" The flight instructor realized that Rudi had only 5 take offs in this aircraft and thought that a wheel landing with a flat tyre was too dangerous, so he fired a green flare. When Rudi saw that, he retracted the landing gear, but almost did not make it because a hydraulic line in the wheel well was damaged and he had lost a lot of hydraulic fluid. At this time the flight instructor received a telephone call from the very irate base commander Col Aue who wanted to know what was going on. After he had heard the situation he demanded for Rudi to make a wheel landing, which he thought would cause a lot less damage to the aircraft if done properly with some luck. Meanwhile Rudi circled around the base and prepared the aircraft for a belly landing.

As he made his approach to land the aircraft, the flight instructor fired a red flare. Confused, Rudi made a second approach, and again he saw a red flare. Well, that obviously meant that he should now make a wheel landing. Rudi now extended the gear -- that is, he was able to get the gear halfway extended, when the hydraulic system which had lost too much fluid failed and would not push the gear any further out. Fortunately he had a mechanic on board who knew what to do. In the cockpit there was a manual hydraulic pump which he now pumped frantically. Luck was with them and with the last drop of hydraulic fluid the gear extended and locked in place. Naturally Rudi was quite nervous, would he be able to get the aircraft on the ground in one piece? Keeping a little power on his right engine as the aircraft stalled in a perfect three-point landing attitude on the grassy part of the field. Other than the blown tyre, there was no damage to the aircraft,. Hooray!

We thought that pilot training had top priority but some high echelon bureaucrats (or maybe some saboteurs (?) as we thought) had a different opinion. In the spring of 1944 an order was issued to all flight training schools that pilots had to have additional infantry training, just in case their base was under direct enemy ground attack and they had to defend the base. We thought this was stupid, but again for the third time we chased an imaginary enemy in a mock battle through the countryside around the base. To give us expert instruction, a 1st Lt. from the Army was assigned to teach us infantry tactics. I could not help but wonder... wasn't there first of all a desperate need for trained pilots in all Luftwaffe combat units?)

Infantry training, with infantry officer in white tunic.

Another unnecessary and time-consuming classroom activity, in my opinion, was the very time-consuming instruction in celestial navigation. I'm sure, very few if any of our group ever had a need or opportunity to use that. Other than long range reconnaissance aircraft or meteorological flight crews far over the Atlantic, we could not use this type of navigation, because the aircraft we used did not even have clear , distortion free glass in canopies to shoot a bearing from the stars. Apparently before the war the USA had sold some instrument flight training devices called Link

Trainer to Germany. Here in a classroom at Brandis sat what looked like a miniature aircraft with stubby wings and a seat for one pilot. Inside the cockpit was an instrument panel with all the instruments the real aircraft had. The pilot closed the cockpit hood and steered the Link Trainer at a certain course at a certain altitude. A wheeled scribe moved over a map on a large table and gave the instructor the information whether or not the student was flying as ordered. The Link Trainer gave us quick familiarization with instrument flying and probably was a lot cheaper to operate than flying the real aircraft. Eight years later when I trained in San Diego for my commercial and instrument pilot's license I again "flew" a few hours in a Link Trainer which looked exactly like our machine in Brandis.

From time-to-time all personnel had to assemble to listen to the latest orders, Squadron, Group or Wing information and the periodical announcements on PARAGRAPH 99, the paragraph in the Luftwaffe law book dealing with any deviation from a given flight order. If a pilot was given the order to fly from point A to point B at an altitude of 3,000 m, he had to do exactly that. If his girlfriend happened to live a few Km from his flight course and he took the liberty to buzz her house he would be in deep trouble, if he were caught. The secret, of course, was not to get caught. If, however, somebody saw the number and type of his aircraft and made a report, the pilot immediately had to face a court-martial. Punishment was usually loss of rank and imprisonment in a military penitentiary.

If an accident happened in connection with the deviation from a flight order the pilot really was in severe trouble. Should it be, that the pilot was killed as the result, he was then buried without any military honours. One would think that, because of the severe punishment that one could expect nobody dared to deviate: Wrong! I remember that once, Horst came back from a cross-country flight in a Ju 86 and had a wire (telephone?) dangling from his tail wheel, although his flight altitude was supposed to be several thousand meters high. Klaus somehow picked up some grain in his engine intake and my flight instructor and I enjoyed a little low-level flying while we were supposed to fly quite high. I still feel sorry for the fisherman who sat in his rowboat in the middle of a lake in Mecklenburg when we thought it would be fun to buzz him. When a big twin-engine bomber came roaring straight at him the man could have had a heart attack while we young pilots stupid as we were, thought at that time that it was funny. Anyway, in spite of all the warnings many pilots disobeyed Paragraph 99 but luckily were not caught.

By this time from the beginning of 1943 until May of 1944, I had been stationed at the Luftwaffen air bases of Oschatz, Fuerstenfeldbruck, Landsberg, Neu Ulm, and Brandis but never experienced a bombing attack. Many German cities like Hamburg, Berlin, Frankfurt and Cologne and all other major cities were already reduced to rubble and many, many German civilians had been killed.

One day the sirens sounded a certain special way, which gave the order: "All personnel clear the base!" Jochen, I, and a couple of guys were too lazy to chase out in the countryside and as the weather was very nice and sunny we all went into the shooting range on the base surrounded by a high solid fence. Here we felt nobody will see us and nobody will kick us out and we can take a pleasant sunbath.

Enemy bombers approaching – tan quickly!
One of the shooting-range targets is visible behind us.

We were stretching out on our blanket when we saw a formation of B-17 four-engine U.S. bombers which changed its course and headed straight in the direction of our base. With some concern we watched as they came closer and closer! Suddenly we saw a large bunch of bombs fall apparently directly towards us, however, the bombs hit the ground about 100 yards from where we were. With a fantastic earth-shaking thunderous explosion and we made one gigantic leap into the dug-out. The ground trembled like an earthquake, had the bombs come a little closer, our jump into the dugout would have been quite futile. As there was no second wave of bombers visible in the sky, we returned to our barracks.

Our bombed out barracks – Jochen and I shared the surprisingly intact upper room on the right.

Now we realized how lucky we were that we had not stayed in our building. About half of our two-story brick building was demolished, but we found the section where our room was located still intact and we could continue living there. The runways were not damaged at all but a couple of the hangars had some damage. Our flight activity, however, was not affected at all and continued as usual.

An aircraft, which we were all hoping to see flying some day, was an odd-looking contraption. It was in size like a primary trainer, but was shaped round, like a flying saucer. When our flight instructor pointed it out to us he said: "This will be the configuration of future aircraft." That aircraft was in a hangar and was badly damaged and had not been repaired by the time we left Brandis.

The Sack AS-6, photographed at Brandis in April 1944

One day when we were on the flight line we thought, "We aren't seeing right": an American B-17 approached our field at an altitude only a few hundred feet high but escorted by two Me 109 fighters. After the air-

110

craft had landed and taxied over to the flight line we had a chance to examine that bird. It was fully intact, no damage anywhere. Apparently the crew had decided to call it quits. Naturally we were impressed by the size of the plane. When we inspected the inside we were amazed by the simplicity. When all of our aircraft had to have all cables and wires in the fuselage enclosed in conduit, the B-17 had simple tie-straps to hold everything in place, good enough we said, why do our aircraft have to perform at 300% above the expected stress level?

A KG 200 B-17 at Brandis.

The Siebel 204 was the newest of the aircraft we flew at the instrument school. There was a lot of glass in the nose section. The Siebel 204 was a fun aircraft to fly; very agile and manoeuvrable, not so heavy like the Ju52, the Ju86 or the Ju88 but more like a sports car. The aircraft had dual controls but some had engine and flight instruments only for the left pilot's seat. The Sie 204 aircraft had two toggle switches for the propeller pitch control located on top of the instrument panel right in front of the pilot in command, but none on the co-pilot's side. In the manual mode the pilot pulled the switches back for a few seconds after take off as the aircraft's speed increased, so that the propellers were given more of a bite. Just a little further forward, but in the same general area were two similar switches, the ignition switches.

One night in June we were all standing at the end of the runway waiting to take our turn to practice night take-offs and landings in an Sie 204. A flight instructor with his student pilot in the left seat was heading down the runway, lifting off, climbing a few hundred feet when suddenly we all heard -- shocking --the engines sputter. Naturally, immediately everybody was worried: What had happened? Then suddenly, the engines started roaring again. The aircraft came around, landed and taxied over to us. The flight instructor obviously still quite shaken climbed out of the aircraft and told us that he had told the student to adjust the pitch of the propellers. Instead of the propeller switches, however, the student had reached too far forward and pulled both ignition switches to the off position. Only the quick reaction of the flight instructor made it possible to recover and get the aircraft safely on the ground. The flight instructor gave us his brief report, and with a very terse "Good night!" left. He had enough of flying for that night.

The instrument landing system at that time was still in its infancy, compared to today's navigational aids. The primary bad weather approach for a landing at a field with a direction finder was the Q.D.M. system. Very brief and in a nutshell: Suppose I'm flying in bad weather somewhere in the East and want to land at Munich airport. First I fly in the general direction of Munich. My radio operator establishes radio contact by Morse code transmissions with Munich Riem. The radio direction finder operator at Riem transmits the direction he "sees" our aircraft. After several corrections my course to the base remains constant, the radio direction finder at the field measures my aircraft heading straight for the Munich Riem base. Now I steer a heading of my established course plus (or minus) 30 degrees for 5 minutes and then return to my original heading. I'm now flying parallel to my original course and wait for the ground D/F station at Riem to tell me that the bearings he gets with his loop antenna change rapidly. That is an indication that I'm really close to the field. I now turn to fly over the field and ask the wireless operator to tell me when I'm over the field. That meant that the man had to step out of his ground station hut and listen for the engines overhead. When he heard the hum he would transmit: "Position message, over the field." Now all I had to do is to fly downwind, base and final and let down. At a certain altitude I should break out of the clouds and have the field in sight. That's all, very simple!

Eight years later, in San Diego when I worked for and received my U.S. Commercial and Instrument Pilot License there was a much more modern instrument landing system in use, the Low Frequency Range. (Today that has long become obsolete and is no longer used in America.)

In June our flight training program came to an end, therefore all of us at Lehrgang 22F had to demonstrate their ability during a final flight test. My check ride assignment was to fly with a Ju 88 from Brandis to the city of Goerlitz. First came the flight planning and the examination of the weather- report. Everything had to be checked and approved by the flight instructor. After take-off a curtain was drawn in front of me so that I did not have any visibility to the outside. It just so happened, that we were flying on top of clouds and the flight instructor too could not see if we were on course or not. After the calculated time had elapsed I was told to drop down to a few hundred meters above the ground. I was very lucky, because when I was allowed to open my curtain I found myself right over the city of Goerlitz. Now I was told to fly a simulated attack on a target in the countryside a few Km from Goerlitz. After that it was, "Pull up and climb to 2,000 Meter!" with the curtain closed again. Then came the next order. "Steer a heading of 270 degrees!" after 5 minutes: "Steer a heading of 350 degrees for 8 minutes!" The flight instructor gave me 5 or 6 different headings to fly at different time spans for each. It was for me important to steer each course precisely and keep track of the elapsed time. After about half an hour "cruising around" the question came: "Where are we?" On my kneepad, I had to calculate which courses I had flown and how long, I then applied the known wind direction and speed and that, all without any help from the flight instructor, without the use of the automatic pilot of course, and as quickly as possible. I must have been very lucky, because after I had reported my calculated position we opened the curtain and what do you know? I really was within a short distance of what I had calculated. After a few more flight examinations and precision approaches and landings my examiner was satisfied and I qualified for the instrument rating. My pilot license states: Checked and qualified to fly combat missions on IFR (instrument flight rules) in Sie 204, Ju 86, Ju 88 and Ju 52 aircraft.

On the first of July, we had a reason to celebrate: we were all promoted to Faehnrich (Officer Cadet, lower grade) a grade above that of a staff sergeant but still under the rank of technical sergeant. Now Jochen went into action. Somehow he had found out that not far from Brandis in an old castle at Pommsen there was a unit of "Arbeitsmaiden" (womens labour detail) who were assigned to work on farms in the vicinity.

Arbeitsdienst (National labour service) had become law some years earlier. Young men and women 17-18 years old were obligated to work for 12 months on national, state or local projects such as digging irrigation ditches, planting trees, building roads, or dikes along the sea shore, etc. Women were usually employed on farms and in other social work assignments. Earnings were minimal but housing was provided, as was food and uniforms. For many Arbeitsdienst girls and boys they had to do work they had never done before or even ever heard of before. It made young people aware of lifestyles, problems and enjoyments in an environment that was foreign to them.

As they lived close together, usually 30 - 40 in a camp, they had to submit to strict discipline, had to keep clean and orderly. They were not issued weapons, but the young men had spades, which they carried like rifles. For men it was in addition to the social work projects somewhat of a pre-military training encampment because they learned how to march as a unit and how to drill. In many aspects it had similarity with President Roosevelt's C.C.C. (Civilian Conservation Corps) programme. Anyway, this group of girls at the Pommsen Castle had no objections to get together with our newly graduated class of multi-engine/instrument pilots in a farewell celebration at their headquarters. We were able to round up some wine for a large pot of strawberry-Bowle (a typical, traditional German summertime drink) and the girls talked their farmers out of butter, strawberries, flour, milk, etc. to bake great cakes. It was a wonderful, pleasant summer evening as we danced to phonograph record music, although it had to be wound up and rewound and rewound again. But everybody had a great time together. Unfortunately we would never see each other again, because a few days later all of us were assigned to combat units everywhere in Europe.

The trip to Pommsen was very easy, just a few miles from Brandis by railroad; however, the return was not that easy. Well past midnight there was no train running and there wasn't any other way but to walk back to the base. "It's a long way to Tipperary," we sang and it sure was a long way. At dawn we finally came close to our base and the first civilian workers on their bikes passed us. As one rider was some 50 feet ahead of us someone said: "Who can still catch up with the man?" No problem, 2 or 3 of us started to dash forward and run after the bicyclist

114

who heard the steps behind him, looked back and apparently got scared and really stepped on it. We made it and all of us laughed so hard because of this ridiculous situation that we had pain in our side.

Jochen, Hans, and Rudi.

Kampfgeschwader 51 / KG 51

Each one in our graduating class received a stamp in the Soldbuch "Einsatzurlaub" (Combat furlough) from July 2nd until July 17 with a free railroad ticket to home. Nobody was told to what unit we would be assigned. For our "Triumvirate" (Jochen, Rudi and Haenschen), the future was very uncertain. Would we be assigned to the same unit? Nobody knew! In Brandis it was "farewell" and there was only the hope to see us again?

I took the train to Hamburg. The streetcar from the main railroad station to our residence on Zimmerstrasse in Uhlenhorst was still in operation; however, more and more of the apartment houses as far as one could see had become huge piles of rubble. I had spent 12 of my 15 days of my leave time in Hamburg, when on July 14, I received a telegram: "Report to Bomber-Wing 51, Edelweiss, at Munich Riem immediately!" Bomber-Wing 51? That's not what I had volunteered for! I wanted to be a fighter, night fighter or maybe destroyer pilot but not a bomber pilot. Well, an order is an order and off I went to Bavaria.

I packed my duffel bag with a few essentials and uniform pieces, grabbed my bicycle and embarked on a train to Munich some 815Km to the South. When the train arrived at Pasing, on the outskirts of Munich everybody had to get off. A year ago when I was stationed at Fuerstenfeldbruck, which is only a few miles to the west of Munich I had visited the capital of Bavaria a number of times. I liked to go to the Operetta Theatre or just stroll through the streets and look at pretty girls. Each time the train took me to the main railroad station in the centre of the city. But here I was now at Pasing, how far is it from here to Munich Riem airbase? A heavy terror-bombing attack had destroyed railroad facilities at the main station and made many streets impassable. That meant that I had to get from the west side of town all the way to the east side. There I saw a man sitting on the front steps of his apartment house. I asked him for directions to Munich Riem. "Well", he said in his really broad Bavarian dialect, which I had never heard like that before, "you won't be able to get through the mess in the middle of town tonight, but you can stay with me and my family and try it tomorrow!" As it was getting dark I gladly accepted his invitation. He even shared some of his scarce food with me and let me sleep comfortably on a kitchen-bench in his apartment. Next morning he gave me directions and I was on my long way to Bomber Wing 51. In many streets I could not ride my bicycle because of all the rubble from the bombed-out houses.

At KG 51, IV Group headquarters at Munich Riem, I reported for duty as ordered and was sent to join the 10th Squadron in Erding (about 20 miles to the East). Great was the joy of seeing Horst, Klaus, and Alex with whom I had been together at Fuerstenfeldbruck and Brandis. However, my close friends Jochen and Rudi, I found out later were assigned to a unit in Denmark to fly patrol missions along the North Sea coast. Six additional Faehnriche joined us; Roland, Walter, Juergen, Ernst, Haenschen J. and Schab who had been through the same flight-training as we, but at different flight schools. Nobody knew what exactly we were supposed to do now. Then finally we were told that we were not to fly bomber missions, (hurray!) instead with the Me 110 or Me 410, we would be flying long-range night-fighter missions. That I liked a lot better!

With great enthusiasm we all turned to our flight training program. Flight training with the Me 110 was a real pleasure. We had no dual control aircraft, so when a pilot familiar with the aircraft checked me out, he sat in the back seat where normally a radio operator/gunner would sit giving hints what to do and what not, flying a few touch and go circuits and a little aerobatics and that was it. I was checked out; I could fly solo and practice all the things for my future combat assignments.

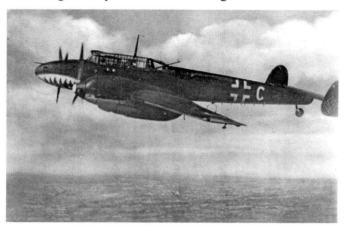

Messerschmitt 110
Made by Messerschmitt Aircraft 1939 Engines: two Daimler-Benz 1,050 hp ea
Weight 13,289 lb Max Speed 336 mp/h Range 680 Miles Ceiling 32,810 ft
5 Mach. Guns, 2 Cannons, Crew 2

I liked the aircraft a lot, especially aerobatics and air-to-ground shooting practice. When there was flight activity at a base we usually -- weather permitting -- stayed on the field near the tarmac and observed take offs and landings.

One day, Walter went up to "wring out" a Me 110, which meant he really should get the feel for the aircraft. He could fly loopings, rolls, Immelmanns or whatever he wanted. We watched him in the distance going through the manoeuvres. Suddenly we were all shocked as we saw his aircraft get into a spin, a manoeuvre where the aircraft turns around the vertical axis. He was quite high so we were only a little bit concerned because we normally did not try to get the aircraft intentionally into a spin. During primary pilots training we were even warned with lots of emphasis that some of the trainer aircraft were very difficult to get out of a spin and a number of student pilots lost their lives because of that. Walters's aircraft spun and spun and lost a lot of altitude.

Pilot Hans Busch in the front office of an Me 110.

The view from the radio operator's position of the Me 110.

Then, finally, the spinning motion stopped, only briefly, and then immediately he went into a flat spin in the opposite direction. Now we really became worried. The aircraft lost all altitude and disappeared behind some hills a few miles to the East. Now we knew that this was the end for Walter and expected any moment a smoke cloud to appear. But no, no fire, no smoke, instead a Me110 hedgehopped over the terrain and landed.

Walter climbed out; he was very pale as he told us of his frantic effort to get his aircraft back under control. He certainly had a guardian angel watching over him that day.

One warm but pitch-dark summer evening Klaus, Horst, Roland, Juergen and I returned from a movie in town and walked back to our barracks. The German movie industry produced films until the end of the war. The type of films, however, was quite different from the U.S. films. There were no hate movies, instead there was light entertainment for people who wanted some enjoyment, some relaxation now that war had curtailed citizens' activity a lot. However, as an indication of solidarity with the soldiers in battles, there was no public dancing permitted. Anyway, here the 5 of us walked through the totally dark streets of Erding and sang some songs. Suddenly we heard from a balcony up there in the dark somewhere applause and some female voices. Naturally we stopped and serenaded the ladies up there, somewhere. Then some lit cigarettes were tossed down – hurray, hurray from the smokers among us (I did not smoke any of the daily cigarette ration during my entire military time). It did not take long and Horst had found a way to climb to the balcony. That really broke the ice and all of us were invited to join them, however, the rest of us walked up the stairway -- that was easier. Five ladies were assembled in the apartment. Mutti Johansen was the oldest and later after we had visited with them a number of times, she adopted us as her sons or new members of the family. Then there was her daughter Inge Johansen and daughter Heli, Margot from Berlin and little Inge from Munich. When we took off or landed at the Erding air base we always tried to fly a little detour so we could rev up the engines over the Johansen house. Each one of us had an identification signal so the girls on the balcony could recognize who was flying in the aircraft; mine was to very slowly rock the wings.

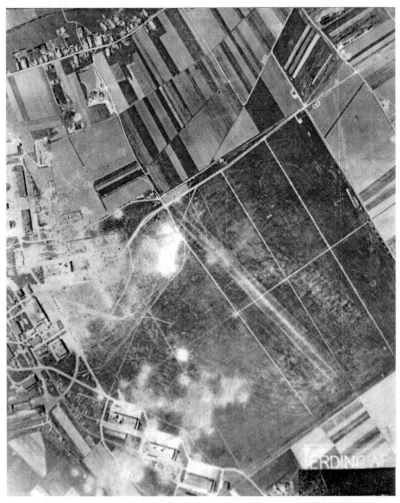

Erding air base, photographed by an attacking American bomber.
Most bombs missed the buildings and only tossed dirt into the air. The storage
and warehouse facilities could therefore later be used by the USAAC

Inge (left 1944) on the right, Hans, Mutti Johansen, and Roland. (1988)

This was the beginning of a very harmonious friendship. We dropped in many times, entertained each other or celebrated a birthday together. Roland and I were very fond of Inge who was the most attractive one of the bunch. However, we both were of the same opinion, for the duration of the war it would be irresponsible to marry or get seriously involved with a woman." We both adored Inge and were ever so grateful if we were awarded an occasional kiss on the cheek.

Gasoline supply was a real problem. We were overjoyed whenever we heard of a railroad tank car that had arrived, but how long can you fly with that petrol when you use it for two 1000 hp engines on each Me 110? To keep us occupied we had to attend "Aircraft Identification" classes. From a slide projector we had to look at silhouettes, front, top and side view of all the Allied aircraft which we might encounter in the sky over Europe at that time. Quite boring, especially when these classes were conducted right after lunch.

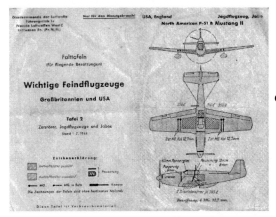

My original "Enemy Aircraft Recognition" booklet and a sample page.

Someone found a bundle of leaflets that had been dropped from Allied aircraft over Germany.

The message was:
"GERMAN PEOPLE, ONLY YOU CAN DECIDE YOUR FUTURE AND THE FUTURE OF GERMANY. IT IS CLEAR THAT NOW THERE ARE ONLY TWO SIDES: ON ONE SIDE THERE ARE THE ONES WHO WANT TO PROLONG THE WAR AND ON THE OTHER SIDE THE ONES WHO ACCELERATE THE ARRIVAL OF PEACE."

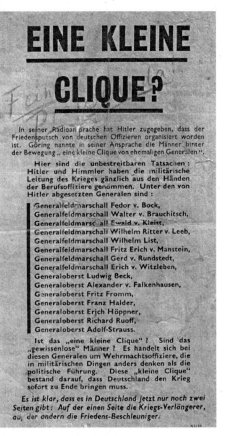

122

I kept two as souvenirs when I found out that it was not illegal as long as they were marked FEINDPROPAGANDA (ENEMY PROPAGANDA). These leaflets were meant to encourage the German people to shorten the war, yet the civilian population had to suffer daily from terrible terror bombings when open cities were destroyed and altogether 1 million people, mainly women and children perished, many burnt alive in Allied terror air raids.

KG 51 ULK Erding

From time to time the Luftwaffe units, Groups or Wings conducted a non-commissioned officer training course-camp called ULK to give soldiers the education to qualify for a position of sergeant or master sergeant. Such a course was in progress at the 4th Group of KG 51. Then someone had the crazy idea, since the Faehnriche (Officer Cadets) have too much free time on their hands, due to the sparse fuel supply, they should participate in this ULK. We were shocked!!! First the basic training in boot camp, then the advanced military training at the academy, then the additional, special infantry training at Brandis the instrument flight school, and now again this stupid idea? Well, whether we liked it or not we had to march, drill and shoot rifles, take guns apart and conduct classes. We were all mad as hell, but what could we do? We submitted our request in writing to be transferred to the "Reichsverteidigung" (Defence of the Reich). We thought, and I am sure we were not wrong, when we assumed that pilots were very much in demand. However, our request went straight into the round file. For us it was: "back to the drill   field."

That's me, looking at the camera

The Spiess Hauptfeldwebel Springer seemed to really enjoy having the Faehnriche under his thumb. One day he ordered the platoon, the Faehnriche in the front rows to practice marching in parade step. When marching and the command "Achtung" (Attention) was given we had to march in "goose step". Here we were marching back and forth on the concrete taxiway in parade step. Continuously he barked, "Lift up your legs - higher - higher!"

Hauptfeldwebel Springer, centre.

We realized that this was really only his chicane to give the cadets a special treatment while he still could, a few weeks later, after we had become Oberfaehnrich, he knew we would give him orders. After a while only the Faehnriche and a couple of corporals were left in the marching unit all the others, one by one were allowed to fall out because they lifted their legs high enough. Very stubbornly we continued to trot casually back and forth until it was time to go to lunch. When a unit marched to the barracks it was customary to march the last 30 steps or so in the parade-step mode. This time too. "Achtung!" And up came the legs in goose step fashion. While everybody lifted his legs high, the cadets now lifted them extremely high. "Abteilung halt!" (Halt). As if stung by a tarantula the Hauptfeldwebel dashed over to me. I, as the tallest, stood at the first row in front. Furiously he shouted: "That high you lifted your legs now," pointing at the height of his shoulder, why did you not do that an hour ago?" "Well, sir, I said, when I know that I have to run 10 miles I ration my strength and energy accordingly."
I don't know if he understood what I had said, but he mumbled something and walked away.

Men of the U L K ERDING

Drill as punishment was forbidden, but one could always say; "This is for training purpose only." "Maskenball" (masquerade party) was one of those "training" exercises. "Now hear this: the unit falls out in sports dress in 5 minutes!" Hurriedly every one changes to sports dress. Naturally there are always a few who are not on time. "Back to your room and return here in 4 minutes in dress blue uniform!" To make it as fast as possible we ripped the sports dress off and put on the uniform. We all tried as hard as we could to be on time but it was not easy. Then came the fatigue, then in swimming trunks and so on. After an hour of this "masquerade party" we had room inspection. Of course nobody had time to put the uniform pieces neatly back in the wall locker, so our room looked like a disaster area. It simply was a mess. All of this "only for training!"

The "old" (probably 25 to 30 years old) soldiers and corporals did not sing with a lot of enthusiasm. Therefore the cadets were given the order to teach them how to sing while marching. The songs that were popular at that time in all of the German military were melodies like "Edelweiss", the little flower on the heath called "Erika", the "Sailing around Madagascar", "The Mill in the Black Forest", etc.; political songs were not in our repertoire. To stimulate soldiers' enthusiasm we came up with a more catching song called "Navajo". Most boys in Germany had read books by Karl May about the American Indians like: "Winnetou", "Old Shatterhand", "The Treasure In The Silver Lake" etc. The topic "Indian" was and still is very popular in Germany. The melody sounds very nice and the soldiers liked especially the part that was just a little bit risqué, which they sang with especially super loud voices whenever we marched through the town of Erding. For the Faehnriche it meant: "Mission accomplished."

Beautiful little town of Erding

For whatever reason the Furier (mess sergeant) at one time distributed to everybody in the entire Squadron a chunk (about 1/4 lb) of "Butterschmalz".

I believe Butterschmalz is a food supplement only known in Southern Germany, I had never heard of it before. It seems that Butterschmalz is regular butter, which has been heated whereby all milk solids have been eliminated. The fatty stuff can be kept much longer without getting rancid and spoiled than regular butter. It is excellent for frying and cooking.

Anyway, the question for us was what to do with it, as it did not taste good as a spread for bread. The answer of course was: let's take it to the Johansens and prepare some potato pancakes with it. Potatoes were still available in rural areas, so we prepared a real feast. Several of us had to peel the potatoes and others had to grate them. My job was to fry them and prepare tasty pancakes. We had so much to eat that for the first time in a long while everybody had his fill, and we all had a great time together.

Then we were billeted in an old building at the edge of town. We liked it there because it did not have so much regimentation and everything was more easy going. On the property next door there was a camp of about 20 standard wooden barracks the same type that was used everywhere in Germany for housing of refugees, military, POW's or "Guest workers" (as they were called at that time, today of course they are called "Forced labourers"). In this neighbouring camp there were foreign workers put up, apparently from Eastern countries. They had no guard or gate so they could come and go as they pleased. One warm summer evening we heard music from the camp. Someone played an accordion,

126

melodies that we had never heard before. At the beginning it sounded very nice until they played one melody that consisted of only four notes. These four notes were repeated again and again and again for what seemed to be half an hour. That's when we thought it would be better if we were staying on the base, at least we would be able to sleep. I'm sure that these workers, who were hired for jobs in Germany, were apparently pretty well off; probably better off than they would have been in their home country.

We were ever so relieved when finally this stupid ULK came to an end. The cadets, after all fully trained pilots felt that someone upstairs did not want us to fly combat missions (hard to believe but...?). But first the conclusion of the ULK had to be celebrated. Some of the members prepared a 27 page "Newspaper" in which many participants and of course the "Star" Hauptfeldwebel Springer were duly ridiculed. After dinner there was a nice get together for which we even had some wine, which happened very seldom. Because the cadets were known for their good singing we were urged to go on the stage and sing something.

Well, that was no big problem and we presented nicely in harmony a couple of catchy tunes. As a conclusion we sang, "It's a long way to Tipperary" (with English text) We were given great applause. The postlude, however, was the stern remark or reprimand by the cadet-training officer when he said at the next training class: "I don't think that British officer candidates would sing German songs at their party!" (Today I have to admit it probably was a little bit in poor taste by us but then ; well we were all young and a bit stupid just like the British Prince Harry when he was photographed wearing a German uniform in 2005!)

KG 51, 11th Squadron Munich Riem

A girl, Sonja was her name, was working as a waitress in the Group 4 officer Casino. When the ten of us transferred to the 11th Squadron, we had our meals there. Sonja had to keep track of our daily food allotment. After a couple of days she knew everyone of us by name. Once I asked her where she had come from. She told me that she was from Ukraine. She spoke German quite well but also English and French. But why did she work here in Germany? "Well," she said, "I got a job working in the mess hall for the Group while the bomber wing was stationed in Russia and Ukraine. When the wing relocated back to Germany I decided to go along, I was treated well and I liked the people I worked for and I liked the work." (Today I wonder if after the war she called herself a forced and slave labourer too?)

When our flight training as a long range night fighter flying the Me 110 or Me 410 had almost reached its goal and we expected to receive our orders any day now, we were informed, "You'll not fly long range night fighter missions anymore as planned. Instead because KG 51 was designated by Hitler himself to fly the new "blitz bomber", the Messerschmitt 262 jet as a bomber." We had heard practically nothing about the development of jet or rocket propelled aircraft in Germany. Now we were to fly the first operational jet aircraft in the world; what a thrill!!! There were no pictures and very little word of mouth information available, after all the aircraft was still considered "Top Secret". (Other aircraft were usually classified "confidential")

Top notch, well-experienced pilots most of whom had flown many hundred missions as a bomber pilot with a Heinkel 111 or Ju 88, were now transferred from the other Groups of Bomber Wing 51 to the 4th Group for re-training. Apparently someone from the Reichsluftfahrtsministerium (RLM – the Air Ministry) thought that it would be best to first familiarize the pilots with a single seat aircraft operation prior to flying the Me 262. These old hands were selected as commanders of a bomber crew, fully in charge and giving orders. However, they were so used to asking the navigator, "Where are we?" or the radio operator, "Get me a fix from such and such station", or "Get the gear out!" But in a Me 262 there was no crew, there was only the pilot. Therefore, as a transitional aircraft, pilots had to fly a fighter aircraft for which a number of FW 190 were made available for flight training.

One of the FW 190 Jabos that we flew at Munich Riem.
Made by Focke Wulf Aircraft Co 1941 engine BMW 1,600hp
Weight 8,770 lb max speed 389 mph ceiling 34,775 ft range 490 mile

Obviously for some pilots flying the single seat aircraft occasionally caused some difficulties. I remember when I watched a FW 190 come in for a landing. The approach and the aircraft attitude was very normal, except when the pilot cut the power the aircraft made a very gentle, very beautiful soft landing, however, without the landing gear extended. The pilot, a captain, was a bit embarrassed when he had to admit he forgot to put the gear out. An experienced master sergeant made a wonderful wheel landing (touching the ground with the main gear only and not the tail wheel, as in a "three-point-landing"). His aircraft rolled and rolled with the tail still up in the air, but finally the field came to an end. It looked like in slow motion the aircraft nosed over and ever so gradually flipped on its back. The pilot was not hurt and his explanation was: "The throttle was stuck and I could not reduce power!" Apparently it did not occur to him that he also had an ignition switch with which to cut power!

We were all very anxious to get a glimpse of this futuristic jet-propelled Me 262. However, that took some more time .

First, my 9 buddies and I transferred from the 10th squadron to the 11th squadron, which meant also relocation from Erding to Muenchen Riem. Much to my enjoyment, we too had to fly a fighter-bomber training program with the FW 190. That was really exciting. The FW 190 was a very sturdy fighter with a radial 1,700 hp engine and a cruising speed of almost 400 mph and a range of almost 500 Miles. I liked to fly that aircraft a lot! I had no problem fitting my 6Ft 2 inches body into the cockpit. Once when I had a chance to sit in a Me 109, I realized that the cockpit was a lot more cramped than that of a FW 190.

Among other things, we had to practice bomb drops with cement bombs onto a target located on the Ammersee Lake. From Muenchen Riem, it was but a few minutes to the lake and dropping the bombs was a simple task. How close did my bombs come to the target? Probably not very close, after all we had no bomb sights and our approach was to be similar to that of the Me 262 tactic, that is a very shallow dive of about 15 degrees, that's all! No dive bombing for us.

What I really liked was "Erfliegen" that is, "Go up, get familiar with the aircraft and wring her out." That was fun. When I wanted to find out how tight a turn I could fly, I banked the aircraft and pulled back on the stick. When I hit my own prop wash I knew that I flew in a tight circle. But as I pulled back some more and some more yet; the aircraft began to shudder, more severely with each moment - then suddenly, wham! The aircraft stalled and made a violent snap roll in the opposite direction of my turn. Now I knew! Until then, we flew in aircraft that had a radio operator on board. All communication was first translated into secret characters then transmitted by Morse code to the receiving station. They in turn had to decode the message into intelligible words, compose an answer, translate it into secret characters and transmit it by Morse code to the aircraft. Then the radio operator had to translate the message into normal words and give the information to the pilot. A rather cumbersome operation! The FW 190, however, had no radio operator. Now all communications were in voice transmissions, which of course was a lot simpler. The FuG 16 radio was located in the rear of the fuselage and the "talk button" was mounted on the joystick. The earphones were installed in the flight helmet (which was made of cloth, leather lined with sheep skin or netting-material each worn depending on the seasonal weather condition) We did not use any hand held microphone. Instead we used two throat mikes buttoned around the neck and throat. This way we did have the right hand on the stick and the left hand on the throttle or cockpit controls.

Our life at the squadron was now very uneventful. We were all housed in the standard wooden barracks just outside the Munich Riem base. At that time there was no radio, no television and no newspapers available. What was there to do during the off duty hours? Play cards with buddies or sleep!

From the Johansens house I borrowed several Eugen Roth poetry books which I found very amusing, so much that I just had to learn many of the poems by heart which I still can recite today. Then, to occupy myself during the off duty hours I decided to build my own FW 190. I didn't have more than a pocket knife and some sandpaper. The size? Well it was a little smaller than the real one -- about 12 Inches wing span. When it was all done I went to the repair shop in the hangar and asked the mechanics, "Would you please paint my aircraft too, next time you have a paint job to do?" Well, of course they did. That's why today I still have a sample of the real paint used on the FW 190 on my desk.

The model I carved of a FW 190, with genuine FW 190 paint.

Hauptfeldwebel Springer was really not very much adored or even respected by the non-commissioned men or the cadets in KG 51. During the time of the ULK, of course, all we could say was "Yes, Sir" whatever the Spiess ordered, we had to do it, but we all despised him. Now at Muenchen Riem, the cadets had to do something to get even with him.

One evening Springer went into town. One of the cadets had the crazy idea: we'll play a trick on the Spiess. Some 5 of us went to work. We somehow got into his room, which was in the adjoining barrack. There we stuffed all of his clothing into one uniform and propped this puppet into the corner. Next we screwed two strong hooks into the wooden ceiling, lifted his bed up and fastened it to the hooks. His bed was now suspended from the ceiling. We moved his wall-locker in front of his door and departed through the window. The room had a little potbelly stove, which we sabotaged by stuffing newspaper into the chimney up on top of the roof. After that we all went to bed. It must have been past midnight when we were awakened by some loud voice. Springer screamed at the top of his lungs because he did not have a bed to sleep in. He never thought that the cadets would dare to do such a thing, but was sure the older NON-COM staff were responsible. So he went over to their barrack and woke them up. Of course they did not have the faintest idea what he was talking about. He gave up trying to find the culprit of this crime.

Next morning Springer told the GVD (Gefreiter vom Dienst) to make fire in the stove of his room. The man did it; that is he tried to do it. He put kindling wood on top of some newspapers and struck a match. The paper burnt and so did the wood, but the smoke did not go through the chimney, instead into the room. He tried it again, but to no avail, the room and the whole barrack became filled with smoke. After some research the problem was discovered, the newspaper in the stovepipe on top of the roof was cleared. Everything was now OK. Naturally Springer was furious, how did anyone dare to do a thing like that to him the Hauptfeldwebel? He talked the squadron commander in to getting to the bottom of this. The whole 11th Squadron had to fall out. Who did this? Step forward! We were not caught, nobody had seen us so we could have just kept quiet and nobody would have been able to prove anything. However, our moral code did not allow us to lie, so all cadets stepped forward. (Although only half of them were involved) We all got a reprimand and the case was closed.

Struppi, the Faehnrich mascot

Airmen of KG51 in an un-dated wartime photograph.

I remember when flying a Ju 88 twin engine bomber how difficult and time consuming an instrument "Q.D.M. approach and landing procedure" was and now here at Munich Riem for the first time we could experiment with radar-controlled approaches. A small 6-8 ft diameter parabolic antenna dish of a Wuerzburg system was set up at the west end of the field. We approached the field from the east. The controller could measure the distance of the aircraft and the approach angle. He would give the pilot that information and the pilot knew from that when he was lined up with the runway and also from the distance to the touch down how high he had to fly.

Code words rather than plain language was used a lot. For example to contact the ground station we said: "This is KAKADU EMIL bitte kommen!" or when inquiring if message was understood we said: "KAKADU EMIL frage victor?" For many situations like, "I have to make an emergency landing" or "Give me a direction to my field," brief statements were used. The maps we used had an overlay of a grid system. For example a large section of 100 Km by 100 Km was named "Dora". That area was subdivided into 9 equal sections named A, B, C, D, E, F, G, H, I. each of these were again divided into nine squares which were named 1 through 9. If the pilot needed to know his position radar control would simply tell him, "You are at Dora Dora Fuenf" which gave the pilot instant information that he was about 20 Km from Regensburg.

The airbase Muenchen Riem was built as a commercial airport around 1937. There was no provision made for military housing. Therefore a number of wooden barracks were constructed in the vicinity of the field and that's where we members of the 11th squadron were assigned to sleep. The barracks were located on a road, which led from the Muenchen-Riem train station to the airport. On the other side across the road there were a number of barracks identical to ours built for Russian prisoners of war. There was one difference; however, one could tell where the Russians were housed as a cloud of Lysol smell always drifted from there across the road to us. Apparently they had problems with bed bugs, fleas and lice and used a lot of Lysol as a disinfectant. Some of the Russians wanted to supplement their food or cigarette supply, so they built crude toys with material they probably could swipe at their place of work. A German soldier escorted a Russian prisoner, as they went through our barracks to offer their handiwork. I think they sold everything because toys were practically non-existent on the market in Germany at that time.

One-day sirens blasted the signal "Raeumungsalarm" (clear the base). The squadron had a truck with which all personnel was ordered to leave the base and drive to a designated area a few kilometres away. Klaus, Horst Alex and I did not like the idea of hiding somewhere in the countryside. While everybody assembled and climbed on top of the truck we hid in our room. Springer could not get his box of paperwork on the truck fast enough so everybody grumbled but had to wait. When finally they were gone the five of us leisurely walked out through the main gate and along the chain link fence. After a few hundred yards we found a patch with grass and as the sun came out we stretched out to enjoy the sunshine. After a while we heard the roaring of a formation of B-17 four engine bombers. We could spot them as they flew on an easterly course to the south of the field. However, suddenly they made a left turn to the opposite direction and now headed west as they were flying over the airfield. The first group dropped their bombs way over the eastern side of the field creating huge fountains of dust and dirt with thunderous explosions. The next group flew parallel to the first group but a few hundred feet more to the north, that is closer to where we were. The bombs of the third group came much closer towards us. Now we no longer laid on our back, sunbathing, instead we rolled over on our bellies and covered our heads with our arms. However, Alex thought, "With the next bombs we are going to get it!" He jumped up and took cover on the other side of a large pile of gravel. Unfortunately the fourth row of bombs hit the ground some 50 yards further to the north. We were caught between the third and fourth row of bombs. It was quite noisy lying there between the many bombs exploding around us. When the noise subsided and we saw the formation of bombers disappearing our first concern was, "What happened to Alex?" We ran up to the top of the gravel pile and looked for Alex.

There he was standing, but the last bombs had fallen very close to where he was laying. Thank God, he did not get killed, but the dust of the pulverized gravel had covered him from head to toe. It looked as if he had just fallen into a box of flour. We were relieved but we were also amused when we saw the way he looked, so we all started a roaring laughter. Only he did not think that it was very funny at all.

With our flight activity we were very happy. Our rank Faehnrich (Cadet) allowed us to stay out until midnight. After duty we took the train to Erding and spent some happy hours with the girls. The last train that we had to take in order to be back in the barracks by midnight was scheduled to leave Erding at about nine o'clock. Of course it was always "decision, decision." If it was especially nice at the Johansens, we were inclined to disobey the midnight curfew and take the first train in the morning, which left Erding around 5 o'clock. We did this many times without ever getting caught. One evening, we were all sitting together with the Johansen family. A Lieutenant from the 4th Group KG 51 was also present, although I don't know who had invited him. Anyway, when the time came to leave to catch the last train before midnight Mutti Johansen said "Why don't you stay until the first train in the morning?" "Well", we said, "this Lt. may tell on us". "I'll talk to him," said Mutti. He then talked to us and said, "I can't give you any permission to stay over curfew, the only thing I can do is not to see you." So the decision was ours! We all agreed: "We stay"! When we returned to the barracks nobody had noticed our absence, we changed, went to breakfast and reported for duty.

About a week or so later we received an order to report to the squadron commander. We had no idea why? He then told us, "On such and such a day you stayed over curfew!" We were brought up, and always believed, that we should tell the truth. So we admitted, "yes we stayed over curfew. "Very well," he said "I'll punish you with 5 days in the brig!" The rule was that the defendant had to accept the verdict, then sleep one night on it and return to the captain the next day for bringing up any comments or excuses, and except punishment. Of course we were surprised as we were not caught when we had returned to our barracks. How did the captain know that we were not in the sack by midnight? It did not take much for us to find out that this certain Lieutenant who said to us that he would not see us, which for us meant that he gave us his word not to report us, was a blabbermouth. When he was sitting together with the other officers he was talking about the cadets being in Erding at midnight. The rest the Captain could figure out for himself. The following day we returned to the Captain, as ordered and said: "Yes, we accept the punishment," but, "we also want to resign as officer candidates." The captain was momentarily stunned. "What in the hell are you talking about?" "Well," we said, "if the word of an officer in the Luftwaffe does not mean anything, we do not want to become an officer!" We then explained the whole situation. The Captain took our punishment papers and tossed them into the wastepaper basket, "Dismissed!" That Lieutenant, however, was transferred to another unit. Our feeling towards officer integrity was re-established!

On the first of November 1944, all ten Faehnriche were promoted to "Oberfaehnrich" (Senior Officer Cadet), which is one grade under that of a Lieutenant. This did not change anything in our duty or daily life, however, our rank now was a notch above all non-commissioned officer ranks and that we enjoyed, especially as Hauptfeldwebel Springer was concerned.

We all went to a professional photographer and proudly had our picture taken dressed up in our uniform with the new rank insignias.

Oberfaehnrich Busch
Senior Officer Cadet

KG 51 12th Squadron, Neuburg a/D

In December of 1944, we had completed our prerequisite flight training with the FW 190, now we ten Oberfaehnriche were to begin flying the Me 262 program at the airbase Neuburg on Donau (Naturally that caused another sad good bye from the Johansen family as we now were stationed some 80 Km to the north, so there was no quick after duty-drop-in any more.)

Hauptmann Bender, our Squadron Commander was a really neat guy. When we reported to him as ordered, he right away told us: "I'm not looking at your personal file until I have had a chance to evaluate each one of you from the way you conduct yourself in my squadron." That was very good, because we were known to be a bunch of wild ones.

Finally we experienced the thrill of our life. We walked up to this mysterious aircraft that we had never seen a picture of and heard that it was still "Top Secret". What an excitement, we were allowed to touch this bird that looked as if it had just dropped in from the future or from another planet. No aircraft we had flown or seen so far looked as sleek or as streamlined as the Me 262. We were allowed to sit in the cockpit but that was all. First there was a lot of learning and familiarization necessary.

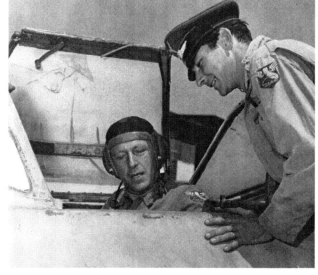

Decades after the war, we re-enacted the event with a derelict Me 262 once owned by Howard Hughes.

Classroom activity was number one on the agenda. We were instructed in all the details of this new aircraft; as there were many things we had never heard of before, which we now had to learn. The propulsion system was the Jumo 004 jet engine, a long cigar-shaped axial-flow turbine which was mounted under each wing required special handling quite different from the reciprocating engines we had flown so far. Adhering to very strict discipline in handling these machines was essential as non-compliance with the operating instructions would likely result in fatal accidents. This propulsion system, of course seemed to be a device out of a futuristic novel. The little booklet Me 262 A-1 Bedienungsvorschrift - F1 issued in August 1944 (Instruction manual) was still considered "Geheime Kommandosache" (Top secret).

The "pilot's manual" of most aircraft were not "Top Secret" like ours!

We were sternly instructed to never, ever talk to anyone, military or civilian about this aircraft. Secrecy was enforced! We used to take pictures of us sitting in all sorts of aircraft or standing in front of one, but with the Me 262 that was an absolute NO! NO! That's why relatively speaking so few pictures of the 262 are available today. Together with expert pilots with lots of flying experience and many combat missions under their belt, we ten Oberfaehnriche formed a flight-training group. Normally we kept track of who would be the next one in line to fly, but from time-to-time an officer pulled rank on us and demanded the next flight. The flight instructor, usually an enlisted pilot, knew the aircraft quite well and was very demanding and critical with his students. He would stand on the wing of the aircraft and shot his questions at us, like: "What is the turbine –starting procedure?", "Where is the electrical master switch?", "Where are the turbine temperature gauges?" "What is the normal operating temperature?" ..and so on. He demanded the answer immediately and correctly ! After all the theory, finally, it was my time to actually fly this great machine. In those days we did not have a two-seat Me 262; later in February 1945 one became available to us.

In December 1944, I was confident to make my first flight because I knew every step, every RPM limits, and every temperature range, pressure requirements etc, etc. Here I sat in the cockpit, parachute strapped on, flight helmet secured, radio - telephone hooked up, throat mike buttoned down, and shoulder/belly straps tightly secured. I could reach to every knob, dial or lever blindfolded. I was confident that I knew what I was doing — Now, "Start the jet engines!"

With other aircraft engines all I had to do was: turn the master switch on, press the starter-switch button and advance the throttle. The starting procedure of the jet engines was a little more involved. A small two-cycle engine, a Riedel motor the size of a large lawn mover motor, was mounted in the intake section of the turbines and connected with a claw clutch to the front end of the turbine shaft. We had electric starter motors for the Riedel motor. Earlier models had to be cranked by hand with a rope, just like a lawnmower motor. With a jack-switch the Riedel motor started and the claw clutch engaged the turbine.

When the Riedel runs properly at about 500 to 1000 RPM it's time to depress the button on the throttle which turns the starting fuel (aviation gas) pump on and begins the ignition process (spark plugs). When the combustion is running properly which is indicated by a rumbling noise, the throttle has to be advanced to the idle position. At about 2000 RPM the Riedel starter motor switch has to be released, which turns the Riedel off. The claw clutch automatically disengages from the turbine shaft. Now the ignition and the starting fuel pump switch on the throttle can be released. The turbine runs at 3000 RPM on jet fuel. During warm-up the engine runs at about 8700 – 8900 RPM. Internal gas temperature should be about 700 degrees Centigrade. Now it's time to check all other critical functions like difference pressure / intake vs. exhaust, fuel injection pressure, oil pressure etc. as well as all electrical systems, hydraulic systems, etc. Flight instruments were practically the same as any other aircraft I had flown. As practiced everything went off like clockwork. What a thrill to close the canopy and taxi to the end of the runway. I looked out the left side of the aircraft and observed the markings on the flaps as they moved in the 20 degree position.

I checked out the engines; 8800 rpm, temperature 800 degrees C, okay, I turned into the wind and stepped on the brakes. At the Erding base and at Munich Riem we flew from a grass field. At Neuburg, however, there was a concrete runway. With full power on both engines the aircraft could still be held in position by the brakes. One last look at temperature, RPM, fuel pressure, difference pressure, etc., and then get off the brakes. Ever so slowly the aircraft started to move forward. By using brakes during the initial take-off run, the aircraft could be held accurately as it proceeded straight down the runway. I was amazed how quiet it was. What a difference to the piston engine propeller aircraft! After a few hundred yards the acceleration increased rapidly. The rudder became effective.At about 4,000 Ft down the runway the aircraft speed indicated about 180 Km/h. Just a little pull back on the stick and off I went. While climbing, "gear in" - "flaps in". At first the aircraft climbed at 300 mph (at an altitude of 10,000m, however, the aircraft would climb at 400 mph) but now I had to look around, "Where am I?" It took a few moments for me to find the base, not being used to flying at such a speed over the countryside. Then I found myself, "Aha! -- that's where the airbase is!" The rest was easy, no problem at all.

The most remarkable difference from all the 15 types of aircraft that I had flown so far was how quiet it was in the cockpit. No roaring engine vibration, only a slight hissing sound. I was so excited I guess I probably screamed in joy; it most likely was the same feeling I had when I made my very first flight at the time I was about 14 years old with the primary glider trainer, the SG 38. Now I headed downwind, reduced power, gear out at about 350 Km/h, flaps out, I turned to base, turned to final and watched the airspeed. It was ever so very critical to remember that the jet engines could not be gunned like the reciprocal engines. If one realized that the airspeed was too slow or the aircraft was too low it was absolutely necessary to ease the throttles forward ever so slowly. Pilots who could not control themselves and added power too quickly experienced a total loss of engine thrust when the turbine compressor wheel or the Zwiebel (restrictor) in the engine tail section disintegrated. Well, I had no such problem.

I lined the aircraft up with the runway, reduced the airspeed to 220 Km/h, full flaps and shot for a nose-wheel-high, gentle touchdown. When the aircraft slowed down, the nose wheel dropped down by itself and I could say, "Earth has me back!" What an experience, what a thrill! When General Galland, the General in charge of the fighter forces, flew a Me 262 for the first time, he exclaimed enthusiastically, "It feels as if angels are pushing!"

By the way, the nose wheel was a weak part of the aircraft. We were careful not to put too much stress on it. It was not steerable; in other words it was freewheeling. At one time when I turned the aircraft at the end of the runway into take-off position I made the mistake and stepped on the right brake just a little too hard. The aircraft promptly swung around, but then it would not move forward anymore. The nose wheel had flipped in a crossway position. "Now what"?

Well, there was nothing else to do but to idle the engines, unbuckle the seat belt, unbuckle the parachute, disconnect the radio, open the cockpit, jump to the ground and kick the nose wheel very hard with my foot until it was in an about 45-degree position.

Then back into the cockpit everything reconnected and now a more careful taxiing in takeoff position. That's the only time that it happened to me, because from then on I was ever so careful not to turn the aircraft too hard.

After the war, this jet from my unit was found at Neuberg.

It was getting close to Christmas 1944 when our squadron commander Capt. Bender prepared for a Christmas party. He wanted to give each soldier in his squadron a little memento. He was able to find little booklets with poetry or short stories. Then he wanted to paste a picture of the Me 262 in the booklet. That however had to be approved by security. When they saw the picture they immediately said: "No way!" So Capt. Bender had a sketch of the aircraft drawn, and submitted that for approval. "It's too close to the real thing!" "Denied". After that he submitted a rather vague sketch of a Me 262, one could hardly recognize it, that was finally approved.

War Christmas 1944

On December the 24th, the squadron had a nice dinner and heard a

few words by our squadron commander who distributed his modest gifts to his men. There was no leave allowed for anyone to go and visit his family or friends at that time. Being in love with sweet Inge I came up with a scheme. I told Capt. Bender that my mother had come down from Hamburg to Bavaria and would like to spend a few hours with me in Erding. Capt Bender was very sympathetic, however, he was not allowed to issue a formal pass to me. He just said: "If you can get to Erding and back without getting caught by the military police -- Go!" Overjoyed, I hopped on my bicycle and headed towards Erding (some 70 - 80 Km to the southeast) .It was a cold clear winter night.

I pedalled and pedalled on roads that I had never been on before. The only thing I knew was that from my experience flying over that part of the country Erding must be located somewhere "that away!" Finally I saw a sign on the right hand side of the road, which read ERDING. Was I glad! It was about daybreak and people were already heading to work. Now I had no problem finding the house and by ringing the doorbell woke everybody up. Naturally, by that time I was a bit tired, so I hit the sack and recuperated. I spent the first and the second Christmas day with the Johansen family. Heli, my buddy Horst's dear love, was a bit disappointed that Horst did not come along to Erding. I don't know why, but the return trip to Neuburg somehow did not seem to be as interesting as the trip to Erding. I decided to take the train instead. I was very concerned that a military police unit might catch me without proper leave papers. To avoid any inquisitors I asked the locomotive engineer if I could ride up front with him? He did not mind and so I threw my bicycle on the coal tender and rode the train to a couple of stations south of Ingolstadt at which time I hopped on my bike and pedalled to Neuburg. At the squadron, I was anxious to find out if my absence had been noticed. Fortunately, no!

Like flying with any aircraft, it's the take off and landing that has to be practiced the most. The "experts", old hands from other units of Bomber Wing 51, some officers and of course the former cadets, now promoted to Oberfaehnrich (senior cadet) were standing in line waiting their turn to fly. In addition to the usual traffic pattern flights we also went on cross- country flights, endurance flights and bomb-drop practices. Remember we were a bomber group. All of us had again and again the same experience when navigating over terrain we were familiar with from our training as night fighter pilots; we did not realize how fast we were now moving over the terrain. I never had a serious problem, which means that I found myself in time and never got lost. One lieutenant, however, was forced to make an emergency landing in a field. Although he flipped the aircraft on its back, he was very fortunate and did not sustain any injuries. Fuel ran out and drenched him, but luckily for him there was no fire. The fuel had such a penetrating ugly odour, worse than that of an outhouse, that we were always careful not to get any spilt on our uniform. When the lieutenant came back to the base, he first took a thorough shower and dressed in a different uniform. At the dinner table he sat next to me and he still spread the very penetrating odour around.

In January 1945, I was assigned to fly a triangular course over beautiful Bavaria, a real pleasure assignment. It was one of those wintry days with lots of sunshine and clear skies. The first leg of my flight was to go to the city of Linz. With a minor deviation from my assigned flight order I made a little detour to fly over the Johansen house at the edge of town in Erding. It was great fun to fly at treetop level towards the house and then pull up and rattle the windows down below. There was no time for a second pass, so I continued per my flight plan.

I had just reached my altitude again, when I noticed that the right engine had lost power. Throttle setting or fuel pumps on and off did not have any effect, so I shut the right engine down. After a bit of trimming the aircraft flew very nicely where I wanted it to go. I was only a few miles from Muenchen Riem, so I thought it best to land there, rather than flying in single engine mode back to Neuburg. The approach was quite normal; however, I realized that the sink rate with one engine dead was considerable higher. I made it over the fence and set it gently on the grass field. After taxiing the aircraft over to the KG 51 hangar, I turned it over to the mechanics and prepared to spend the evening with Johansens. Next day the aircraft still was not ready yet so I was "forced" to spend some more time in Erding.

The following day the aircraft and I were ready to fly back to Neuburg. During take-off, suddenly the left main gear brake froze and I decided to abandon the take-off. Everything would have been fine, if I had been able to stop the aircraft before I had reached an open bomb crater. With the last momentum, very slowly, the left landing gear skidded into a crater.

The mechanics now had to have more time for the repair of the aircraft, so I took the train back to Neuburg. The manpower shortage in the 5th and 6th year of war in Germany was very acute. As able bodied young men were drafted into the military, male Luftwaffe personal whom women could replace, were reassigned to some infantry unit on the Eastern front. For example we had girls who re-fueled the aircraft, cleaned the windscreen or handed the mechanics a tool.

KG 51 Me 262 A-2a jet bomber and an Me 163 B rocket interceptor.

500 KG bomb in front of an Me 262 A-2a.

The mechanics were not too happy as they then had to work with totally inexperienced helpers. We, my buddies and I, found that a much more pleasant arrangement. With a nice girl, we could chit chat while the tanks were being filled up or have a little get-together after duty hours. I struck a little acquaintance with a nice-looking, young woman who did not like her assignment because she would much rather be in classes studying to become an actress.

One day my buddy Horst was sitting in his aircraft while a girl had the re-fuelling hose in the forward tank just in front of the cockpit but got carried away with her talking to the pilot. Suddenly the tank was full and fuel was overflowing. Instead of stopping the fuel flow first she just pulled the hose out of the forward tank and put it in the rear tank (900Ltr) in the rear of the cockpit. Unfortunately that gave Horst a quick shower of the smelly J 2 fuel. She was very embarrassed and he was not very happy with his " eu de cologne".

The Me 262 had a fuel capacity of almost 2600 Lt. (700 Gal), for the two jet engines plus some 30 Lt. for the Riedel starter motors and the fuel for the initial starting phase of the jet engines. We had some fun with all the helpers who were as a rule not too mechanically inclined, but tried to do the jobs assigned to them. For the duration of the war, public dancing was not allowed. Naturally many a soldier at home on furlough would have liked to enjoy himself, but then again it was considered unfair to all the many other soldiers who were deprived of such entertainment wherever they were stationed. Alcohol was a rarity. From time-to-time a little booze like brandy was distributed which sometimes came to the unit in a barrel. Because we had no bottles or any other container we received our share in our two-quart field aluminium mess tins. One day we had just picked up our ration and taken it to our rooms, and the group commander announced at dinner time: "Tomorrow we will have a "Herren Abend" (Gentlemen's Evening) at the officers' casino, please keep your alcohol for that night!" We cadets, however, did not want to "waste" our ration at a dull evening with senior officers so we went to the group commander and said: "Sir, we have received our ration and consumed it already".
"Well, then you'll have to drink beer tomorrow!" was Major Barth's reply. In reality we still had our alcohol, waiting for a better occasion to use it.

Next evening, after dinner everybody relaxed in the casino with a drink, a glass of wine or so, except the cadets, who were given a glass of weak, thin beer. Klaus went to the casino sergeant and asked him if he did not have something better than beer? "Well", he said, "I'll fix you something; I still have a couple of bottles of vodka which we brought back from Russia"! The next "beer" really was a mixture of 1/2 beer and 1/2 Vodka. It looked like a harmless drink, but it was a lot more than that. It did not take too long and the noise level at the cadet's table was considerably higher than at the other tables, which prompted some older gentlemen to remark: "Look, nowadays, the young ones cannot even handle a glass of weak beer anymore". Little did they know!

**Knights Cross holder
Gruppen Major Barth,
Gruppenkommandeur, IV/KG
51**

**Sharing a drink with Major Barth and Roland Gruhn
at a reunion for Me 262 pilots (1992)**

The evening turned out to be a very nice party. I remember that someone got up, climbed on his chair and gave a speech. He said a few "Apropos" words, but then he told a couple of funny jokes. One was this:

He imitated the voice of the minister of propaganda. Dr. Josef Goebbels:

"My dear countrymen and women: If ever a British aircraft should fly over German territory, we will retaliate and fly over there with 50 aircraft.. Should they fly over here with 100 aircraft, we will fly over there with 1000 aircraft, if they ever fly over here with 1000 aircraft, well, then we won't fly anymore!" Obviously a very true statement, the way it finally turned out to be.

Our supreme commander of the Luftwaffe, Hermann Goering, was many times referred to as "Mr. Meier". The reason was this: In America we say: "If so and so happens I'll eat my hat." In Germany one says, "If so and so happens my name shall be Meier." Goering made such a boastful statement when he said at the beginning of the war, "If ever enemy aircraft fly over Germany, you can call me Meier!" Well, that's why many times he was referred to as "Meier ordered so and so", or "Meier said". Because of his overweight condition, he was also referred to as "the fat one".

One joke circulated when Mrs. Emmy Goering gave birth to a baby girl which they named Edda. Supposedly the name Edda was selected because it is the name of a collection of 1000-year-old Germanic epic poetry; however, we said Edda is an abbreviation and means E = Emmy D=dankt (thanks) D= dem (the) A= Adjutant (adjutant). We did not think that Meier was capable of producing a child.

Somebody else told the story imitating Hitler's voice: "In order to alleviate the critical manpower shortage we have here in Germany, I have decided after a considerable in-depth study, to shorten the pregnancy period of women from nine months to seven months!" "Sieg Heil"!

On our level, we did not ever have the feeling "Big Brother is watching you" and said whatever was on our mind. For instance sitting at a desk in the middle of the night while on guard duty we tuned in a radio station with the best music. If it had Glenn Miller melodies or any other music we liked which came from a foreign station, we turned it up and enjoyed it. I have never heard of any complaints about violating a government order, "Not to listen to foreign broadcasts!"

When a couple of aircraft had to make an emergency landing because the loss of engine power, it was thought that perhaps there was fuel contamination. Everything was checked and rechecked which meant that all aircraft were grounded. Fuel for aircraft which needed high-octane gas became more and more difficult to get, our diesel-type fuel, however was not nearly as difficult to obtain.

We were wondering, and today I'm still puzzled, "Why did the Allies not bomb and keep bombing the hydrogenation plants that produced gasoline out of coal in Germany which would have stopped all German military activity, as without fuel no war?"

One day we were informed that engineers had built a highly developed REVI, EZ 42 (Reflex vizier = gunsight), which was supposed to give a pursuing aircraft in a dogfight situation the ability to hone in, that is to correctly lead on his opponent even in a tight turn. The device was installed in a Buecker 181, which we were then to fly and try it out. After having flown so many much heavier aircraft we enjoyed for a change to fly this 85 hp primary trainer again. We tried out the REVI and found that it was very easy to use.

The Allied Bomber command at that time could fly over Germany at will and drop bombs on any city. That, I believe was foremost on my mind and on many Luftwaffe colleagues too: "We have to do something to stop the killing of so many thousands and thousands of innocent women and children." But how can we do it? Obviously the air raids were not primarily directed towards the German aircraft industry because in the year 1938 there were only 8,000 aircraft manufactured and in the year 1944 aircraft production in Germany rose to almost 40,000 in spite of raw material shortage, manpower shortage, food shortage and air raid interruptions. Of course U.S. production was 90,000 aircraft that year. Many engineers were searching for ways to stop the bombers. I remember when we observed a test of a procedure to attack the U.S. bombers with bombs.

The experiment was this: a Ju 88 flew overhead, at a few thousand feet altitude and a Me 262 with a 250 Kg bomb on board flew above the Ju88 and dropped the bomb so that it would fall down near the Ju 88.

The bomb had a percussion-vibration-triggering fuse which would then activate the bomb. The explosion if it happened in the middle of a bomber formation of B-17's probably would eliminate some aircraft.

For that approach, only the Me 262 would have been able to evade the fighter escort and fly near the bomber formation because of the much higher speed. Tests were also conducted at our base at Neuburg to extend the range of the Me 262. We watched as test pilots took off with a Me 262 which had a device, a large fuel tank with stubby wings, attached to the tail of the aircraft with a long pole. It looked like a V1 pilot-less bomb and was attached with some sort of a pipe. Take offs that I observed were broken off before the Me 262 became airborne. Porpoising seemed to be one problem. If I remember correctly the code name for this project was "Deichselschlepp" (pole-tow).

My Guardian Angel

On January 13, 1945, I experienced the most dramatic, and devastating episode in my entire aviator's life. This is what I wrote in my diary in 1945: On Sunday the 13th, I was scheduled to go on a cross country flight. About 13:00 the aircraft 9K + I W (Werk # 170049) was refueled and everything was ready for takeoff. My takeoff runway was east. When I had already accelerated close to take off speed the aircraft wanted to brake out to the right. Applying the left brake did not correct the "off course" direction. I had lost power on the right engine. Now what? I had reached the critical point where I had to decide: If I brake off the take off now, will I be able to stop the momentum of the aircraft or will I plough right through the farmhouse at the edge of the field towards which I was now heading? -- Or perhaps if I'm lucky I'll get the aircraft to fly in spite of the reduced power on one engine? I thought that I would have a better chance if I attempt a take off. As I was lumbering over the frozen grass the speed increased ever so slowly, 170 - 180 - 190 Km/h The farmhouse became larger and larger. Now I was probably only some 100 yards from the building when I pulled back on the stick -- and the aircraft responded, lifted off and flew! Hurray! I made it! I cleared the roof of the farmhouse, not by very much, but I made it. Then there was a road with tall trees I barely made it over them. Then I was shocked - the aircraft rolled to the right, it did not respond to the controls and I saw the ploughed field with snow covered on one side of the furrows coming straight at me. Now everything went by in a matter of seconds. The aircraft touched the ground with the right wing and began to cartwheel, while disintegrating, piece-by-piece. One of the 900-ltr fuel tanks exploded, blew the canopy off and surrounded me momentarily in a ball of fire. Then everything suddenly became quiet. The fire gave me the awareness that I had to do something. I unbuckled myself and stepped from the cockpit right onto the ground. There was only one thought on my mind -- "Fire!" Somehow, I was under the impression that any moment now a big explosion would happen. As fast as I could, I limped away from the cockpit.

The rest of the aircraft was scattered over a wide area on the field. Then I sat down and laid back. Am I still alive? Can I still move my arms? My legs? Am I badly injured? I was very surprised that I was able to move all limbs; the right knee hurt a little bit, but I could move it.

Then a group of Flakhelfer (teenage anti aircraft gunners) showed up who were sure that the pilot of this aircraft could not be alive anymore. When they saw me they placed an overcoat under me and I laid back and contemplated my situation. A Sanka (Sanitaetskraftwagen = ambulance) arrived and the medics wanted to place me on a stretcher and haul me to the base. Now I was able to stand up and insisted to ride back to the base sitting next to the driver. As we drove near an aircraft which was being readied for take off I saw Ernst Kinscher standing there staring at the ambulance. I waved at him, but he just stood there and looked with a very blank expression on his face. Later, he told me that he had observed my takeoff and when he saw the explosion and the column of smoke rising up, he knew that Haenschen was just killed -- he could not believe that Haenschen had survived that crash. He already was contemplating, so he told me later, that someone had to deliver the message of Haenschen's death to his parents and as he had a girlfriend in Hamburg he would volunteer for that mission. Fortunately for me and unfortunately for him the trip to Hamburg was not necessary.

At the base hospital I was checked out. When I looked into a mirror I realized why Ernst thought a ghost was sitting in the ambulance. My face was black, my hair was scorched and I had some first-degree burns in my face. My right knee was banged up, but that was pretty much the extent of my injuries. The Doctor could not find anything seriously wrong but told me: "If you have any feeling of nausea or any internal pain, see me immediately!" With that I was bandaged and released. When I returned to my room I cleaned myself and dressed in a clean uniform. I could not understand how it was possible for me to survive such a crash.

The flight helmet had built-in earphones. Two microphones were buttoned around my throat, and an oxygen mask was hooked to the flight helmet in front of my nose. Everything was firmly in place.

The cord from the flight helmet to the radio set was customarily first wrapped around the belt as a bailout safety precaution I now realized that the flight helmet and oxygen mask had disappeared but the telephone cord was still wrapped around my belt under my flight jacket. How can that be? How can the explosion rip the helmet off my head without ripping my head off also? I believe that my Guardian Angel was there at the right time and held his hand over me and protected me.

Theoretically, I should have been killed, but the dear Lord kept me alive for future assignments.

There I sat in my room waiting for some feeling of nausea or some internal pain. When my buddies came in, there was a big 'hallo' and congratulations. This was what we called a "Flyers Birthday" which had to be properly celebrated. To this day I still celebrate my second birthday each year on January 13.

A bottle of Cognac was somehow quickly available, and a sincere toast, first to my Guardian Angel, then a "thank you" to Willy Messerschmitt who had designed an aircraft with a cockpit that some day was to be pressurised and was therefore constructed especially sturdy. Finally of course, a "Prosit" to the lucky "13" -- which I have since considered my favoured number. I'm sure we did not run out of reasons for many toasts, and when finally I crawled in my bunk I was a little tipsy. Apparently, I had a couple drinks too many. I felt sick! Juergen immediately thought that I was sick because of some internal injuries from the crash, so he quickly ran over to the first-aid station to talk to the Doctor. Fortunately he was unable to find the Doctor. The night went by -- I had no internal pain and woke up the next morning with a little headache -- not from the crash! It was never determined what caused my crash. Maybe fuel starvation? Maybe? maybe?

Another mysterious fatality happened when Lt. Elter, while in a formation flying exercise, suddenly spiralled down to earth. He did not bail out and was killed. We all wondered what might have been the reason.

Given enough time everything will heal. My hair grew back, so did my eyelashes and eyebrows. The burns in my face blistered and dried up. My right kneecap, however, took a little longer to heal. Bending the knee was quite painful and therefore I had difficulty using it for flying.

Duty as usual

In a discussion someone brought up the news that Allied aircraft machine gunned German pilots or aircrew members who had bailed out and were hanging on their parachutes. We were all appalled and could not believe it. Would anyone of us do such a thing? -- no way! We considered such a thing as pure murder. Many years later I discussed the subject with a former pilot of the US Army Air Corps and a pilot of the U.S. Navy and both confirmed that an order was issued to try to "eliminate" any bailed-out German jet flyer.(*A clear example of an Allied War Crime –Ed*)

Of our flight group of 10 Officer Cadets, Alex, Walter, and Hans Jaskolla had completed their Me 262 flight training and were transferred to the first group ,KG51, to fly bombing missions on the Western front.

About this time Schab had a potentially dangerous flight. He was cruising along at about 15,000 Ft when suddenly his left engine was on fire. He had no other choice but to bail out. With a red lever on the right side the canopy should be jettisoned. Schab pulled the lever but nothing happened. Meanwhile he had pulled the nose of the aircraft up to reduce the speed for his bail out. In vain he tried to release the canopy. The flying speed of the aircraft rapidly reduced to near stalling speed, when he decided to open the cockpit the normal way by tilting it to the right side.

Thank God at least that worked. He unbuckled himself and stepped out of the cockpit. That's as far as he was able to go because by that time the aircraft had stalled and gone into a flat spin. Although outside of the aircraft now, he was not able to free-fall away from the aircraft. The centrifugal force of the spinning aircraft glued him on the wing root on the side were the engine was on fire. With all his strength he pushed and pushed against the fuselage while sitting on the wing, very close to the burning engine. With the last hard push he fell through the flames but at least he was free. He pulled the rip cord of his parachute, "Oh my God"; he thought as he held the handle with a piece of wire attached in his hand, "I must have ripped the wire off, now the parachute will not open!" Frantically, he reached for his back trying to find in vain the broken end of the release wire. Then a little jerk, he looked up and saw that he was safely hanging on the parachute floating slowly to the ground. He was taken to the airbase Fuerstenfeldbruck, where he stayed overnight and returned the next day with a student pilot in a primary trainer aircraft back to Neuburg.

In February, Ernst, Juergen, and Schab were also transferred to the I/KG 51 to fly bombing missions at the western front. One day Horst had a very exciting flight. When he was taking off, and was in a climbing attitude, suddenly, without warning, with a loud bang the canopy ripped off and blew away. It was unfortunate that the canopy hit him on his forehead and the guide wire sliced his throat. For a moment he was dazed but he was able to regain control of himself and his aircraft just in time, and he flew the traffic pattern and landed safely. He gave the ground crew quite a shock when he pulled up to the flight line because blood was pouring over his face and from his throat. He was very lucky because his injuries were not life threatening and after a few days he was back on duty.

Now Roland, Klaus, Horst and I were left. We continued the prescribed training flights, which for the most part were very enjoyable.

My close friend Horst, shortly after his close call. The injury was minor and he soon returned to duty.

I loose my friend Horst

On March 2nd Horst was supposed to fly an endurance flight, which was to be at about 12,000 Ft altitude. At that altitude it was required to breath oxygen so he had to check out an oxygen mask. Horst wanted to check out an oxygen mask at the parachute / oxygen mask department. However, the sergeant in charge could not be found.

Instead of waiting and postponing his flight, he took off without the oxygen mask. Therefore he had to fly at a lower altitude, which caused him to use more fuel, which forced him to reduce his airspeed to be able to fly his course and still make it back to the base. He was just cruising along and was only some 30 miles away from Neuburg when four P-51 Mustangs in a dive caught up with him and shot him down. Apparently he attempted to bail out, unbuckled his seat belts but because of a bullet which had pierced his hip he was unable to lift himself up and out of the cockpit. At 09:35 near the small town of Dillingen the aircraft hit the ground and Horst was catapulted out of the aircraft and his body was found several hundred feet from the crash site.

Horst and I shared a room and a wall locker. We were very close friends and I was deeply sorry Horst was no longer with me. For me now it was required to return his flight equipment and material back to supply and pack his personal belongings to be sent to his parents in Bielefeld. With the first part I had no problem, however, when I bundled his letters and notes I felt that it was not proper for me to look at them or read them. I therefore bundled everything and deposited it for shipment at the orderly room.

A few days later I was summoned to the squadron commander. Capt. Bender had on his desk the package to be mailed to Horsts' parents. He did read Horst's letters, as he was supposed to do, and found that Horst's girlfriend had written: "Horst, why did you not claim that your mother was visiting in Erding as Haenschen did, so you and I could have spent some time together?" That was my pretext to get the squadron commander to allow my trip at Christmas time to take the bicycle ride to Erding. Now, on top of Horst's death I felt very bad that I had deceived my squadron commander.

Horst was buried at the cemetery in the city of Neuburg. Only Roland and I stood at his gravesite with a very heavy heart to bid him farewell. At the beginning of March, Roland was transferred to the first Group KG 51. Now I was the last of the Mohicans of our tightly knit Cadet Bunch.

Destruction of Neuburg Luftwaffe Base

In the first days of March, on a Monday, the USAAC attacked our base. There was some damage to some of the buildings but my barracks was still very much intact. Overall flight activity was disrupted only slightly.
On Wednesday the same week the sirens sounded "evacuate the base" alarm. "Well," I thought, "our comrades with the other postal service number" (an expression often used when speaking of enemy soldiers) were here only a couple of days ago, they would not drop bombs on our base again, or would they?" This time most likely the target will be the city of Neuburg a few miles to the west. I took my time, nonchalantly

pedalling my bicycle towards the Danube River. I had not made it too far from the base when a loud hum, the thundering noise that many big aircraft are making approached our base from the East. The hum intensity grew louder and louder by the minute and there I could see a formation of B 24 bombers heading straight for our base. Now I stepped on it to get away from the target area -- maybe it was our base? -- as quickly as possible. I had not reached the stand-by area yet where I was supposed to go to, when the first bombers dropped their bomb load causing earthshaking, thunderous explosions. I found a shallow trough and hugged the ground, making myself as flat as possible. Formation after formation of the bombers discharged their deadly cargo. Each time when the dust had settled a little bit I observed that my two-story barracks was still standing. However, after the last of the about 300 aircraft had flown away to the west, my barracks disappeared. After the sirens sounded the "all clear", I returned to the base.

As the U.S. bombers had dropped their heavy bombs on the base's facilities, they also dropped many small anti-personnel, shrapnel bombs on a wide area all around the base, which were to target our aircraft parked in protective earth boxes and our soldiers who had disbursed some distance from the base to be safe. When the all clear sirens sounded I pedalled back. I had never seen such thorough destruction at what used to be the base. It looked like a moon crater landscape. Apparently what one bomb had thrown that away, the next bomb threw back this way. It took a lot of imagination to determine where each building used to stand. I started to dig and search in the rubble that used to be my barracks hoping to find something of value of my possessions, but there was nothing left. The fact that I lost my uniforms and a few personal items, I could accept. But I thought that it was not very nice of the USAAC to drop a bomb on my barracks just as I had one of those rare allocations of Brandy in my wall locker. One full bottle, gone!

As I was poking around, suddenly there were three men in striped suits like the one prisoners wear they walked by escorted by an elderly Luftwaffe soldier. Naturally I was curious who they were and what they were doing there. The guarding soldier did not mind when I asked them some questions. It turned out that they came from a concentration camp called Dachau, a few miles to the south.

The word "concentration camp" I had heard somewhere, sometime before to mean a prison for political prisoners But of course I had never heard any details about such a camp. The purpose of the camp was to collect and isolate anti-government, leading Communists or Social Democrats. In America it was sufficient to have the appearance of a Japanese person to be arrested and confined for the duration of the war to a concentration camp. The British used such concentration camps during the Boer war in South Africa back in 1904.

Back to the three prisoners. Why had they come to the base? They were volunteers to come to our base and defuse bombs that had not exploded. They were not forced to do it but did it because they received as compensation some extra benefits, which any German soldier would also receive. Usually that consisted of cigarettes, brandy, food and "brownie points" for good behaviour. All three men had been brought to Dachau around 1934 because they were prominent members of the Communist and Socialist party. As they were very much opposed to the new regime, the National Socialist Party, they were considered a threat to the security of the new government. To get them out of circulation they were simply arrested and confined at Dachau

They told me that life for "us old-timers" is bearable as we can receive food parcels, an occasional bottle of wine or brandy and we can see our wives and families from time-to-time. However, people who arrive there only to be transferred to somewhere else a few days later are very hungry, and are starving." It was only many years later I was to read that some concentration camps were established to annihilate Jews.

After the total destruction of our base, all personnel now had to be billeted somewhere else. I really was very lucky because I was assigned to a room at a butcher's house in a nearby village. When I arrived and introduced myself, I was given as a welcome greeting a huge plate with samplings of delicious sausages, wonderful Bavarian farmers' bread and of course a mug of tasty beer. This proved to me again, "everything has it's bad and everything has it's good side".

During the last air raid there were many, many fragmentation - anti -personnel bombs dropped in a wide area around our base. The purpose, most likely was to damage or destroy our aircraft, which were parked in "shrapnel protection boxes", as well as killing personnel dispersed some distance away from the field. Yet we still had some flyable aircraft left! It was strange that after so much total destruction the runway was still intact. So I continued to fly.

Neuburg during attack

A Mission?

One Sunday; I had just completed a prescribed flight and was now being refuelled for another take off, when I heard in the distance in the general direction of Ingolstadt, and about 20 Km to the east, the rattling sound of machine guns. There was nobody with authority around who could give me an order to do something or prohibit me from doing something. I thought that here now I had a chance to investigate and perhaps disturb some enemy activity. Both fuel tanks are full, start the turbines, disconnect the battery wagon, check once more engine temperature, pressure, oil, fuel etc. and off I went. The take off was to the east, so first I climbed in a wide arc towards the south to gain altitude. Then I veered towards Ingolstadt where I spotted some smoke. As I came closer I saw a bunch of P-47 Thunderbolts diving towards some targets on the ground firing their guns, flying a 180 degree turn, climbing and again turning 180 degrees to line up for another shooting spree. I approached quite fast and out of the sun so it seemed that they did not spot me. I switched guns "on" and lined up with the aircraft which was almost ready to dive, right in front of me. When I was only a couple of hundred feet away I pulled the trigger. A loud burst of firing four 30mm cannons is what I expected to hear, but instead all I heard was a clicking sound in my earphones. By now I had come so close to the P-47 that I almost rammed it. As I zipped over it the pilot looked up at me and I looked down at him he immediately started a split ass manoeuvre, while I climbed away. Frustrated I activated again and again all control buttons and switches but to no avail, not a single shot fired.

Later I realized how lucky I was that the P 47 pilot went into a dive instead of just lifting up his nose and firing his guns at me while I was passing over him.Now what? I certainly did not want to return to base as I was expecting the P-47 to cruise around and wait for me to land. I would have been an easy target in my final approach landing at Neuburg. I thought that it would be best to conserve fuel and wait for those guys to buzz off. I climbed to 30,000 ft and received continuously the Ami position reports from the ground radar station. When those "Indians" had moved to the north, there was no more threat for me from them during my landing approach. I returned to base. Naturally I was mad that the stupid guns did not work. It turned out that there were three electrical wires that were disconnected causing the guns not to fire. This was my only opportunity to shoot down an aircraft. Today over 50 years later, I feel very happy that I did not kill anyone during the war -- especially myself, of course.

On Monday, around 3pm, my aircraft was reported to be ready. I thought, "Today I will have a better chance to shoot an aircraft down because the guns will definitely work!" But no! There came an air raid warning, signalling, "Clear the Base". I did not have a chance to leave the base in time so I ducked behind the wall of an aircraft fragmentation bomb protection box. This time a formation of about 100-twin engine Marauder aircraft approached from the west and dropped their bomb load on only the concrete runway. With that, my wartime flying came to an end. All facilities, the tarmac and the runway were destroyed, although there was still the grass field next to the runway. The few of our aircraft that were still serviceable were turned over to the JV 44 (Jagdverband 44) with which General Galland and his top notch aces flew combat missions until the end of the war.

Now that everything was reduced to rubble, we thought that we would abandon this base and select a stretch of the Autobahn straight and long enough from which we could operate. Unfortunately that would have been too logical. The order was given: "Repair and reconstruct the runway!" What a Herculean job that was from, 07:00 until 18:00. All available manpower was assigned to work on the runway. Along with us there were some Russian soldiers-POW's, civilians, Hungarians, or workers from OT (Organization Todt, a Government construction team) or other military personnel, all busy shovelling and filling up bomb craters in the concrete runway with dirt, and a patch of new concrete. Progress was not very encouraging, so an SS officer took over the command. Of course that did not change anything at all either.

Meanwhile, American forces were already moving towards Southern Germany. Day after day we worked to repair a few hundred yards of the runway. We realized that we most likely would not be able to finish the job and therefore would not be able to use it to fly from it again. We really saw the futility of our effort when we saw that the section of the runway that was completed was also being prepared for destruction because alongside the runway a number of 500lb bombs were deposited which could later, when the enemy approached be used to blow up the runway again.

Sometimes American fighter aircraft showed up -- maybe they wanted to inspect our rebuilding progress? Anyway they did not come too close, as there were still some light flak guns around. From time-to-time a formation of heavy bombers flew by, but no one was allowed to leave the shovelling job unless the sirens sounded the "Raeumungsalarm" (clear the base). When that happened the "construction site" was evacuated in a matter of minutes. At that time I thought that our future looked very bleak. It was not only the fact that it seemed hardly possible for Germany to win the war even if suddenly "Wunder-Waffen" (Wonder-Weapons) should become available. Rumors circulated that the Allied Forces were determined to annihilate Germany. To begin with, they were not interested to negotiate a peace, but instead demanded nothing less than "Unconditional Surrender". Stalin, it was reported, wanted to randomly shoot 50,000 German officers and Roosevelt wanted to modify that by shooting only 49,000*. I too had the feeling that I might just as well continue to fight than throw in the towel and face starvation and death after the war. Henry Morgenthau, Roosevelt's Jewish Secretary of the Treasury, prepared a devilish plan, which Roosevelt totally supported, which in essence demanded that Germany would be turned into a "pastoral country". All industry and mining was to be destroyed. The Germans had to live off their land. There would be massive starvation as only 60 % of the Germans of the German population could support themselves on food stuff grown on German land, which meant 40 % would die. All the barbaric Morgenthau Plan details I found out many years later. Here a few weeks before the end of the war, rumours could not possibly grasp the real danger Germany was facing. Fortunately there were still enough level-headed people, especially in the U.S.A. and England, to not implement and enforce this sadistic Morgenthau Plan**.

*Editors note: Remarks and "jokes" of that nature were in fact exchanged between Stalin and Roosevelt at Yalta
**To this day it remains a matter of speculation if it was level headedness, or the necessity of the "Cold War" that caused a change to this most monstrous proposal of future Allied policy.

Defending a bridge

I don't know for sure, but I don't think too much of the runway was repaired. For me flying from this base was over. I and personnel from our 12th squadron, clerks, mechanics and a few pilots were now given a new assignment. Near the base there was a village with the name Stengelheim. We were ordered to prepare for the defence of a small bridge over a little river near this village as infantry soldiers of course. We were given old Italian rifles, which looked like American Civil War issues, some hand-grenades, one MG 15 and some "Panzerfausts" (Bazookas). We practiced with our new weapons a little bit and started to dig foxholes. Nobody was very enthusiastic about this suicide mission, because we all realized that the Americans would have no problem wiping out our improvised "Siegfried" defence line. Our action plan was this: two 500lb bombs were placed under the bridge to be detonated as soon as one or two US tanks had crossed it. With our Panzerfausts we would then take the tanks out of commission. Out of our foxholes we then would stop the following US infantry,...and then what?? We were all aware that the slightest resistance like our heroic effort would immediately trigger a massive artillery or fighter-bomber barrage. My pilot buddies and I thought that this would not be a very good way to end the war or to die as an infantry soldier. However, we followed orders and hoped for a better way out of this 'infantry assignment'.

Kommando Bienenstock

One day a message came to us, "Who wants to volunteer for the "Kommando Bienenstock?" Initially, we thought it was called "Kommando Totenkopf", which would have been more appropriate.
Nobody had any idea what that was, but when we heard that this was an assignment that had something to do with flying, we pilots immediately said "Yes! We volunteer." The worst flying job we thought would still be better than this suicide mission on the ground!
The next day we heard what we had volunteered to do. At some of the primary flight schools there were still a number of small single engine

trainers around. We were to load up the aircraft with a bunch of explosives and take off with an army expert just as it became dark and fly over the enemy line and attempt to land the aircraft somewhere on a field or meadow. The infantryman would than take his explosive material and head for his goal -- a bridge, a fuel or ammunition dump, or whatever target he was to blow up -- while the pilot was to take off from that dark field and head back to base. "That simple!" Well, that certainly did not sound very inspiring to us, but then again it beat the certain death of the infantry mission. Next day we received written orders to report at Fuerstenfeldbruck airbase, my great alma mater from the good old days at Luftkriegsschule 4. Each one of us had a small bundle of personal things, uniform pieces, flight gear etc, which we hung on my bicycle so we did not have to carry anything. Then off we went heading south. To Fuerstenfeldbruck it was about 40 to 50 miles - a long way to Tipperary! Whenever a vehicle stopped and asked us if we needed a ride, we always declined as we weren't in that much of a hurry to get to our new assignment.

We had not gone too far, when it became dark and we asked a farmer if we could sleep the night in his barn. No problem! We had not fallen asleep yet, when artillery shells started to burst nearby. We thought that it was too close for comfort; we packed our things and walked a few miles further to find another barn where we could sleep. Next day we continued our march, or better said our nonchalant stroll. Somewhere along the road I had picked up a stick, maybe about three foot long and 1 inch thick, which I used as a walking stick. As we came through one village, suddenly an army soldier rushed up to me, saluted and said: "Sir, the General wants to see you!" Of course, I was perplexed, "Where, what General?" I did not see any military activity but was led to a Gasthaus (inn) and a stern looking General. I saluted and asked him what he wanted. The General gave me a lengthy speech about military conduct uniform code and that it was not becoming of an officer to set bad examples and walk in uniform with a stick in his hand. What can one say? "Yes sir, yes sir, and yes sir!" I'm sure he would have liked to assign me to his command but fortunately I had my written orders to report at Fuerstenfeldbruck, so he could not very well shanghai me. Meanwhile I was wondering if that General did not have anything better to do but to reprimand some Luftwaffe soldier for improper uniform code at a time like this when our whole world was falling down around us.

When we were a few miles from Fuerstenfeldbruck we decided to have one of us take the bicycle ride to the base and explore the situation. We drew matches and the "short" match had the job. Meanwhile we went to a village Gasthaus and found something to eat. Suddenly a troop of about 30 soldiers walked in. They looked strange because they all had their hair cut very short -- they looked bald. We then found out that they were of a SS military penal unit and were now on their way towards the combat area. When we asked them with what they intended to fight as they had no weapons; they said they had to find some weapons first. We were glad that we did not have their assignment. (Perhaps "my General" would have been glad to recruit them. I wonder if he would have commented on their non regulation haircuts)

Then an American tank rolled in at the most northern end of the village...we quickly packed our things and helter-skelter dashed out of the village at the southern end. We had not walked too far when our "Reconnaissance-Scout" came riding towards us and reported the situation at Fuerstenfelbruck. The Kommando "Bienenstock" had requisitioned all available flyable aircraft and sent them on their mission. The night before the last one had left and none ever returned. Later I was told by Col Hajo Herrmann that a number of missions were flown against the Russians from Austrian bases with some actual success reported. But where do we go now? Out of this hopeless atmosphere came several last-minute, desperate projects, attempts to stave off the daily flood of allied bombers and perhaps saving a few lives of some German civilians, mostly women and children.

Col. Hajo Herrmann

When in April 1945, when my flying had come to an end at Neuburg and I volunteered for the Kommando Bienenstock. About the same time Jochen heard of a very special mission in North Germany.

Only volunteers were accepted; the mysterious name was "Sonderkommando Elbe". The objective was to keep Allied Bombers out of the sky in the area of East Germany, long enough for the German army to stop the advances of the Red Army towards the centre of the Reich. Jochen thought that all that was necessary was for him to say: "I volunteer!", but that was not so. First there were some psychological examinations, then some physical tests with strength and endurance, he had to prove himself and show that he had courage. Finally he was told, "You are accepted!" Now the candidates were introduced to the details of the mission. He was to fly with a Me 109 together with three other aircraft towards the Allied bomber formation. He was to avoid the many Allied fighter escorts and break through to attack the bombers. As a last resort he was to ram the bomber and make him crash. His chance of survival probably was not too good but it could mean a blessing for a German city. Jochen contributed with a report about his experience of his first and only mission with the Sonderkommando Elbe to the book "Das Bittere Ende Der Luftwaffe" ("The bitter end of the Luftwaffe", written by Erich Saft).

Jochen wrote:
"Around noon on April 7th 1945, only 36 German fighters were available in the general area of Verden – Soltau to attack the 13th Allied heavy bomber wing. Lt. Thiel and Ofhr. Jochen Boehm were the only two of his Schwarm of 4 aircraft to get off the ground. My aircraft apparently was a very lame bird because I fell more and more behind. I was unable to speak to Lt. Thiel, because none of the aircraft had any radio gear installed.
Suddenly my windshield was covered with a thick black coat of oil. There I sat in the dark. I did not see any enemy fighter aircraft anywhere around me so I assume an oil line of my engine had ruptured. Of course with an aircraft in this condition I could not possibly attempt an attack.
I looked for a suitable place for an emergency landing which was not easy with zero forward visibility. In a steep dive I focused on a meadow down below through a blurry view in a side window of the cockpit. I was approaching the field with a speed of 400Km/h, when I had the field in sight- but -suddenly with a thunderous bang. I crashed through a group of trees which I had barely seen a glimpse of in the last second. The aircraft, now totally out of control somersaulted, flipped on its back and finally came to rest upside down in a ditch.
The extremely high centrifugal force caused my left upper arm to pierce

the hull of the aircraft, causing it to break in five places. Badly injured, bleeding from numerous wounds, I was hanging by my seatbelt harness upside down in the ditch. A man with a little boy who were fishing in a nearby lake ran over to the wrecked aircraft and tried to pry the canopy open. They were unable to do that, therefore the boy ran off to summoned the village blacksmith. With all the effort, it still took them three hours to free me out of my cockpit. The helpful people tried their best; finally they laid me stretched out on my opened parachute in the green grass of the meadow. After what seemed to be an awfully long time, I was taken to an emergency hospital in Doenitz and shortly thereafter to the general hospital in Ludwigslust. All this time I remained fully conscious. In the hospital, just before I passed out I heard the doctor talking. "He is so very young, we have to try to save his left arm, if necessary we still can amputate at a later time." My arm was saved and eventually all of my injuries healed too.

As an epilogue to my ordeal in 1945: It was 48 years later that I visited the crash site and even had a chance to meet one of my rescuers, the then 9-year old boy who ran for help and got the blacksmith to the crash site. This kid, now a farmer, presented me with one blade of my Me 109 aircrafts propeller which he had kept for all these years on his farm. It was a very emotional gesture for me!"

All that remained of Jochen's fighter – a single propeller blade – and Jochen!

Now What ?

Our assignment fizzled out. Therefore, I took possession of my bicycle and pedalled to Erding. Now I was a bit concerned that some military police unit could pick me up because I was heading in the wrong direction per my orders. As American forces were advancing quite rapidly, I contemplated that perhaps it would be best to let them capture me in Erding at the Johansens home. What a surprise when I came to Erding and found Roland had also come to the Johansens! He reported that in Holzkirchen, south of Munich, a number of KG 51 personnel had congregated. We decided to join them so we said "Auf Wiedersehn" and pedalled to Holzkirchen. Surprise, surprise, the "heroes" with whom we should have defended that little bridge near Stengelheim had wisely retreated and they were now in Holzkirchen. Roland and I reported for "duty". Someone had assigned KG 51 personnel to form a military police unit and control the traffic in this small provincial town. All I had to do was to check trip tickets of military vehicles, of which many were occupied by women and children and had large bundles tied to the roof of the car. The authorization to drive the vehicle to the Swiss border was properly signed by some General, so I had to wave them on. In spite of all the commotion and the overall state of confusion during the last days of the war the bureaucratic apparatus seemed to still function. A message was received that announced that Roland and I as of March 1st 1945 were promoted to the rank of lieutenant.

After a couple of days with about two dozen other soldiers we formed a unit under command of First Lt. Kuhn, equipped with a couple of Kettenkrad's, a heavy three-axle truck, an Opel Blitz truck, a couple of Mercedes passenger cars, a couple of heavy motorcycles with side cars and a few smaller motor-cycles; in other words a nice contingent of usable vehicles. The order was: "Move to a small village in the vicinity of Kitzbuehl in Austria," and, "Stand By for further instructions!" We started the trip of about 80 miles at night; of course, it was too dangerous to drive during the daytime because of the "Tiefflieger" (low flying enemy aircraft). In Kufstein we made an overnight stop. Again a brief traffic control assignment. A strange episode happened to me on the road south of Kufstein. I checked the papers of some military personnel when suddenly two men in a German uniform but with an Indian turban came by. With a little bit of German and a little bit of English I found out, that they had volunteered to fight against Communism on the side of Germany, but were now on their way back to their home country India, on foot.

In St. Woergel, at the military supply depot, we requisitioned for our troop whatever we felt we needed, like flour, canned food, and other goodies. Unfortunately, there was no Brandy or anything substantial to drink available, only a few cases of Triple Sec, a sweet orange liqueur, of which I could not drink more than a couple of shots without waking up the next morning with a booming headache.

I was very interested to see for the first time in my life the beautiful Bavarian / Austrian high mountains with snow on their peaks close up from the ground. However, as our convoy moved along the winding roads, I was very disappointed to see no mountains, because low clouds restricted the view in all directions. On the other hand, the clouds gave us protection, because we did not encounter any Allied strafing aircraft. We arrived at our destination; a very small village called Flecken and arranged sleeping quarters for everyone with the farmers. We did not know if we were supposed to function as infantry soldiers or what? Obviously flying was no longer expected of us. "Stand By"! was the motto. We really had nothing to do so we did some target shooting practice and threw some hand grenades in the lake (although not very nice, but we were young and it resulted in the catch of some fish.) Other than that, we waited.

So, this is the enemy we surrendered to

One day we heard the roaring hum of a tank. We watched as an American tank drove from the main road on the narrow road towards our village. Apparently the driver did not watch where he was going and managed to get his vehicle stuck so that he could not move forward or backward. At first we were a bit apprehensive; as we did not know what to expect from the first U.S. military vehicle that came to our village. When we saw his predicament we walked over to the frustrated driver and asked him: "Do you need some help?" -- Of course he did, and said so with expressions and vocabularies that I had never heard before in my six years of English language instruction in school. However we were able to communicate with the man so we hitched our heavy truck with a chain to the tank and pulled him out. That was my first contact with the American Forces.

Although these G.I.'s were quite friendly they just had to brag to us that at home in New York the skyscrapers were higher than the mountains in Austria. (about 6,000 Ft)   With a little bit of envy they told us that we had it made, because we could go home now while they would not know when they would see their families again.   An American officer came to our "headquarters" and inquired who we were and what we were doing. There was no search for weapons or inspection of our equipment. Nobody bothered us, even though we still had all sorts of weapons. After that a small U.S. army unit moved into the village and took quarters in the western section of the village. A couple of days later an American Captain came to us and asked us if we would like to perform military police duties for the U.S. Army? We discussed the offer and all agreed "why not"? We were now given white armbands with large black "MP" letters and underneath in smaller print "Luftwaffe". We were given gasoline for our vehicles   Enlisted men could keep their rifles and officers their pistols. Each one of us received a "Pass" printed in German and English so we could identify ourselves. Sub-machine guns and hand grenades we had to turn over to the Americans. Now we found out why there was no hostility between the American soldiers and us. Initially the mountain area was supposed to be defended as the last bastion of WWII. Fortunately on May 7th, the German General Kless and the American General Devers of the 6th U.S.- Army Group negotiated a surrender of all German troops in the mountain region. The very next day the war was over!

German - Luftwaffe Military Police

Our duty was, "To keep law and order!" which we did by driving our motorcycles or Mercedes Kuebelwagen through the beautiful Austrian mountain region. If we had seen any German soldier walking home from Italy or where ever, we were supposed to pick him up and deliver him to a POW camp. Strangely enough, we never saw a single one!

Including three gliders, I had been checked out to fly a total of 19 different aircraft. I felt quite confident travelling through the air. However on the ground, I could only ride a bicycle. I had never driven a motorcycle or an automobile. Now was the time to catch up! A sergeant sat next to me in an open Mercedes Kubelwagen and I took the wheel. With "do this", "do that", clutch, gas pedal, brake etc. I cruised through the countryside. I have to admit, when I shifted into second gear, I thought that was too fast for me and then when I was driving in third gear it was even scary. Well, after a few excursions, there was hardly any traffic in those days, I felt quite confident that driving a car was just as easy as flying an aircraft and the next best thing.

The same was true with the three types of motorcycles, a 125cc Gillett, a 480cc BMW and a 750cc Zuendapp with sidecar. Naturally our whole "duty assignment" was a lot of fun. One day, two young men strolled into our "headquarters". They were sharp looking and about our age. They did not wear uniforms. As we started talking we found out that they were members of an SS unit that had retreated way up into the higher region of the mountains. We invited them to a drink - our terrible sweet Triple Sec. We all had a great time together. Both of them had been members of the famous Skorzeny outfit (commanded by the SS officer who liberated Benito Mussolini in a daring mountain top rescue mission). Both of them spoke Hungarian, Bulgarian and what have you. They told us of their escapade when they were dropped off behind the Russian lines, swiped a Russian tank and roamed around for several weeks, then made it back to the German line. When they wanted to walk to their hiding place, Roland and I, as authorized German military police (who could drive a motor vehicle even at night regardless of curfew) would not let them walk; we insisted that we drive them. When our Mercedes would not go any farther on the dirt road which became steeper and steeper we let them off, said good bye and planned to visit them soon at their hiding place. A few days later, when we went up there to visit with them, we first met a young man who appeared like a kid herding some cows. It turned out that he was one of them and was the advanced watch-out. We made it to their camp and had a chance to meet the group leader. This SS Captain was a really easygoing officer. He was an old man compared with us, but ever so relaxed and nonchalant. He had been in a combat unit since the war began. They told us about their last major combat engagement, when they had to fight the Russians near Stettin: "The Russians were hurling mortar shells at us and everybody stuck his head into the ground. Then the Captain rose to his full height, looked through his binoculars, while mortar shells were exploding around, and very calmly gave orders for the machine gun to shoot where he had detected the mortar position." Of course, the Americans were not aware of our fraternization with SS soldiers.

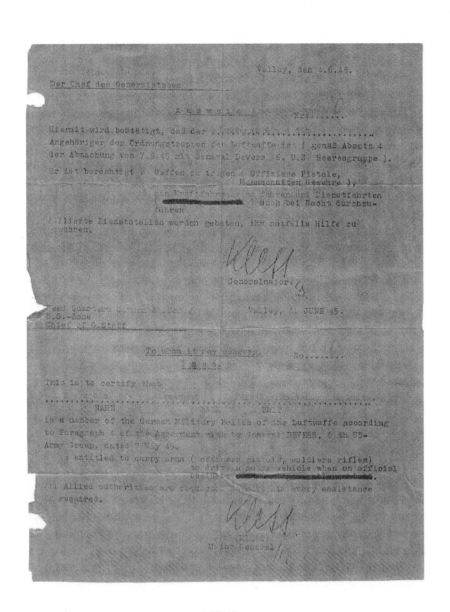

Valley, den 4.6.45.

Der Chef des Generalstabes

A u s w e i s.   Nr......

Hiermit wird bestätigt, daß der ....
Angehöriger der Ordnungstruppen der Luftwaffe ist (gemäß Absatz 4
der Abmachung vom 7.5.45 mit General Devers 6. U.S. Heeresgruppe).

Er ist berechtigt : Waffen zu tragen (Offiziere Pistole,
                                        Mannschaften Gewehre),

                     ein Kraftfahrzeug zu führen und Dienstfahrten
                     (~~~~~~~~~~~~~~) auch bei Nacht durchzu-
                     führen

Alliierte Dienststellen werden gebeten, ihm notfalls Hilfe zu
gewähren.

Generalmajor.

Head Quarters ....   Valley, 4. JUNE 45.
U.S.-Zone
Chief of G.Staff

To whom it may concern.   No......

I.A.S.C.

This is to certify that

....
      NAME   RANK   UNIT

is a member of the German Military Police of the Luftwaffe according
to Paragraph 4 of the Agreement with by General DEVERS, 6 th US-
Army Group, dated 7 May 45.

Is entitled to carry arms (officers pistols, soldiers rifles)
                           to drive a motor vehicle when on official
                           ~~~~~~~~~~~~~~~~~~~~~~

All Allied authorities are requested to give him every assistance
required.

Major General

MP Pass

On one pleasant warm pre-summer evening we were all sitting together enjoying the fact that we were alive, we sang some folk-songs, nothing political or so, just old favourites like "May time is here" or "On the heath of "Lueneburg". Then a Lt. Col. who had joined our group (he did not belong to KG 51), walked over to us and started yelling! How dare we sing when American soldiers were close by and could hear that, where we try to provoke them? Fortunately the war was over and we did not have to snap to attention and say "Yes Sir!" instead we said "Fly a kite!" and continued our singing. The Americans never complained or even mentioned our singing.

In June, all German military personnel every where in the mountain region of Austria were to be relocated to Bavaria, especially around the newly established discharge camp at the former Luftwaffe air base Bad Aiblingen. We, the Luftwaffe MP's, continued our very important duty and made sure there was "law and order". We had a lot of fun riding our BMW motorcycle through the countryside around Bad Aiblingen. One day when I drove near the main gate of the base an American soldier saw that I had my side arm ,a 7.65 Walther pistol, on my belt he asked me: "Do you want to sell your pistol?" First I was a little perplexed but then I told him that I did not want to give up my dear 7.65 Walther pistol, but if he were interested I would return the next day with a pistol he could buy. Well, yes, he was interested. As agreed I went back to the gate the next day and sure enough my G.I. customer was waiting for me. He was ever so delighted when he saw that I had brought with me a 08 Luger. I think that I traded the gun for a carton, 10 packs of cigarettes, for which the G.I. had paid $1.10, but which was worth on the black market DM 500.
When we realized how much in demand German pistols were , little by little, traded all of our service guns for cigarettes, soap, chocolate, etc. because we knew that sooner or later we would have to surrender all of our weapons anyway, so, why not "dispose" of them this way? Naturally, whatever we traded for we divided fairly among our group.

Our MP unit still had a number of other military property items that we did not want to throw away or turn in. I was not interested in office material and equipment, but there were two large table radios, AM, FM, short wave, of which I wouldn't mind having one. We raffled the radios off and I won one. As a "law and order" police unit we practically had nothing to do, but we were the "Authority". One day I was called to a small lake nearby where a soldier was causing a little disturbance. When I arrived I saw a stark naked man walking like a rooster on a manure pile between women and children, sunbathing on a meadow at the edge of the lake. I called him over and asked him why he walked around in his birthday suit? I'm not ashamed of my body, sir! "He even stood properly at attention. Of course I bawled him out and told him to go to the other end of the lake and show his body that he was so proud of to the birds and the bees - which he did. End of problem! There are odd people everywhere in the world!

Discharge from the German Military

At the end of June 1945 Roland and I decided to resign from our military police job. First we wanted to know the Luftwaffe discharge-procedure. We drove to Bad Aiblingen and heard: "nothing to it -- all we had to do is: report to the base, and a few days later get the discharge paper", a fast and simple procedure. First, however, we had to do a little planning. We needed transportation when we were discharged. So we swiped the 380cc BMW motorcycle, that is we "stored it" for safe keeping in a barn of a farmer we had become acquainted with. For some food-stuff, we traded a bicycle and of course we kept our MP identification papers. Now we reported at Bad Aiblingen air base. The discharge camp was to process daily many German soldiers from the "Austrian Surrender Area" that were now staged in villages around the base. It was considered very important to have a properly issued "Entlassungsschein" the piece of paper with which one could prove that the American military had released the soldier from the German military service. That was of special concern for those returning to their home in the British, French or Russian occupation zone of Germany. No one wanted to be picked up again and end up in a slave labour camp for years. (The Russians kept German P.O.W.'s for up to 10 years after the end of WWII few of whom came back with their health intact)

As we checked in, Roland and I were assigned to a group of a couple hundred German soldiers, Army and Luftwaffe, who were directed into a barbed-wire-enclosed compound. An American officer addressed us and gave instructions. Of course all military equipment, weapons, binoculars, watches etc., had to be turned in. Then, at night we prepared to sleep. There were no beds; there were no tents or barracks, just the grass ground of the airfield. Fortunately Roland and I were prepared. We had brought blankets along so the cool night did not bother us and luckily, it did not rain.

The next day a repeat of the announcements from the day before. I was amazed that some soldiers still came up and turned in their watches or other utensils. Roland and I had nothing to turn in, as we were prepared. Although food and water was very scarce we were very fortunate to be discharged at Bad Aiblingen, as we later heard the German prisoners at Bad Kreuznach or several other "death camps" were not so fortunate. No food and water, no sanitary facilities, no tents or housing of any kind, with men sleeping on the muddy Rhein meadows, exposed to the elements which caused hundreds of thousands to die.* Again we had planned ahead, as we brought with us a couple of loafs of bread. After a day or so, although we did not understand the reason, we all had to move into another compound. Surprise inspection! All soldiers had to stand in line and spread their belongings out on the ground in front of them. A young American G.I., a private, accompanied by a Luftwaffe major, the compound elder, walked from soldier to soldier, poking with a stick into the belongings and ordered this and that to be confiscated. Next to me stood a Captain who was a Dentist. The U.S. private did not know what to do with the many dental tools and ordered: "out, pick it up!" The Major did not object with one word, but there also was also a Luftwaffe Major, a former airline captain who had flown many times before the war many the route to London and who spoke English fluently.. He jumped in and loudly said: "Can't you see that this man is a dentist who needs the tools if he wants to treat anyone with a toothache!" The young private, although perplexed immediately agreed, and moved to the next inspection.

The airline captain told me that he still had his military wrist watch, not on his arm, of course, but hidden in the bottom of a can of liver sausage. Again we moved. Roland and I thought that we would probably get our discharge papers now. As we walked past some compounds there were soldiers who had been there for some time who stood and watched us. Some asked: "Do you have something to eat for us?" Well, we still had some bread, so we tossed it to them over the fence. Little did we know that from now on we too would be hungry, as the discharge took several more days. After almost two weeks, finally the day came for the discharge processing. In one of the aircraft hangars a number of desks were set up, behind which an American civilian employee sat. We, the dischargees, had to form a line and stand at a distance of about 30 ft from

* Editors note. Some reports give a figure as high as 1 million German POW's that were starved to death in Eisenhowers "Hunger Camps" and illegal slave labour programmes . See James Baque : "Other Losses"

the desk. The inspector a former German Jew who spoke fluent German, and who had immigrated to the U.S.A., jovially waved for a soldier to step forward. The soldier had to make a very snappy salute and if the interrogator was not satisfied with the salute the soldier had to go back and stand at the end of the line again. Obviously the inspector enjoyed his "power". When it was my turn, he asked a few questions, like where were you born, what you did in the military, etc. Apparently he did not have any problem with my answers, so my interrogation was fairly short. If a soldier was a former Waffen SS member, he was immediately separated and assigned to a special compound; regardless what rank or what unit he had been in. It seems that the Americans were looking for certain persons, because all soldiers with a "wanted" name were also locked up in a separate compound. It was like having all men with the name of Mueller or Schmidt in one compound) waiting for a more detailed interrogation. Then came the physical examination! Well, of course things had to be done properly! A German military doctor sat behind a desk and asked: "Sind Sie gesund?" ("Are you OK?") Naturally everybody said "Yes". With that he scribbled in my Soldbuch: "Untersucht!" (Examined!") That was it!

Now we were directed to walk to the main gate where a number of GMC 2 1/2 t 6x6 trucks were lined up to transport the discharged soldiers to areas close to their home. The tailgate was down but it was still quite high to climb onto the back of the truck. There were some soldiers who thought that now they were safe, as they were released, they could put their wristwatch back on their wrist. Unfortunately there were G.I.'s just waiting for the moment when the sleeve pulled back and the wristwatch became visible. Immediately that watch was confiscated. Some G.I.'s proudly showed 10 or more wrist watches on each arm that they had stolen from the German soldiers. The truck carried as many soldiers as were able to stand on its back, squeezed together like sardines. Roland and I only wanted to go only a short distance, so we jumped off and walked back to our MP Headquarters. Next day we collected all of our belongings and said, "Goodbye," to everybody. Now we had to figure out how we would best proceed to Erding. We ended up putting the large radio on the back seat of the BMW motorcycle along with our duffel bags. We also found a rope about 20 ft long -- which we fastened to the rear of the motorcycle. Then our odd team began to move. One of us (we switched after a while) drove the motorcycle and the other one on the bicycle held on to the rope being towed behind. We drove only on secondary roads and fortunately there was no vehicle traffic and we did not have too far to go to Erding. Several times G.I.'s from a road checkpoint flagged us down and inquired who we were and where we are going. We had not turned in our "Feldjaeger Identification papers", so we could present our pass and were promptly cleared to continue. I'm sure those G.I.'s thought that the German Military Police were a bunch of oddballs.

Back in Erding

With no problems we made it to Erding and reported at the Johansen family. We moved the motorcycle down into the basement. After all it was really Luftwaffe property and we could not drive around with it yet. Later we thought we perhaps could perhaps legally register it in our name. Unfortunately that misfired. Although the U.S. occupation forces prohibited fraternisation between their soldiers and German civilians, none of the American G.I.'s paid any attention to that order. Sergeant Franz Schmidt had become acquainted with the Johansen family and that's how we met him. When we told him about "our" BMW he immediately was excited about driving the machine. We thought that he would drive it a little bit through the city of Erding and then return it to us. Unfortunately some of his buddies, (he was an MP of the US Army Air Corps,) confiscated the vehicle to use it as a toy for everybody to drive around in it. That's how we lost the motorcycle that we had swiped so cleverly.

Roland and I could not very well become a burden to the Johansen family, so we had to find some employment. We thought that food would most likely be a major problem in the winter of 1945. Where is the best place to get nourishment? -- on a farm, of course. In the vicinity of Erding, there were a number of small and large farms. We applied as farm-hands and were accepted. As a boy I enjoyed working on a farm, but our situation was not exactly ideal. We were given a simple, maybe a rather primitive room with two beds. We did not get paid, instead worked for food only. On weekends we visited with our "Family". We tried to get some foodstuff from our farmer, but he was not inclined to give away anything. As chickens have the habit to build a nest somewhere hidden in the straw of the barn, we found a couple of them and "confiscated" a whole bunch of eggs which we proudly donated to the Johansens.

Now it was harvest time for wheat. Three mowers cut the grain with scythes and we followed to bundle sheaves and set them up like little houses. There was a lot of thistle growing in the field which made our

175

arms a bit bloody after a while. When all the grain, wheat, oats and barley had been harvested, the turnips followed and then, the potatoes. Thereafter it was time to prepare the fields for winter. With two horses we ploughed back and forth for weeks. Around this time in the year, work on a farm slows down. We had both hoped to have a safe place with food for the wintertime, however, now the farmer said: "Goodbye", to us, "I don't need you any longer!" What shall we do now? Roland wanted to go to his family in Dortmund and I went to Hamburg. In the fall of '45 there were no bus's or passenger transportation by railroad. The only mode of transportation was "Per Anhalter" (hitch-hike). Many people were on the road to get to their loved ones somewhere, somehow. Most truck drivers who had room on their vehicle took hitchhikers along. I remember how slow some of the vehicles were moving. As gasoline or diesel fuel was not available vehicles were propelled by wood. German ingenuity had invented the "Holzvergaser" (wood-carburetor) and the device functioned like this: a large steel kettle about twice the size of a 55 gallon drum was mounted on the back of the truck. On top was an opening through which wood chips about the size of one half of a hand, were dumped into the container. A lid tightly closed the top of this "Holzvergaser". On the bottom was a small opening through which the wood chips were ignited. The wood chips inside then started to smolder. An air pump sucked the fumes to the motor and with that the engine was running and the vehicle moved. Holzvergaser did not run as fast as a diesel or gas engine, because the system did not develop as much power as gas or diesel, but they moved! The truck driver had to calculate the distance he intended to go and take sufficient wood chips along to make it home again. On longer hauls the truck's load capacity was reduced considerably to allow space for the wood chips fuel to carry.

Enjoy the war, the peace will be terrible!

My travel to Hamburg, only about 500 miles to the north, took several days on many different vehicles, but eventually I made it. The last stretch, I was able to ride on a freight train, which carried coal to Denmark. Miserable rainy, foggy, typical Hamburg weather made the city look even more desolate after so many terror bombings.

The house on Zimmerstrasse 3 was spared. It had survived, but not too many houses on the block were intact.

"Enjoy the war, the peace will be terrible!" was a slogan we had said jokingly during the war. Now, living in a big city, life really was terrible. From the year 1945 until the middle of 1948, Germany was subjugated to physical and emotional trauma, something that had no comparison in history. The victorious Allied Forces (Communist Soviet Russia, the USA, Great Britain and France) agreed at conferences held at Yalta and Potsdam that the German Reich was to be dissected into four military occupation zones and the capital city of Berlin split into four sectors.

It is interesting how world politics manipulated the life and death of so many millions of innocent people. When, after WWI at the Versailles Peace Treaty, it was dictated that the Danzig corridor was to be established, the ground work was laid to assure that a new war would be started, sooner or later. Nobody with a little bit of intelligence and looking for a durable peace would have made such stupid arrangements. A traveller who wanted to go from central Germany to the German state of East Prussia had to go 100 miles through the sovereign country of Poland or take a ship on the Baltic Sea. From October 1938 until March 1939, German and Polish delegates held meetings to resolve this impossible situation. Several sensible proposals were discussed and considered in good faith by both parties until England interfered and persuaded Poland not to come to any agreement with Germany. It was not until then that Germany initiated the invasion.* When Germany invaded Poland 1939 to resolve the corridor problem, Soviet Russia invaded the eastern part of Poland, yet Russia was never accused of starting a war and to this day has not returned to Poland most of the territory she had conquered in 1939. On the other hand, East Prussia, Pomerania, Silesia, etc., were all amputated from Germany. For the sake of justice Russia should also finally accept responsibility for the murder of 15,000 Polish officers -- which for many years was falsely blamed on Germany.

In the British occupation zone at the beginning of 1946, the situation became so bad that Field Marshal Bernard Montgomery sent a wire to the British Foreign Office in which he demanded that the food rations be increased considerably. *"If we do not do that, the result will be death and misery and we will be remembered in history with dishonour and at the same time give the indication that we are against any effort to establish a democratic Germany."* Nevertheless food rations in the British Zone during winter and spring 1946 / 1947 were only 1,000 calories per person - a sign of starvation. Herbert Hoover explained to the current President of the United States: "1550 calories are not enough to keep a human being healthy". For a long time the food ration in the US occupation Zone was

1275 calories per day. All this had nothing to do with any shortages of food worldwide.

Occupied Germany in October of 1946 had 65,000,000 people (per the census of the Allied Control Commission) The total of the German population in 1950 should have been 73,000,000; however, the census of the German government listed 68,000,000 a difference of almost 6 million. Starvation affected especially older people. Combined with the lack of heat or at least some warmth, many people just died of exposure. There was no wood, coal or gas available for heating. Electricity and gas was allowed to be consumed at a certain small amount, but not enough for heating. If the allowed quantity was exceeded in a given month the gas / electricity meter reader would turn the meter off for a certain length of time. Many people walked early in the morning through the streets which had large trees and picked up any small branches that had fallen on the sidewalk. As I did not like to live in a cold apartment -- in the evening, after curfew, I took a saw and climbed up a tree lining the street. First I cut some smaller branches, then later bigger and bigger ones and dragged them into the living room of our ground-floor apartment. Father did not like it at all, because this was an act of citizen insubordination to the authorities. But then again he was glad when the next day we were able to have a little fire in the kitchen stove.

When mail was being processed again I wrote a letter to my good friend Rudi, whose parents I knew lived in Possenhofen, south of Munich. Shortly thereafter I received a reply not from Rudi but from our third buddy in our "Triumvirate". Jochen wrote that Rudi was missing after a combat mission against the Russians over Hungary, in April 1945. This is when I learned that Jochen had miraculously survived a terrible crash in a Me 109. As his home was in Breslau / Silesia, he could not go home because all Germans were expelled from there by the Russians. It was great news, that at least Jochen had survived and had a place to stay with Rudi's parents.

In Hamburg, all three of us (father, stepmother, and I) were constantly hungry. Sometimes we were able to get turnips from somewhere. Cooked with some meat, potatoes, vegetables, etc., I liked them, but we did not have any other ingredients. We could only cook them in water with salt and artificial pepper; that was it! But it was something to put in the growling stomach. At one time we got some sunflower oil; it looked almost black like old motor oil. We thought if we added some to the turnips stew maybe this would add a few calories, as bad as it tasted. One time I went to the "Black Market" where one could buy anything if one had enough money or cigarettes or gold, or other treasures. For my last 70 Marks I bought a ration coupon for a loaf of bread. Then I went to a bakery and for one Mark purchased the bread, went home, sat down and ate almost half of the black bread. Oh, did that taste good, better than the best cake. The remainder I gave to my parents.

During the first three years after WWII the distribution of foodstuff was very problematic. As there is always, a greedy entrepreneur around to take advantage of the misery of the people, the black market boomed.

Weekly Food Rationing in Germany 1940 vs. 1947

Weekly allocation of:	1940 Quantity	1947 Quantity
Meat, or meat products	14 oz/500 g	3.1 oz/91 g
Butter	4.5 oz/125 g	.4 oz/10 g
Lard	2.2 oz/62.5 g	.4 oz/10 g
Margarine	2.8 oz/80 g	.4 oz/10 g
Jam / Marmalade	4.0 oz/100 g	1.4 oz/40 g
Sugar	9.5 oz/250 g	2.8 oz/80 g
Cheese	2.2 oz/62.5 g	.49 oz/14 g
Eggs	1	0
Not rationed in 1940		
Bread	-	62 oz/1,869 g
Flour / Grain products	-	9.5 oz/287 g
Whole Milk only for children rationed according to age		
Skim Milk	-	0, 24 Qt
Fish	-	4.4 oz/119 g
Potatoes	-	62 oz/1,869 g

[A standard letter weighs about one ounce]

I was ready to get a job and work, any work. With some connection, I lined up employment as a long-distance truck driver. (I had never driven a big truck, but I thought: if I could fly an aircraft I certainly could drive a truck.) It seemed to me that a long distance truck route would bring opportunities to find food somewhere. That sounded very promising to me. The procedure required me to go to the "Arbeitsamt" (City labour office) and fill out the appropriate forms for my job application. The man looked at my form and harshly said: "You were not a truck driver before the war?" Of course I had to say "No, I was still a student!" "In that case, you are assigned to clearing of bomb rubble debris." -- "But, sir", I said, "I was not a bomb-debris-remover before the war either!" -- "Don't get fresh with me", was the only comment from this "Bureaucratic-Authority". The job I had found for myself was denied.

A few days later a notification from the Arbeitsamt came by mail. "On such and such a day at such and such time and place you are to report for work for rubble removal. This is an assignment by the British Military Government; non-compliance will be severely punished except by the death penalty!" I did not want to work in the ruins of the bombed-out city. I therefore had to leave if I did not want to be arrested. Certainly they would not issue any ration cards to me. I packed my little bundle and headed south. I thought, "Maybe I'll get a better job in Bavaria, in the American occupation zone." There were still no passenger trains going from Hamburg to Munich. The first stretch was from Hamburg to Bielefeld. I thought it would be a passenger train, when I bought a ticket at the railroad station. The train, however, was a long line of empty open boxcars that came back from Denmark, having delivered coal (even though no coal was available in Hamburg). It was a cold night. About 30 people huddled together on the front end of the boxcar to get out of the draft. The wind, however, still whirled around and blew fine coal dust in my eyes. On another stretch, I was delighted when I saw it was a very old, but real passenger train. I was very disappointed, however, when I found out that all compartments were brim-full. This was one of the old railroad coaches which had running boards outside, the length of the car. I decided to do what others next to me did: I stood on the running board and clung to the entry handle. At first that seemed to be not too bad, but soon I realized that the coldness and the wind when the train was in motion made me more and more numb. How long would I be able to hang on?

When the train made a stop I collected all my strength and opened the door to the next compartment. Someone almost fell out and several voices said: "Don't you see it's full?", but I was at that time desperate and just pushed with all my strength and made it inside.

The next part of this train ride was not exactly comfortable because there were so many people in the compartment sitting and standing that I was able to only find room for one of my feet on the floor. In addition I was not able to stand up straight because there were so many bags and packages stowed away topside. But it was warm! It took a long time, but finally I arrived in Munich and from there made it to Erding at last.

My first employment.

The most important thing for me now was to find a job. At the time when we were proud pilots of the Luftwaffe, my buddies and I were always welcome guests at the Johansen family. Now we had been replaced because some American pilots had made the acquaintance of the Johansens and visited with them frequently (ignoring the US military "non- fraternisation order"). When I met these men and became aware that they were pilots we immediately had a good understanding. When pilots meet, regardless from where and from what country, there is always contact between them. We just understood each other and after a few drinks, which they provided, as there was no alcohol available on the German market, we could see the world much more clearly. Here is an example of the futility of this stupid war. These young men, about the same age as I were ordered to go to Europe and do their best to kill as many German pilots as possible. German pilots on the other side were ordered to shoot down as many of the U.S. pilots as they could. The war was over and we found out that we all really had no animosity; we did not hate each other. If only all the politicians of all the countries would get together to work out their problems at the conference table, and if they cannot do that, then get guns and shoot it out without involving everyone else! The famous German General von Clausewitz once said: "War is the continuation of politics by different means". If politicians did their job right, they would accomplish their goal with diplomacy, not bullets.

One young U.S. pilot I liked especially well was named First Lt. Bob Schillinger. One day he asked me, "Haenchen", (he could never say "Haens'chen" correctly) why don't you get a job at the Erding-airbase?" This was the Luftwaffe- Flugplatz where I flew the Me 110 in preparation for long-range night-fighter missions many moons earlier. The base was taken over by the U.S. Army Air Corps and re-named "European Air Supply Depot" APO 207. As the base was not destroyed, nor hardly damaged by bombing, the warehouses, hangars and shops were ideal for support of the US Army Air Corps. This is where Bob was the personnel officer.

Bob Schillinger in Erding

I needed a job, but what work could I do? There certainly was no pilot job in Germany anywhere. I went to Bob's office at the base and we looked through the lists of job openings. Auto-mechanic we agreed would be something I could do and what I didn't know, I could learn. Since I was already contemplating to go to the U.S.A., I thought one should know something about automobiles anyway. After I had filled out the job application forms I had to be interrogated by a U.S. intelligence man. Apparently this man too, like the one at the discharge camp, was a former German citizen, a Jew, who of course spoke fluent German. He asked all sorts of questions, what I thought about this and what I thought about that, whether I had been a member of the NS Party, the Jungvolk or the Hitlerjugend. I answered all questions truthfully without any reservations. Then Bob stuck his head in the door, listened for a moment (he thought that I probably was too honest with my answers) and abruptly said to the interrogator: "I think you have enough information on Mr. Busch! -- Let's go Haenchen!" With that I was hired.

Now that I had a job I was also entitled to a place to live. With my proof of employment I went to the "Einwohnermeldeamt" (Erding district housing control office). I had no problem and was given an address in Moosen, some 15 miles from Erding. One bus drove out there each day. I went to the address and introduced myself. The lady living there gave me a long dissertation why she could not take me as a roomer. What could I do? Of course I just said thank you and returned to the Einwohnermeldeamt in Erding. Apparently situations like this happened often so they now gave me three addresses to check out. The first one I went to the next day was in the village of Hubenstein a mile from Moosen. I was lucky this time and right away I was given a large room upstairs. It had a bed, a little too short for my 6ft 2in height, a night stand a chest of drawers and a chair. I was allowed to use part of a clothes-locker and I even had a washbowl on a wash-stand. My handful of personal belongings I could store in an old suitcase under the bed. That was it! There was no bathroom or toilet facilities inside the house. The outhouse was across the yard next to the large manure pile. To use it in the wintertime in the middle of the night took a lot of self-overcoming.

The Haider family were really nice people. In addition to Mrs. and Mr. Haider, there were two 7-9 year old kids (a boy and a girl), and a domestic servant Marie. They had a small farm and a little grocery store. Although they were all Catholic like everyone else in the entire area and I was a Lutheran, I still had good rapport with them. There were still some people around who had the dislike of all "Prussians" (that is, everybody north of the river Main), a similar situation as in the U.S.A. with the "Damn Yankees" and the "Rebels", but although I was born in Hamburg I had no problem with anyone in the village. The Haiders were so nice to me that I can really say "I had it made!" When I came home in the evening there was always food from their dinner meal set aside and kept warm for me. Often, Mr. Haider enjoyed sitting with me for a while and discussing "World Affairs", while enjoying a smoke. Of course, I'm sure for the Haiders it was easier to have to take a single man into their house instead of perhaps a large family of refugees; maybe some displaced people from Silesia or somewhere in the East.

The American forces had no difficulty recruiting workers in the villages around Erding. There were many, many refugees living everywhere in the district of Erding or for that matter in all of Bavaria or rural West-Germany. The victorious Allied Forces had agreed at Yalta and Potsdam to the largest Ethnic Cleansing operation the world had ever seen. Fourteen million Germans who had lived for centuries in Balkan countries or in Eastern Germany or Eastern Europe were forced to leave all their belongings behind and walk to the west. Some 3 million -- mainly women and children -- died in this cruel inhuman operation. How long can a mother carry her three- or four-year-old child? How long can a child trot in severe winter weather without food? (I don't recall that there was ever a claim for restitution filed, at least not in the following 50 years for just reparation of their losses.)

The base in Erding sent out every morning a fleet of GMC 2 ½ t 6x6 trucks to bring workers to the base and return them at night. Sometimes the trucks did not have a tarpaulin covering the back where some 50 people had to sit, which was especially uncomfortable on freezing winter days. One G.I. assigned to be the driver of the Hubenstein route, who called himself "Danny Dimwit" showed that he was very tense, very much afraid to even talk to anyone. He always locked the doors of his cab and let nobody ride up front as other drivers did. One evening the engine of his truck seemed to have a problem. It had lost some power and ran very rough. Now Danny Dimwit really was in trouble. He was sure that someone would come and stick a knife in his back. When I got off he mustered some courage and asked me what I thought why the engine had suffered such a power loss; as he knew that I worked in the motor pool. It turned out to be only a minor problem; I think a spark plug wire had fallen off. Boy! was Danny (whose real name was Harold P. Siewerth) relieved. His grandmother had come from Germany he told me and still preferred to speak German. That was the beginning of a great friendship. He later talked about how he was "brain washed" with movies and other propaganda so that he had to think that all Germans were bad and he would be in grave danger of being killed.

"Danny"

Being employed, I also had a room. I tried to get Jochen to come to Hubenstein too. Jochen had very graciously been given a place to live with Rudi's parents. So far, nothing was known about Rudi's fate a year after his capture by the Russians and a year after the end of the war.

Because of the strong friendship between Jochen and I, we decided to find a way for us to live closer together. Jochen tried to get a job at the Erding U.S. air base, but the Jewish interrogator apparently did not like that Jochen had been a leader in the Hitler Youth and, of course, he did not have Bob Schillinger standing by. He was rejected. But he found employment with the "Fernseh GmbH" in Taufkirchen a few miles from Hubenstein. It was great to be together again.

At night, Danny did not mind when Jochen hopped aboard his truck for the last few miles from Taufkirchen to Hubenstein. The three of us became such good friends, that Danny visited with us on weekends and went with us to Munich and Possenhofen. Jochen's civilian clothing was about his size, so we dressed Danny up like a genuine German, he really liked that.

Work at the 3rd and 4th echelon vehicle motor maintenance shop was not difficult. A crew of about 15 German mechanics, who were experienced and knew what they were doing, were working under an American Staff Sergeant. Five or six American G.I.'s were also assigned to the shop but they hardly ever did any work, except to test drive the vehicles. We worked mainly on Jeeps, Dodge 3/4t trucks and weapons carriers and 2 1/2 t GMC 6x6 trucks. After I had a chance to participate in a U.S.-sponsored training program for several weeks in Esslingen I specialized in "Carburetor and Ignition". Now that I had a little bit more knowledge about automobiles, I was assigned to be the German Shop Foreman. The German custom was, and probably still is, to be very thrifty and not waste any material. Naturally, when we changed an engine in a truck and found the clutch pressure plate in very good condition, we saved it and stored it in the shop, instead of throwing it in the trash; as the stockroom would not take it because it was used. Then one day there was inspection. "What is this? you're not supposed to have that in the shop!" We had no choice but to haul all the still good spare parts to the dump. Pity we thought! Then over the next few days we needed parts which were on back order in the supply department, we drove to the dump and retrieved our discarded parts. The G.I.'s only said: "Macht's nix, haben viel!"
Another method to save good parts was to load them on a truck, then we wrote a trip ticket to another base and when inspection was finished we brought the parts back to our shop.

Part of my job assignment was to be an interpreter, because of the German crew, very few spoke any English. All Germans employed at the base had one very important advantage. The Americans served at noon each day a warm meal, and without ration cards! The food was not fancy but in my opinion, it tasted quite good.

Mechanic Hans Busch

Shop Xmas party

Many American soldiers were very busily involved in Black Market business activities. For example 1945 – 1948 cigarettes were very much in demand as there were none available on the German market. G.I.'s could buy a carton of 10 packets at the P X store for $1.10 and sell the pack for RM 35.-. In 1948 the price per pack had gone up to RM 350.-. But there were other opportunities to make a lot of money. One G.I. collected a truckload of tires, new and used, prepared a fictitious trip ticket, drove the truck through the main gate and rendezvoused somewhere with a German black market businessman where they exchanged money and merchandise. When the supply department threw several thousand flashlight batteries in the dump because they had reached their shelve life date, a G.I. picked them up, hauled them to Munich and sold them on the black market. In Munich on the Moehlstrasse one could buy and sell anything that was not otherwise available. Everybody in town knew about it and went there to buy or sell, butter or stockings, foodstuff or perfume or whatever.

From time-to-time the police made a raid and arrested some people; however, a few hours later it was "business as usual". Obviously the police were not very much concerned, and some were involved. Strange things happened . One Sunday afternoon a Jeep pulled up to the farmhouse where I lived. When I heard a horn honking I checked who it was. My friend Bob Schillinger, with a buddy of his came out to Hubenstein to do some target practice with what I thought was an awfully big pistol, a 45. "Come on Haen'chen hop aboard, we'll drive into the forest." There we found a rusty old tin can, put it on a tree stump and fired away. First Bob fired three shots and missed each time, then his buddy shot and missed, then they gave this monster of an automatic sidearm to me and what do you know my first shot hit the target. At this time I should have said: "You guys are just not in my league!" and stopped shooting. Instead I continued shooting and proved that I was just as bad a shot as the other two. The first hit was only beginner's luck.

Towards the end of the year Bob's time was up and he was scheduled to return back to the United States. One day he asked me: "Haen'chen would you like to fly my P-51 Mustang?" At first I thought he was kidding, but he wasn't at all. Gee, what an offer! Of course I would have liked to fly the P-51, but then I thought what if anyone should see me? What could they do to me? Nothing or nothing much. On the other hand I was certain that Bob would have been court-marshalled and that certainly was not worth one joy ride by a former Luftwaffe enemy in an American aircraft. So I declined!

My friend Bob

My friend Bob.

During that time I already had hopes to emigrate to the USA and fly commercially. Bob had great sympathy and we devised a scheme how I would sneak aboard an American freighter and as a stowaway illegally start a new life in the "Land of unlimited opportunities". Again my Guardian Angel protected me, because Bob and I just could not get together -- He was in Bremerhafen and I was in Erding, then I went to Bremerhafen to meet with him, while he came down to Erding to look for me. That plan did not work out! (My Guardian Angel had better plans for me.)

The last time I saw Bob was when he came to Hubenstein to bid Jochen and me his farewell. This time he did not come by Jeep but instead flew over Hubenstein in his P-51. The first passes he made over the village looked to us "old pilots" like dangerously low. He had his canopy rolled back and waved to us. Then he retracted Flaps and gear and performed for the two of us, Jochen and me, a private air show. With loops, rolls, split-esses and Immelmanns, he really wrung the aircraft out. Of course we were thrilled and watched the performance from on top of a large wood pile in the middle of the village. At the end of the show Bob flew at an altitude of a few hundred feet over the terrain in slow rolls back to the Erding airbase. When Bob returned to his hometown Liberty N.Y., he immediately sent me the first of many food packages with all the things we did not have. Many years later, I was very sad when I found out that Bob had died in an aircraft accident near Liberty, NY.

Jochen and I enjoyed living so close together; he had a room at the village wheelwright a few hundred yards from where I lived. We could see each other daily and spent hours talking and planning for a great future. Priority #1 was to get out of Germany where the future looked very bleak. We thought that perhaps we could find a job flying airplanes somewhere? Rumor had it that they were looking for pilots to fly nitroglycerin over the Andes Mountains in South America. It was a bit risky but it paid well. Unfortunately or fortunately it was only a pipe dream, we were unable to make any firm contact. Jochen was born in Breslau, Silesia where his father had a business downtown, right in the middle of the city. When the Soviet army occupied Silesia his father and mother grabbed a few personal belongings, whatever they were able to carry and escaped further West. Magdeburg was the end of the line. Somehow Jochen was able to make contact with his parents. Great joy! Now perhaps Jochen and I were willing and able to visit with Boehms in Magdeburg? There was a good reason to make this trip from Bavaria to Magdeburg because it was the Boehms' silver wedding anniversary. Why not? Of course it was a little adventurous. There was no train going into the Soviet Occupation Zone. At a small railroad station close to the border we got off and walked east. Pretty soon we realized we were in no- mans-land, no mines and barbed wire "Iron Curtain" yet but an area patrolled by Soviet troops. Just like in our infantry training in the military we crawled under roads through culvers, dashed from one cover shrub to another, always on the lookout for Russian soldiers and after several hours arrived at a small railroad station from where we could take a train to Magdeburg. I remember the compartments were quite crowded, so we thought the fresh air will be good and remained on the platform, but then we found out why there was still room on the platform. In the Soviet occupation zone there was no hard — or pit coal, only soft — or brown coal. When the steam locomotive was fired with brown coal it rained sparks on the open platforms and one had to be very quick brushing the sparks from your clothing or get holes in it. We finally made it to Magdeburg, found the address and had a wonderful family reunion. The Boehms, his two sisters and Jochen, were all thankful that they made it through the war alive and now had found each other. We celebrated, stayed a few days but then we had to return back to Erding.

As we had no map we had to ask people for directions to take the shortest way to the British Occupation Zone. Naturally the directions we received were not always consistent. "Follow the patch of young pine trees", "No, no look for a hill with a bunch of oak trees!" and so on. After we had walked for quite some time we saw a group of women with children guarded by some Soviet soldiers. Naturally we did not want to be captured by those guys and bolted sideways which promptly made the Russians shout: "stoy!!" Jochen was still not physically healed from his wartime wounds, so he stood still and raised his arms. However, I thought that I can run faster than the Russians and continued. After one more " stoy" they fired their guns at me (I heard the bullets whistle by) then I too graduated from my quick course in the Russian language. I dashed under some small trees and waited. It did not take very long and a young, short Russian saw me laying there came over and kicked me with his boots and gesticulated for me to get up. He took a couple of steps back when he saw that I was by one head taller than he. But he recovered quickly, after all he had a machine pistol and I had nothing. Jochen and I as well as several other people were gathered and placed on a large log and interrogated. Jochen and I answered their questions and some young German border police men assisted the Russians. We told them, that we did not fight in Russia; instead we were anti aircraft soldiers in Germany during the war. When we did not change our story even after we had been slapped in the face several times they told us to go back to where we had come from, thinking that we were on our way to come to the Russian zone. We were glad to go West, at least now we knew which way to go. The group of women and children with their luggage that the two Russians had stopped and guarded when they saw us and chased us were quickly rescued by some people from the British Zone who were watching this border activity. Naturally the Russians didn't like that as they, I'm sure, were expecting to find some valuables in the luggage. That was the end of our brief Russian language course. We caught a train from the British Zone back to Bavaria.

Two Musketeers, waiting for word of the third.

Still we had a great time together. As there was no entertainment of any sorts we thought we should do something. But what? Jochen and I liked to sing together, so we sometimes on warm evenings sat under a big Lime Tree in the middle of the village Hubenstein and sang, and sang, and enjoyed ourselves. Then we thought how would it be if we organized for the village people in Hubenstein a folksong-choir? The word got around and we assembled a nice group of young people to sing with us on evenings in the local inn.

When Christmas time came around, we thought we should do something special for the village. At work I had access to little automotive light bulbs. I brought a bunch home and we soldered them together on a string of wire and created our own homemade Christmas lights. With the lights we decorated a tree in the middle of the village. Village people really enjoyed our Christmas decoration. Another involvement in the village life was our role as "Knecht Rupprecht and Santa Claus". We were in a costume appropriately dressed and had requests from families to visit with them and inquire if the children had been obedient and listening to their parents. I remember in one house the whole family was assembled in the living room and the children were lined up to report to Santa Claus that they had been good kids. There was one little girl maybe 5 years old who stood in the rear and always kept her hands behind her back. Her grandmother asked her: "What do you have there?" She admitted that she had a knife. Of course grandmother wanted to know why she had a knife. "Well, if Knecht Rupprecht puts me in his big sack, I'll be able to cut a hole in the sack and get out." For the village kids, Jochen wrote a manuscript for a little children's play called, "Little red riding hood". The kids loved it and we too had some fun with it.

We built simple radios which we sold to the people for cigarettes or some food stuff. When the American occupation military came to the village of Moosen they made a proclamation to the local population: "All weapons, all binoculars, all cameras and all radios are to be turned in." Naturally law abiding and obedient as German people are it was done as ordered. That's why radios were very much in demand. In 1945, the entire economy had come to a standstill. Whatever was produced was not sold on the open market. For the purchase of clothing for instance, a special authorization ticket was required and even with that one could not be sure that merchandise was available. A good example how the military government controlled the smallest detail of the economy: Jochen at his job at the Fernseh GmbH the company, which was "allowed" to regenerate radio vacuum tubes, had this experience. One day a commission of half a dozen military government officers showed up unannounced. They had to check if the right types of tubes were worked on and not tubes that were not on the authorised list -- I'm sure that Germany would have been able to get the economy going again years earlier if Allied restrictions had not been imposed on the country at such detail.

Meanwhile Jochen and I were still sitting in Hubenstein, keeping our eyes and ears open for an opportunity to find a flying job somewhere in the world.

Of our triumvirate Rudi had to suffer the most. WWII had been over more than a year already when Rudi's parents finally received a very brief message from him from a Soviet prisoner of war camp in Stalingrad; no details but at least the word --thank God -- he is alive. However, it was not until August 1948, three and a half years after the war, when we received the great news: "The Soviets had released Rudi and he had returned to his parent's home in Possenhofen -- a skeleton of our buddy Rudi." We were very happy that now all three of us had survived this 6 year long war in which more than 11 million Germans died, 3,250.000 of those were combat soldiers and additional 3,242.000 soldiers died in Allied prisoner of war camps during and after this unnecessary war. International laws stipulate that enemy soldiers taken prisoner should be repatriated after hostilities ceased. However, none of the victors complied with that. The Soviets did not release most German prisoners until around 1950, five years after the war.

A brief excerpt from what Rudi told us what had happened to him in 1945

"After completion of fighter flight training all my buddies transferred to a combat unit except me. I was directed to be a flight instructor. Now that the German bomber units were no longer able to function because of the overwhelming air superiority of the allied air forces and because of the severe shortage of fighter pilots, it was decided to reassign bomber pilots to become fighter pilots. My job now was to familiarize experienced bomber-pilots with the operation, the handling, the do's and don'ts of flying a fighter (the Me 109). Then I received the order to report to a fighter unit in Hungary. There I flew several reconnaissance missions without having contact with the enemy. Then, a couple of weeks later (in April 1945), our Schwarm was attacked by a squadron of Russian Yak 3 aircraft, which came out of the clouds above and hit us. There was no dog fight, but my aircraft was hit, was on fire and quickly went out of control. I was still able to get my Me 109 to go into a steep dive and somehow was able to bail out. There I was, dangling on my parachute and looking down at the beautiful countryside of Hungary. Then bullets which zipped past me shook me back to reality. A nice strong breeze was the reason why Russian infantrymen who tried to kill me were not successful, Thank God! I landed safely in a field where grain already had been harvested. Now from all sides Russian soldiers approached me —- there was no place to go, no place to hide and no chance to just run away. When they had me surrounded I threw my pistol on the ground. The Russian soldier closest pointed to me to pick up the weapon and give it to him. Next he demanded my wristwatch. (The same thing American and British soldiers did with German POW's) Then they took me in their midst to guide me to the nearest road). The 20 or so Russian soldiers all stared at me as if I was a strange animal. I had to walk in their midst to the nearest road.

Then some non-commissioned officer on horseback showed up who obviously wanted to take me away as his "trophy". After an excited argument, he won. Angry that I was no longer their property they punched and kicked me with their rifle butts. I had to walk really close to the neck of the horse so that the sergeant could protect me by hitting the soldiers who attacked me. At the edge of the field a Jeep was parked with two officers who had great difficulty to take me away from the sergeant but finally I sat in the Jeep, not without a hefty farewell kick from the boot of the sergeant. With all of the excitement I hardly noticed the pain of the hits and kicks I received until next day when I saw all the black and blue marks on my body. The Russian military unit kept me for 2-3 days. They moved from village to village, took over farms, butchered what animals they wanted to eat, and established themselves in the best available quarters while the farmers had to live in the barns or stables. One day a Captain who spoke fluent German interrogated me. I wanted to say only my name and rank but the Russian brusquely snapped: "Young man, quit this nonsense. Look here, you are young, you want to live and whatever you know we know already for a long time. We have captured your comrade Harbig and interrogated him; you were in JG 51 and everything else we know too. You see, my grandmother was German, so you were lucky this time, but when you are interrogated again don't be so stubborn and stupid as you were today, things may go badly for you."

After that I was transported for a whole day on top of a tank and dropped off at a prisoner of war camp. Again I was interrogated and this time beaten until I became unconscious three times. My P.O.W. time as a captive of Soviet Russia began in March 1945 and ended in August 1948 — almost 3 ½ years. When I became a prisoner I was in excellent physical and mental condition, I weighed about 160 lbs. War is a miserable thing of which we young fellows knew very little. To me it was more like a sporting competition. The ugly side of war we did not see until we were on the ground together with the poor, worn out, disillusioned, exhausted from 4 – 5 years of combat, army soldiers who now had to surrender to the unbelievable harsh conditions which Russia had for her prisoners.

I was regarded as a spy and transported to Focsani in Rumania on the Black Sea. This camp was a large meadow, no tents or barracks. Fortunately the weather was bearable. From there we were shipped with 3,000 P.O.W.'s on board a steamer to Novorossisysk. All we had to eat was rusks and water. In a railroad boxcar we travelled to Stalingrad. After 4 days the door was opened for the first time and some food was distributed. Also the first four dead soldiers were taken out. From then on every day a bucket of soup was placed in the boxcar. There were so many soldiers in the boxcar that it was impossible for all men to stretch their legs at the same time. In the middle of the floor of the boxcar was a hole the size of a standard piece of writing paper, that was the toilet. It caused indescribable consequences for the soldiers laying nearby.

Most of the prisoners had diarrhoea. By the time we reached Stalingrad, which took about three weeks, an additional six soldiers had died. Finally we were at Stalingrad. Groups of 100 men were formed regardless of their military branch. Officers were housed in a separate barrack but had to work the same jobs as enlisted men. I did all sorts of jobs in Stalingrad. Brick cleaner, plasterer, oven builder, arc welder, raft worker on the Volga river. Soon my weight dropped to 100 lbs. After one year I had learned enough of the Russian language that I could communicate with the Natschalnik, the boss of the construction project about the assessment of our work quota. At 80% we received 700 Gr of bread, at 100% 1,000 Gr and at 120% 1,200 Gr per day. Every day there was a battle with the Russian construction boss about the fulfilment of the quota. Sometimes we experienced some expressions of hate by people who might have lost some relative during the war. Usually it was just some swearing, physical abuses happened seldom. The system was inhuman under which the majority of Russian people had to live and under which they suffered. One has to remember that at the time of the Tsar the average Russian was but a Muschik, a farm labourer, uneducated, good-natured and meekly without any individual thinking or initiative of his own. Then Lenin and Stalin came with the Communists and Muschiks became workers at the Soviet collective farm, living the same dull life as the Muschiks had before. In this climate prisoners of war tried to survive. Russian citizens too had nothing of their own. Housing was very critical. Generally about 10 people shared a 538 sq Ft apartment. They were always in fear of the secret police NKVD. Today many, the silent majority, live the same life as before, many even worse off as before. It will probably take several generations before there will be a drastic change, until the masses will think for themselves and become articulate.

Our clothing naturally was totally inadequate; all we had was old Russian military junk shoes made of fabric with wooden soles and foot rags, which caused many blisters. Our assignment was to rebuild Stalingrad as long as our strength lasted. To work at minus 20 F, half starved to death, out in the open chipping mortar off old bricks is a job nobody will be able to do very long. When the question was asked: "Who can do plastering work?" I immediately raised my arm although I did not have the faintest idea about plastering. However I reasoned that this work couldn't be done in freezing temperatures. By mere chance I became arc welder at a construction site where we had to move large steel beams, a heavy and dangerous job. Unfortunately I was exposed to too much arc glare and had a temporary blindness. I had to remain in camp and take the Russian cure: "Lay slices of potatoes on the eyelids and keep quiet for 2 – 3 days." (3 days of food allocation without having to work!)

For a while I was raft worker on the river Volga, a job somewhat dangerous. Then there was the unloading of a cement cargo from a ship on the Volga. Cement sacks had to be carried some 900 ft uphill to the truck loading dock. At 4pm, it became clear that it would take at least 3 – 4 hours to finish the job. The Russian guard said that he too could not go home until the ship was unloaded. A typical situation of Russian mentality. So we let our most tired workers continue to carry cement bags off the ship, and with 8 or 10 men we disposed of cement bags through a hole in the hold into the river. The guard knew exactly what we were doing but he did not object; he did not care because he wanted to go home too.

The food situation was not always the same, usually, however, we were hungry. Sometimes when we had enough to eat, we ate too much and became ill afterwards. At one time when we were really hungry we found a dog at the construction site. We killed him and cooked him in a bucket of water. We ate him without any salt or seasoning. Once, when we had to unload a ship with a cargo of tomatoes we were no longer hungry but very sick afterwards. Every night about 30 prisoners waited around to unload bread from a truck, although only 3 or 4 were really needed. When the loafs of bread were passed from one man to the other we learned to chip just a little bit off from each loaf, but not too much to be noticed. That gave each one a chance to eat maybe two pounds of bread that night. It was important not to be caught while chewing.

We were housed 300 men in a loam bunker and slept on wooden plank beds. Two large stoves were on each end. We had to scrounge firewood every day because there was not enough issued to us. Two reasons to be excused from working were fever or diarrhoea. Fever could easily measured with a thermometer; diarrhoea had to be presented with a sample.

In 1945, 50% of all trucks in Stalingrad were made in the USA. Large quantities of foodstuff like Oscar Mayer canned pork meat and various other foods from America was available on the market. Without this American aid most likely many Russian people would have died of starvation, but also many more German P.O.W.'s. My lowest weight was 90 lbs. I had dysentery. I resigned and accepted my condition because it was said that with such low weight you had a chance to go home as you were no longer able to work. On the other hand the question was very much on my mind, "Will I last long enough until a transport will go back to Germany?" Of everything that makes P.O.W. confinement so unbearable is first of all the feeling of uncertainty. "Will I ever see my family again? Will I be able to survive? How much worse will it get? How long will it be?" Not being able to write or receive any mail from the family for 2 ½ years certainly added to the feeling of severe depression. Then I had a break, I was transferred to a different camp where -- how could I be so lucky — I got I job in the camps kitchen. That was like paradise! I was aware that I really had a guardian angel. Meanwhile I had learned enough of the Russian language that I became the Russians camp doctors' interpreter. After a few months he became my fatherly friend. Nine months later he was assigned to accompany a transport of German P.O.W.'s back to the German border. This was the time he could do something for me. He issued a medical certificate for me to go home. During this railroad journey to Germany he and I had some very interesting discussions. He told me that his father owned a farm when the communists came to power. That was reason enough for him to be executed. He, the Doctor, as the son, was banned to Siberia. After years in forced labour camps he was able to study medicine and became a Doctor. He freely admitted that he hated communism but was confined to this system from which he could not escape. At the German border where we had to say goodbye, I really had some mixed emotions. I was looking forward to join my family and he was forced to return to the "Working mans paradise" which I knew he hated so much. That, then, is the story of my time as a Soviet captive.

Ofhr Rudi and his sister (a nurse) in happier times.

What a God-sent solution

In Hubenstein, my life as a roomer at the Heiders was really very pleasant. (Except that there was no heating in my room nor indoor plumbing in the house, which was very uncomfortable especially on a cold winter night around midnight.) One day as I was going up to my room I heard piano playing in the downstairs living room. Mrs. Haider used this opportunity to introduce Mr. Busch to Miss. Rennschmid, the local school teacher, and Haider's daughter Angelika's piano teacher. I was very pleased to say the least to make the acquaintance of the most beautiful woman in Hubenstein, in Moosen, heck in the whole world! After that I occasionally saw Ms. Rennschmid on her bicycle pedalling by, all I could do is say: "Hallo!" wave and she was gone. In those post WWII years there was no entertainment available for people living in the rural areas in Germany. No radio programs that we could listen to (radios had been confiscated by the US Army), no magazines, no newspapers. Occasionally an entrepreneur came to the village Gasthaus (Pub) and set up the dance hall for a movie showing. One of those shows, I even re-member the title "Sag' die Wahrheit" ("Say the Truth") that I went to, I immediately spotted Miss. Rennschmid in the second row, sitting next to her mother. Naturally, in spite of my shyness I daringly asked: "Miss. Rennschmid, may I sit next to you?" Graciously she answered: "Yes, Please!" I still remember a good part of the movie but I certainly remem-ber what happened after the show. When the last scenes of the film phased out bright lightening and very loud thunder told us that there was a thunderstorm moving through. Nobody was prepared for rain! -- This was for me the opportunity to swing into action. "Mrs. Rennschmid, Miss.

Rennschmid, please wait a moment, I'll be right back with an umbrella".
It was but a couple of hundred yards for me to dash to my landlady. Mrs.
Haider not only had one umbrella, but two. That was extremely wonderful, because now I could offer one umbrella to Mrs. Rennschmid and offer
to take Miss. Rennschmid under the other umbrella to her home in
Moosen (about one mile). That was the most beautiful stroll in the rain
that anyone could experience. Close together, under an umbrella one has
to be as close as possible to avoid getting wet; I think we both enjoyed
this walk.

At the doorsteps of the schoolhouse I politely said: "Good Night,
Fraeulein Rennschmid," and went home. When Mrs. Rennschmid,
Fraeulein Rennschmid's mother, came home she was surprised that her
daughter had not offered me something, at least a cup of tea. This short
walk under the umbrella certainly was for both of us the beginning of our
great love affair that lasted, for the following 56 years.

Change of plans

When Jochen went to Munich one day he had the God-sent experience of his life. He ran into Mariettel, the girl who was his dance course
partner and whom he dated back home in Breslau when he was a teenager.
What an exciting surprise. As the proverb says, "Alte Liebe rostet nicht"
(old love does not rust), Jochen and Mariettel really fell in love and decided to get married. Of course that changed Jochen and my plans for
immigration etc. But then again we both, had the God-sent solution for
our life. Jochen found his Mariettel and I found my dream girl Marianne.
We both now had definite plans for marriage. In 1948, finally the
Reichsmark was replaced by the new Deutsche Mark. For the German
people this meant that for a second time within 25 years all savings were
wiped out. First the terrible Inflation 1923 and now the thrifty saver
turned in his hard earned money and received only 1/10th of the new
Deutsche Mark. On the other hand the change to the Deutsche Mark propelled the German economy over night into action. Suddenly goods and
merchandise became available on the market, no more need for barter

trading. My opinion is that Germany would have progressed 3 ½ years sooner if that had been allowed by the victorious Allies.

On October 1st 1949, my darling Marianne and I celebrated our engagement to be married. I'm sure it was a sad day for Marianne's father , who was naturally very concerned about his daughter's future. My plans were not very sure at that time, although mother wrote that it would not be difficult to find employment in the USA as a pilot, but really there was nothing sure about it. Marianne accepted a teaching position in Munich and a dream job potential in the Bavarian school system as school psychologist. I quit the Erding motor pool job and we both moved to Munich.

```
          7213TH MAINTENANCE SQUADRON (VEHICLE)
                 ERDING AIR FORCE DEPOT
                 APO 207  US ARMY

                                           10 January 1949


SUBJECT:  Letter of Recommendation


TO:       Whom it may Concern:


        Hans Heinrich Busch has been employed by the undersigned since
March 1946 as automotive mechanic. Hans's first assignment was 014 in
second echelon shop. He developed interest in automotive mechanics and
was later assigned to a field maintenance shop. Due to Hans's initiative
and capabilities he was assigned to the Theater Ordnance technical school
for instruction in carburation and ignition. In July 1948 Hans further
advanced to foreman of a Lubrication Department in a fourth Echelon Shop.

        Hans has demonstrated that he is a capable automotive mechanic, a
good foreman, willing to work extra hours to get the job done, and can
supervise and control subordinates. He is young, energetic, and willing
to learn. He studies American automotive literature and is constantly
developing himself.


                                    JAMES F. COUCH
                                    Captain, USAF
                                    Shop Officer
```

Letter of Recommendation

Emigration

1948 was the year when general immigration to the USA was allowed again. I had written to Uncle Willie (mother's brother) in California to ask if he could sponsor me. He sent me the required notarized Affidavit of Support which I had to submit to the US consulate in Munich, together with my application for a visa. A sponsor obligated himself to care for, and support, an immigrant if necessary for five years. Bureaucracy always and everywhere moves ever so slowly. For me it meant waiting. Maybe my guardian angel helped, a quick visa would have not made it possible for me to meet my love Marianne? We were engaged to be married in October 1949. Then on November 18. 1950, we had a beautiful wedding in downtown Munich in the century old Dreifaltigkeitskirche.

Our wedding picture

For the US consulate, however, I now needed an affidavit of support for me and for Marianne. That meant "Uncle Willie, please send me another affidavit" (To immigrate was not as simple then as today's illegal immigration by millions of people from Mexico to the US. No affidavit, no visa application, no sponsor, just walk over the border and live in the USA for a few years and wait for amnesty.) I now had to submit in addition to the sponsor's affidavit a health certificate and from the police department a certificate that I and Marianne had no criminal record. After that it was waiting, waiting, waiting. When year after year nothing happened, people said to us: "You'll never get to the USA; you'll not make it!" Marianne's Father especially was not very happy at all, as a matter of fact he was very sad to see his beloved daughter leave. It is understandable that he was very apprehensive that we were leaving for the USA. After all, his treatment by the Americans in 1946 (they arrested him and locked him up in a concentration camp without ever accusing him of anything and starving him) was still very fresh in his memory. "And think Marianne, you don't know how the New World is and you, perhaps, will hate it over there. Always remember if you would rather live here in Germany, I'll send you the money for the return trip immediately".

Finally in September 1951, Marianne and I started our journey from Munich to San Diego California. On the 15th of September 1951, Hans and Marianne Busch finally embarked on the steamer "Homeland" in the harbour of Hamburg. The ship went first to Southampton, then to Cherbourg, to Halifax in Canada, and then finally to New York. That took eleven days, of which Marianne was ten days seasick, the poor girl, and nothing could be done about it. I, on the other hand felt great, and as five of our eight passengers at our table for several days in the Atlantic were seasick, I could eat whatever I liked best and there was plenty of it on the dinner table.

Onboard the Homeland

A new life in the New World

Our plan was to take a Greyhound bus from New York to San Diego, a long way to Tipperary. A very eager beaver taxi driver offered his services and took us in a few minutes to the Bus station on 51st St and charged us $15. We thought that it was quite expensive to ride the taxi in America, in Munich it would have cost us maybe $2. When we purchased our Greyhound bus ticket we mentioned: "it's amazing that a bus ride all the way from one end of America to the other costs less than $100 and a short taxi trip costs $15!?" The counter-clerk was amazed and said that should have cost but a few dollars, do you remember the number of the taxicab? Of course not! Who comes to another country and remembers the Taxi number?

Our first impression of America was that the country is immensely huge. For hours and hours, the bus went on a highway straight as an arrow all the way to the horizon. To the right and to the left as far as one could see grain fields, unbelievable! What a difference to the countryside in Germany. We climbed aboard a bus and headed West. One strange sight to us was that the houses in the urban area of cities had lawns in front of the houses, but none had a fence or wall around their property. That certainly has changed in the 50 years since. We were amazed that villages and cities all had a dense forest of TV antennas, power line masts and telephone lines, something we had never seen before in Germany.
When the bus stopped for lunch, we too went in the next door restaurant for a bite to eat. We had no problem ordering some food. However, what do we drink? As we would have done it in Munich we ordered a beer. Sorry, said the waitress, we don't serve beer; perhaps you would like a Root Beer? What's that? We did not know. It's what the guy over there is drinking she pointed out. That looked to us like dark beer, so we agreed to have a Root Beer. That's when we received the shock of our life, when we had the expectation and were prepared for the taste of beer, well dark beer, instead surprise, surprise we experienced for the first time in our life the taste of a sweet, strange but indefinable liquid. It was not beer at all. That's the only sip of root beer that we had for the rest of our life.

Of our ,until then, unknown family branch, uncle, aunt and cousins, we were accepted at once as part of the family and later, when Marianne felt a little homesick Uncle Willy was her fatherly friend who could always encourage her and cheer her up.

Celebrating our arrival with family in Tijuana

I had been told that there was no problem to find employment as a pilot with any airline. I did not expect that my German pilot license would be valid here in the USA, so I visited the Federal Aviation Administration to obtain an American license. "Sorry, we can not issue a pilot license to you because you are not a US citizen." It takes 5 years to become a citizen! Now what? What am I going to do in those 5 years? Checking everywhere and talking to many people, including a Senator, I finally did find out that it was possible to get a pilot license if the Civil Aeronautic Board waives the citizenship requirement. Quickly I sent a letter to the CAB and what do you know, I did get a reply promptly. I had to submit a few answers to their questions like where did you arrive in the USA, when did you arrive, what is your immigration visa number etc. In a short time the CAB sent me a letter: "We waive the citizenship requirement for any airman certificate you may qualify for." Now with that the FAA was able to issue me a student license, after I presented my medical certificate. With the student license, I went to a flight instructor at the National City airport to check me out. I rented a little Aeronca and we took off. After one hour and thirty minutes, during which he had me perform a number of flight manoeuvres (no aerobatics) and a few takeoffs and landings, he apparently was satisfied with my flying ability so he signed me off to fly solo.

Flying is like riding a bicycle, one does not lose the skill. After all, my last time since I had flown an aircraft was in April 1945, some 7 years earlier. Now I had to apply myself really hard to study for the commercial written examination. I had no problem to pass the four part test (Meteorology, Navigation, Airframes and engines, Civil Aeronautic

203

Regulations) and could prepare myself for the flight test. After about four hours of flight time, during which I got the hang of flying several types of awfully slow aircraft (compared with my last flight in a Me 262), an FAA examiner went up with me to check out my flying skills.

There were only two manoeuvres which I did not know by the English name, but after a brief description, I understood what was required. I passed the commercial flight test examination. With that I had accomplished all the requirements and the postman delivered a few days later my Commercial Pilot License. Immediately I went to commercial airlines in San Diego and Los Angeles in expectation of finding employment. They looked at my application and records and said: "Wonderful you even have flown jet aircraft, h o w e v e r, you are not a U.S. citizen! Sorry we can not hire you!" Devastating news. It takes 5 years to become a US citizen.

At the time when Wernher von Braun and his rocket specialists came to the USA, there were also many experts and craftsmen in numerous fields brought to America. One of these was a superb craftsman, an outstanding master scientific glassblower, who was hired by General Dynamics to oversee and direct the glasswork of a new invention, the Charactron tube. Unfortunately, Karl could not communicate in English very well, only in German. Through the grapevine, the word spread that there was a young German who could speak English and German and perhaps would work with Karl? Well, that's where I came in, as assistant of Karl mainly as his interpreter. The Charactron project was classified secret; therefore all employees working there had to have a security clearance from the US Government. But Hans Busch was not even a US citizen yet. Well, where there's a will there is a way. A member of the management team , "good ol' Ernie" (who became a dear friend of mine and later our girl Renate's godfather) had to escort me to the military security department at the Rock -- the Convair administration building -- to process my secret clearance application. An employee there reviewed my papers and had a few questions. "By the way, you were a pilot in the Luftwaffe during WWII?" "Yes sir"! I said (at this time some people in the office raised their heads and listened.) "You know", he continued, "I was also a pilot, that is in the US Army Air Corps during WWII. What aircraft did you fly," he asked? –- "The last aircraft I flew was the Messerschmitt 262," I told him. (More people listened and looked over). Then I asked him what aircraft did he fly? "I flew a B-24 bomber, but I was shot down by a Me 262 over Germany and became a POW," he said. "By any chance did you fly in the area of Nuremberg?" I said, "Yes," because I was stationed at Neuburg not far from Nuremberg. — "When were you shot down?" (At this time everybody in the office turned to us and anxiously listened in.) "In April of 45 — could it be that it was you who shot me down?" he asked. (Now there was high tension in the room) "Sorry, but no, it could not have been me because I was a bomber pilot and not a fighter pilot." End of the thrill for all in the office! I still got my secret clearance without being a US citizen.

Charactron glass work

Meanwhile I was still in hopes to find a job in commercial aviation or maybe as a test pilot with Convair. No luck! Then I read that a pilot in Czechoslovakia stole a Russian Mig 17 aircraft and delivered it to the US military. He received a bundle of money and became an American citizen immediately. I tried to find out if I, who had not stolen an aircraft, could not get my citizenship in less than 5 years time? No! was the answer even when I begged a Senator in Washington to help me? Then I thought, perhaps, if I can not fly in the USA, maybe I could go back to Germany and apply for a position in the at that time newly-reformed German Air Force? I wrote a letter and I received an answer. Fill out the lengthy questionnaire and return it to us. No, we are not able to give you any travel expense assistance. In other words: we are not too interested in your application. Years later I had occasional thoughts like: Should I have pursued the new Luftwaffe in Germany? Was it right to give up my dream? The job as Research and Development Technician was interesting but did not have a good chance for advancement. Again dear friend Ernie was able to help me. Ernie had left the Charactron project and was now working at General Dynamics Astronautics. As Ernie has the ability, always with a smile, to make friends easily, he kept looking around at Astronautics for a job that I could fit into. Sure enough, one day he made arrangements for Jay Mumford, Ernie and I to go for lunch together. Well, that was the beginning of my employment at General Dynamics for the rest of my working years, (retired in 1991) and that was the continuation of a great friendship to this very day.

My flying in California.

A funny incident happened when I was trying to generate interest in the community for the Youth Glider Program. I talked to a reporter from the San Diego Union newspaper to publicize the glider flying program. During the discussion he asked me: "Did you fly gliders?" I said "Yes I did". He wanted to know when and where and made a few notes. He found it interesting that I had been a pilot in the German Luftwaffe. At that time, I thought for sure he realized that I was joking, I said: "The fact that in March 1945, the U.S. Army Air Corps dropped bombs and pulverized our air base at Neuburg I can accept -- after all it was war -- but did they have to do it just when I had received an occasional ration of liquor, a whole bottle of brandy in my wall locker? I can not forget it, I hated them for that!" I did not see him writing any notes and so I did not think he would print this remark.

Next morning I was sitting at my desk at Convair plant 2 when a colleague whose desk was but a few feet from mine came over and said: "I think I owe you a drink!" I didn't have the faintest idea what he was talking about. He then explained that he had read the morning edition of the San Diego Union-Tribune, and that he was sure that it was he who dropped the bombs on our Luftwaffe base Neuburg in March of 1945. I was dumbfounded and did not know what he was talking about, because I had not read the newspaper article that quoted me saying I hated the U.S. Army Air Corps because they destroyed my one bottle of liquor supply. But he certainly had papers to prove that it was him. He unfolded a large piece of paper, a flight order with all the detail information, like pilot in command Hal Heist, co-pilot, bombardier, how much fuel on board, how many bombs, etc., and there it stated, "09:39 bombs away over Neuburg." But he had more proof. He had several photographs of our base taken at exactly that moment as the bombs hit the ground. I could point out to him where my barracks was before it disappeared. What a coincidence. When the reporter called a little while later and told me that his boss inserted my remarks as a human interest story I told him that I had not meant to publicise that little episode, but then again it was good that it was printed because now I know who dropped the bombs on my brandy. Of course I had to explain.

He then insisted that the three of us and a photographer meet after work at the Cotton Patch Restaurant and have a drink together

H.B. and Hal
Heist

DEBT PAID—Repaying a debt of 19 years, Hal Heist, right, buys the drinks and buries the hatchet with Hans Busch, a former Luftwaffe pilot. Heist was navigator on B24 raid over Germany that de- stroyed Busch's barracks and liquor supply at Neuburg Air Base. The two have unknowingly worked within view of each other at General Dynamics Aeronautics. News story brought them together.

Tribune Story Gets War Foes Together as Friends Here

Commercial flying in the USA is not possible for me.

But back to my primary purpose to come to the U.S.A.. During the five years of waiting to become a U.S. citizen I wrote many letters and applications to other companies that had something to do with flying (including flying oil pipeline patrol for the American -- Arabian Oil Co.) But no job. Finally, after having been in the U.S.A. for five years, I could apply for citizenship. I wanted to make very sure that I would not flunk the test at the INS; I therefore learned by heart almost the entire citizen instruction booklet. I could answer all questions and passed with flying colours.

"Now that I am a citizen I'll get a flying job," I thought. Wrong! Equipped with all my documents I went to all major commercial airlines. Each time it went like this: "Aha, you have a commercial pilot license with an instrument rating, you are an American citizen but -- so sorry -- you are 32 years old we do not hire pilots who are older than 29 or 30 years of age." That was such a devastating blow; all my dreams drowned, the future looked very bleak. As time went on I had a constant feeling as if I was sitting on a raft in the middle of a stream without a paddle and drifting towards a waterfall. My worries then caused my stomach to develop stomach ulcers. But, to return to Germany? When Marianne and I thought that now, that our first child, Christian, was born, and now that I had a good job with General Dynamics and now that we had already purchased a house, maybe we had better stay here (and not having to listen to friends and family members in Germany saying: "See -- We told you so!").

San Diego Man New Citizen

HANS BUSCH

HANS BUSCH, cathode ray tube technician in the developmental tube facility at San Diego and a wartime lieutenant in the armed forces of Germany, acquired a new title this month:

Citizen, United States of America.

Hans came to America in October, 1951, with two ambitions—to become an American citizen and to become a commercial pilot.

He now is certain that the time necessary to achieve the first goal has made him too old (32!) to try for the second. His plans are for a continued career with Stromber-Carlson—San Diego.

Hans was graduated from Gruestrow High School in 1943 after special study in English, French, Latin, German, physics and biology. He immediately entered the German air force and served successively as a glider pilot, a pilot of single engine, multi-engine and twin-jet (Me262) aircraft.

After serving as a German M.P. under the U.S. 6th Army Group, and for three years as shop foreman and interpreter for the U.S. A.F. European Air Depot, Hans came to the U.S., with his wife, Marianne, a former German school teacher.

Mrs. Busch, now a teacher in San Diego schools, received her U.S. citizenship at the same time as her husband. The couple has one child, a boy, 3; and is expecting another.

Further episodes in my life

My interest in flying stayed intact and over the years, I met several famous airmen. At an autograph-signing party at Virginia Bader's fine art gallery, I met the legendary leader of the German fighter force, former General Adolf Galland.

General Galland and Lt Busch.

For several years, I had been corresponding with Hans'l Baur, Hitler's personal pilot who lived near Munich at Lake Ammersee. Now I had a chance to meet him personally and talk about the old times. At one such visit, we were just enjoying a glass of good Bavarian beer, the world renowned British historian Mr. David Irving showed up.

With Hans Baur and David Irving

During vacation time we explored a bit of Italy, Austria, Hungary, and after the "Iron Curtain" fell, also East Germany. We drove through the Mark Brandenburg and Berlin where we picked up some chunks from the infamous Wall and toured to the village of Zuehlen some 50 Km West of Berlin. Lonely, a bit removed from the village, we pulled up to my grand-parents' farm, that I had last seen more than 50 years ago. The dwelling was in a fair condition but barn and stables were very much deteriorating. I had to say a prayer for my Aunt Guschen who was beastly murdered with her 10 year-old-daughter, my cousin, by the invading brutal Soviet soldiers back in 1945. The area had been a part of "East Germany" since way back when– although East Germany is really a misnomer because the area is situated in the former Central Germany. The original East Germany was Pomerania, East Prussia, West Prussia, and Silesia which were taken over by Russia and Poland after WWII.

At the beginning of 1991, I retired at the ripe old age of 67. Initially, after we had been in Munich a few months, we thought that we might some day retire in Germany, perhaps in a small village in a beautiful Bavarian mountain village. As time went on, however, we realised that we had been grown accustomed to the friendly, tolerant, pleasant life we had experienced in all the years we lived in California

Then, it was time for a quick return to Germany to be reacquainted with some of my friends from my Luftwaffe days. The number of friends and buddies with whom I had the great opportunity to fly the most advanced aircraft in the world, the legendary Messerschmitt 262, is day-by-day decreasing. The year 1992 was the year in which we had a good reason to see each other because it was the 50th anniversary of the first flight of a Me 262. On July 18 1942 Flugkapitaen Fritz Wendel took off for the first time with two Junkers turbines propelling his Me 262. From our former Luftwaffen unit Kampfgeschwader 51 there were only some 24 pilots who showed up, and since then several friends have passed away.

My old C.O., Major Barth on the right.

50 Jahre
Messerschmitt Me 262
1942 – 1992

Am 18. Juli 1942 – vor 50 Jahren – startete der Messerschmitt-Versuchspilot Flugkapitän Fritz Wendel auf dem Luftwaffenflugplatz Leipheim mit der Me 262 V-3 erstmals mit Strahlantrieb durch zwei Junkers-Jumo-004-Turbinen-Luftstrahl-Triebwerke (TL). Dieser erste reine Strahlflug der Me 262, des ersten serienmäßig hergestellten und eingesetzten Düsenflugzeugs der Welt, gilt als der entscheidende Durchbruch im Jet-Zeitalter.

Die Me 262 war aus Studien unter der Projektnummer P 1065 hervorgegangen, die im Messerschmitt-Projektbüro bereits 1938 begonnen hatten, als erste Hinweise auf die in Entwicklung befindlichen Strahltriebwerke der Firmen Heinkel, BMW und Junkers bekannt wurden. Die Entwicklungsaufträge für die neuen TL-Triebwerke waren zunächst zum Teil auf privater Basis (Heinkel, Junkers) erfolgt und später vom Reichsluftfahrtministerium (RLM) offiziell erteilt worden. Während die Heinkel-Entwicklung mit der He 178 bereits im August 1939 und mit der He 280 im März 1941 in die Flugerprobung gehen konnten, erteilte das RLM der Firma Messerschmitt erst im März 1940 den Auftrag zur Entwicklung und zum Bau von drei V-Mustern Me 262 zur Erprobung der BMW- bzw. später Junkers-TL-Triebwerke.
Da die Entwicklung bei BMW mehr Zeit in Anspruch nahm, als geplant, wurde die Me 262 V-1 zur Vorerprobung der Flugeigenschaften am 18. April 1941 in Augsburg zunächst mit einem konventionellen Motor Jumo 210 eingeflogen. Bei einem Flug am 25. März 1942 waren in die Me 262 V-1 zusätzlich zum Mittelmotor Jumo 210 die ersten verfügbaren BMW-003-Strahltriebwerke eingebaut, die jedoch versagten. Da zeitraubende Konstruktionsänderungen an den Triebwerken notwendig wurden, mußte die Erprobung auf die Junkers-Strahltriebwerke umgestellt werden. Diese ermöglichten dann den erfolgreichen Flug vom 18. Juli 1942. Die daraufhin vom RLM bestellten 10 V-Muster flogen bis zum Frühjahr 1944.
Ein Vorserienauftrag des RLM vom 25. Mai 1943 über 100 noch bis zum Ende des Jahres zu liefernde Me-262-Jagdflugzeuge konnte nicht eingehalten werden, da zu diesem Zeitpunkt bereits die firmenseitigen Forderungen nach Facharbeitern für den Vorrichtungs- und Serienbau vom RLM nicht mehr erfüllt werden konnten. Außerdem gab es schon kriegsbedingte Engpässe, besonders für Rohstoffe und Spezialteile. Diese Probleme hatte auch der Triebwerkshersteller Junkers, bei dem außerdem die Entwicklung der Jumo-004-TL-Triebwerke noch nicht abgeschlossen war. Zu diesen Verzögerungen kamen andere Erschwernisse hinzu, darunter die Forderungen der obersten Führung, die zunächst die als Jagdflugzeug konzipierte Me 262 ausschließlich als Schnellstbomber eingesetzt sehen wollte.
Der Serienbau der Me 262 begann mit ersten Auslieferungen im März 1944. Die ersten hundert Maschinen waren im Juli ausgeliefert. Bis Kriegsende wurden 1433 Me 262 gebaut, wovon etwa 700 bis 800 der Luftwaffe erreichten.
Erste Jagdeinsätze mit der Me 262 erfolgten im Juli 1944 von Lechfeld aus, wo sich die Messerschmitt-Flugerprobung befand und wo die ersten Erprobungskommandos für den Jagd-, Bomber- und Aufklärungseinsatz mit der Me 262 etabliert wurden. Sie waren die Vorläufer der ersten Luftwaffengeschwader mit Strahlflugzeugen.

Full of enthusiasm I look forward to the day when one or two maybe all five Me 262 which are in construction in Seattle fly in formation over the skies of America. A very sincere "Hals – und Beinbruch" to all of the lucky pilots who can fly them!

A standing-room-only and appreciative crowd listen intently to Mr. Busch's comments about flying the Messerschmitt jet.

In 1999, the owner of the "Planes of Fame" museum planned on having a symposium to showcase his Me 262, the very same one that I had been shown during the 1970's. Over the years, it had been lovingly restored and on that day, well over a hundred people came to see the beautiful Me 262. Mr. Mahoney sat next to me and I spoke about my flying experiences as well as the characteristics of the first combat jet.

Afterwards, I sat in their Me 262 in the sunshine and gave the museum staff a walk around "pre-flight", as if I was going to fly it. All four of our children attended, giving them a chance to hear stories that I had kept somewhat private over the years since the war. Afterwards, we watched a fully-restored Bf 109 E fly around the airport and were able to examine it up close.

This then brings to a close my recollection of my full life. The Busch family is now happily together again in beautiful California. Christian still single and with his fiancé Bonnie. Rainer with his beautiful wife Jackie and their son Nicky. Renate with her handsome husband Jeff, son Lucas and daughter Lindsey. Normann and his fiancé Debby. We all enjoy celebrating birthdays, Christmas or Easter together. There is no end to this story as our family continues on.

Richard Lutz and Hans Busch meet at the cockpit that Mr. Lutz restored in the "Planes of Fame's" Me-262. Oct 2, 1999

Our Mexico Cruise-October 2003

Shelf Books specialises in the publication of books dealing with various aspects of World War Two, and associated topics. If you have a manuscript you would like us to consider then please contact us at:
shelfbooks@yahoo.co.uk
or visit our website
www.shelfbooks.co.uk

Breinigsville, PA USA
29 October 2009
226669BV00002B/4/P